# Change
# your
# life
# right
# now!

# Change
# your life
# right now!

## Breaking down the barriers to success

## Dr Sidney B. Simon

## Thorsons Publishing Group

*To my wife, Suzanne Simon, for loyalty beyond the call of love*

First published 1988 by Warner Books Inc., 666 Fifth Avenue, New York, NY 10103, as Getting Unstuck

This edition published 1989

Copyright © Sidney B. Simon 1988, 1989

British Library Cataloguing in Publication data.
Simon, Sidney B.
    [Getting Unstuck.] Change your life now!
    1.   Self-realisation.
    I.   [Getting unstuck.] II.  Title
    158'.1

ISBN 0-7225-2106-5

Published by Thorsons Publishers Limited, Wellingborough, Northamptonshire, England NN8 2RQ

Printed in Great Britain by Mackays of Chatham, Kent

10 9 8 7 6 5 4 3

# *Acknowledgments*

The ideas for this book were hammered out in a hundred Values Realization Workshops and dozens of classes at the University of Massachusetts. I am grateful to all those students and workshop participants and to the myriad people on my life's bumpy path who taught me what I had to learn. I am also indebted to the people whose stories illuminate this book and whose "unstuckness" graces these pages.

I am especially grateful to those adults who used to be our children—John Simon, Douglas Simon, Julianna Simon, Matthew and Carie Lee Bernard. Unstuck themselves, they gave me bountiful inspiration.

I feel a deep gratitude to the members of the Values Realization Institute for what their commitment taught me about getting unstuck. In particular, my thanks go to Michael Wenger, the guiding star in the process that made the Institute a reality.

To Susan Meltsner, my deepest thanks for her brilliance, drive, and follow-through that made the pages mount. It was just a hat full of workshop ideas until she lent her art to my craft and got this book unstuck.

A warm thanks to Cathy Hemming, a shepherd in sheep's clothing. Without her vision, support, guidance, affirmations, and hopes, I might still be on the other side of the barriers to change.

A high-energy thanks goes to Nancy Kalish, my editor. She is so wise, so ebulliently positive that one could never be less than brilliant in her care. My thanks as well to someone who was significantly supportive and who early on had a profound faith in this book, Joann Davis of Warner Books.

There were so many others. To name just a few, let me thank Howard Kirschenbaum, for his always practical insights given with full integrity, and Lee Silverstein, friend and encourager when courage was needed. Also thanks to my sister, Dorothy, who is always in my corner; to Sharon Lumbis, who manages the miscellaneous in this office with sensitivity and efficiency; and to all those other people who cared at the right time.

But let it be known that Suzanne Simon, my everloving wife-partner, never, never wobbled in her utter faith. She, noble woman, lives what getting unstuck is all about.

Finally, let me acknowledge and thank you, the reader, who intuitively knew that something important was waiting for you when you chose to pick up this book. I pray you learn what this teacher deeply believes he has to teach.

*Hadley, Mass.*
*April, 1988*

Publisher's Note

CHANGE YOUR LIFE RIGHT NOW! was first
published in the United States as GETTING
UNSTUCK and contains numerous references
reflecting this title. To avoid interference with the
sense of the original text these references have not
been removed, and should not prove an obstacle to
your understanding or appreciation of the book.

# 1

# *What It Means to Be Stuck*

STUCK IS . . .

. . . setting goals and making plans but putting off the first step until tomorrow or next week or next year or the moment after the rest of your life is in perfect order.

. . . making promises—to stop drinking, quit smoking, spend more time with your family, bring down your credit card balances, exercise regularly, or be more assertive— breaking promises and feeling guilty.

. . . taking no action to prevent dire consequences to your health or well-being despite repeated warnings from your doctor, your boss, your family, and your friends.

. . . waiting for a catastrophe, a sign, an offer you can't refuse, or until you absolutely, positively cannot "take it" anymore before doing what you knew all along you should and could do.

STUCK IS NOT A COMFORTABLE, SATISFYING PLACE TO BE. When you are stuck you do not feel content. You do not think clearly. You doubt your abilities and dislike yourself. Most notably, you cannot move toward your goals or out of unpleasant, unhealthy situations.

This book is about getting *unstuck*. It will acquaint you with the psychological obstacles, emotional barriers, and practical considerations that thwart your best efforts to change. It offers guidance, ideas, and tools you can use to push through the blocks to change. By the time you reach the final page, you will be well on your way to a more satisfying and re-warding life.

However, before you begin your journey, you need a clear understanding of exactly what it means to be stuck. Your first inclination may be to avoid looking at what it means to be stuck. You may want to deny your feelings, ignore the signs and symptoms and refuse to examine what being stuck means and how it affects you. But examine it you must. Recognizing and understanding what being stuck means is a first step toward getting unstuck.

In this chapter you will find both general descriptions of being stuck and detailed profiles of people who are stuck. *You* may not be as stuck as the people whose personal stories appear here. *All* the signs and symptoms of being stuck may not apply to you, but I urge you to consider them anyway. You are embarking upon a journey that many people have taken before you. You can only benefit from their stories of getting unstuck. The ultimate destination of this odyssey is arriving at the life you truly desire and deserve. You cannot plan such a trip or begin travelling until you find the starting line. Stuck is the starting line, and you'll soon recognize that you are not the only person standing on it.

EVERYONE GETS STUCK. Everyone. There are no ex-ceptions. Think about it. Think of the people whose lives seem to be charmed—people who have and do everything you wish for yourself. Do you honestly believe they never have a moment of doubt or insecurity? Do you think they never came upon an obstacle they believed to be insur-mountable or found a frustrating, seemingly intractable barrier interrupting the path to success? Of course not. Try as you might, you will never find anyone whose life was exactly the way that person wanted it to be from the day he or she was born until death.

No matter how rich, powerful, intelligent, beautiful, famous, successful, or admired you are, you can take a wrong turn, lose your way, skid off the road, and find yourself knee-deep in quicksand and sinking fast. At least once in a lifetime, and more likely many times, you and I get stuck.

- Dynamic, talented, self-confident singer Tina Turner spent years and years married to a man who physically and emotionally abused her.

- Former first lady Betty Ford, a woman admired by millions and a role model to many, got stuck in a dangerous addiction to alcohol and prescription medicine. It took years of suffering and painful confrontations by her family to get her to change and on the road to recovery.

- A child star who grew up to be a renowned and respected actress, Patty Duke got trapped on a roller coaster ride of mental illness.

- Billy Joel, the popular music recording artist, now married to one of the most beautiful women in the world and an adoring father, once considered suicide.

Everyone gets stuck—even people who "should" know better. Even a university professor who lectures and leads workshops and writes books about getting unstuck.

In 1980 a newspaper article titled "Lifting the Barriers to Personal Success" appeared in the *Arizona Republic*. It was written by columnist Ginger Hutton, who had attended a workshop I led in Scottsdale, Arizona. In the article Ginger presented in a general way the eight blocks to change you will read about in this book, and which had been the foundation of my workshop that weekend in March. Seeing my ideas about the subject of change in print for the first time started me thinking about writing this book.

I told myself the book needed to be written and that I was the one who could and should write it. I thought a great deal about writing it and told many people of my intentions. But for seven years, I did not write it. I procrastinated. I rationalized. With my busy schedule I could not find time to write a book. I was waiting for the perfect moment; I had to be sure I had enough material. I had to see how more workshop attendees responded to the ideas. I had to be sure no other author had written a book like it.

A dozen times I started the project only to abandon it. The irony did not escape me. I wanted to write a book about change—yet *I* was stuck.

Between 1980 when I initially considered writing this book and 1987 when I finally wrote it, I re-experienced, in a very personal way, the blocks to change and rediscovered how to push through them. I was humbled by my own resistance to change—a resistance I thought I had got over years ago. But most importantly, I dramatically reaffirmed the principle upon which this book is based:

EVERYONE GETS STUCK AND EVERYONE CAN GET UNSTUCK

Any choice you face—from quitting smoking and getting your hair cut to accepting a marriage proposal or job offer—can confuse you, frighten you, and get you stuck. One of the most obvious and painful places to be stuck is when we have got ourselves into frustrating and self-destructive situations. They are all too familiar and all too painful:

- bad marriages

- dead-end jobs

- feeling alone and isolated in a new town

- experiencing physical illness or severe depression

- being unable to escape physical, emotional, or sexual abuse

All the ways you can get stuck have one element in common. Change is required—but you can't seem to make change happen. Whether you want to stop biting your nails or whether you have endured a decade of abuse from a spouse or parent, *when you are stuck your ability to do anything about your situation seems to disappear.* Nothing seems able to get you moving, not your desire to be better, not your treasured goals and aspirations, not even the pain you feel. Threats, bribes, and impassioned pleas are not enough to move you.

---

## STUCK IS A CAR IN THE MUD
## WITH ITS WHEELS SPINNING

Carol, a forty-eight-year-old social worker, is stuck in an unsatisfying, dead-end job.

"I don't work with people anymore," she groans. "I work with paper. Forms. Files. Memos. The name of the game is 'cover yourself.' No one cares what you do with your clients as long as the paperwork gets in on time. I took this job because I wanted to serve children, but I ended up serving the system and it's a cruddy system at that. If you started out caring, the system beats it out of you. They pile on the unreasonable demands until they bury you. Then they top it off by taking away whatever dignity you have."

Carol's tirade against the child welfare agency where she works can go on for hours. Complaining about the system is what Carol does best these days—and she does it often.

Like most people who find themselves trapped in an intolerable situation, Carol did not get to the end of her rope overnight. She had slowly painted herself into a corner by

the choices she made, the real injustices and indignities of
her job, and all she did and did not do to turn things around
earlier in her career and in her life.

The mother of three, Carol returned to the work force
when her sons were still young. She held a bachelor's degree
in social work, wanted to work with children, and needed a
part-time job. The county agency was the only place that
offered what she thought she wanted. In the beginning, things
went well, but as her children got older and more independent, she began working full-time. For unrelated reasons,
Carol's husband left her, and she turned to her work and her
co-workers for emotional support.

"I have such powerful ties to this place because the
people here pulled me through the divorce. They are my
closest friends. I made them my extended family," Carol
explains. More than emotional ties bound her to the agency.
The job also gave her the stability and security of a steady
salary. "I'm not a high-risk person. I take as few risks as
possible. My number one responsibility is to my kids. No
matter how bad things get, leaving the job is never a serious
option. I can't risk losing that salary."

Carol's financial needs increased as her sons became
teenagers and her child support cheques appeared less regularly. To increase her earning power she went back to
college, earned her master's degree, and took the first super-
visory position that became available. Ironically, as she
earned more money, she stopped having direct client contact,
even though working with children and families had been the
only aspect of the job she liked.

"But I keep plugging away," Carol continues. "I moved
right on up the paper-pushing ladder—even though I am
dissatisfied and feel trapped."

Thinking that working with people again would make
her feel better, Carol started a private counselling practice in
addition to her full-time job. "I love counselling. But with
my private practice, the agency, and raising three teenage
boys, I'm giving, giving, giving, twenty-four hours a day."

It does not occur to her to leave the agency and concentrate on her private practice. "It's that salary thing again," she sighs. "I don't think I can make it on my own. I can't take the chance."

Feeling more and more pressured, Carol took a friend's advice and began swimming each morning to relieve stress. Carol believes the physical exercise and the "high" it produces keep her from "going over the edge."

Because Carol swam in the morning, she got to work late. Because the job made her crazy, she left early and took long lunch breaks. Because she was not the only worker suffering from burnout at the agency's expense, the agency cracked down.

"We were told to be at our desks at eight-thirty and not leave before four-thirty in the afternoon. They refuse to make any exceptions, even when I offered to work late to make up the time I spent swimming. They are totally inflexible. I have to give up the one thing that helps me survive and I'm furious.

"Then they moved me into the basement. Here I am, the most senior worker in the agency, and I'm stuck in a basement office with a smoker no less! They won't budge on anything. They won't even let me use an empty office on the first floor for the summer while the students who use it during the school year are on vacation.

"I've been with this agency for fifteen years, and believe me, I gave it a whole lot more than it gave me. But it's too late to start over. I'm forty-eight years old and two of my kids are in college. So now I'm just doing time. I do as little work as possible. I take as many sick days as I can get away with. I sneak out of the building and go shopping for a couple of hours. I bitch about the agency all the time."

Carol also notices herself yelling at her kids more, spending her weekends in bed, and having nightmares about the job. "It's a living hell, but what can I do? At this point I'm probably not capable of being anything but a powerless bureaucrat anyway."

What can I do?
I made my bed, now I have to sleep in it.
How can I risk losing what little I have?
There's nowhere to go.
I'll get by somehow.


Sound familiar? Those are the sounds of resignation, of settling for the way things are, of putting up with jobs, relationships, and circumstances that are less than you desire—or deserve. In Carol's story you can practically hear the sound of car wheels spinning in the mud. The car won't move forward, it won't back out. You're afraid to abandon it and don't know which way to walk to find help. Not strong enough to push the car out of the mud, you hold no hope of being rescued. Frustrated, you push down harder on the accelerator and dig in deeper.

## STUCK IS ...

... seeing few or no alternatives to your current situation.

... allowing fear of failure, disappointment, rejection, loss, or change to keep you from taking risks.

... fatigue, depression, and decreased productivity—at first only in relation to the aspect you can't seem to change, but eventually in many areas of your life.

... complaining more often than you used to; seeing only the dark side, taking every opportunity to point out how bad things are; believing all available options are doomed to fail and rejecting them outright.

... starting projects, diets, exercise programmes, or any ful consideration or planning, pursuing the first alternative that presents itself.

... starting projects, diets, exercise programs, or any other self-improvement effort and abandoning it soon after you begin, halfway through or one step before you reach your goal.

STUCK IS FINDING YOURSELF BACK AT SQUARE ONE
(and wondering if you have the strength to start over).

Over a six-month period, a nationally franchised diet
centre's structured weight-loss programme helped Karen lose
thirty-five pounds. Less than a year later, the thirty-three-
year-old secretary has regained all thirty-five pounds and
returns to the diet centre. She sits across from a reed-thin
counsellor whom Karen sees as a slender, condescending
judge.

The counsellor closes the worn manila folder and peers
at Karen. "You were doing so well," she says. "What happened?"

Karen cringes. "I was completely humiliated to be in
that office at all. I was back at square one. Again. I could
hardly face the thought of another diet, and this lady—who
probably never dieted a day in her life—wants to know what
happened! The same thing that *always* happens. I diet. I lose
weight. I gain it back. It wasn't the first time. Sometimes I
think I should just give up, throw in the towel and resign
myself to being fat for the rest of my life. I looked at that
counsellor, with her collarbones and her skinny legs, and I
wanted to throw up my hands and admit that when it comes
to dieting, I'm a big, fat failure."

Overweight since childhood, Karen has tried many diets
and lost many pounds, only to regain them. Sometimes she
gets back on track before too much damage is done. Sometimes she puts on more pounds than she lost. She is well
aware of the health risks she faces by being overweight—
as well as the damage the yo-yo effect that going up and
down the scale can have. Her roller coaster ride of valiant
attempts and seemingly inevitable setbacks does considerable damage to her sense of self-worth and emotional well-
being.

Karen is bright, witty, and articulate, and her inability
to sustain a weight loss stands in direct contrast to her other
achievements. She has risen from the typing pool to being
an executive secretary, consistently receives high praise from

her boss, as well as large pay rises. Warm, caring, and open, Karen maintains supportive friendships, has close ties to her family, and pursues diverse interests. Her passions range from flower arranging to rock and roll music.

Yet, when she struggles to lose weight only to gain it back again, all successes are diminished in her mind. "None of the good things in my life seem as good when my weight is up. I lose my perspective. All I can see is the problem and what a weak, incompetent, unlovable person I must be because I can't get this one area under control."

Perhaps you never needed to, wanted to, or attempted unsuccessfully to lose weight, and Karen's *experience* seems foreign to you. Her *feelings* should be familiar, however. The emotions she feels crop up whenever anyone is stuck in any way. Perhaps you have tried to quit smoking, drinking, or biting your nails. You may have been determined to better manage your time, stop yelling at your children, patch up your relationship with your parents, or bring down your credit card balances. Maybe you've been telling yourself you *will* join a health club, take a course, or ask for a rise. You take the first steps toward your goal. You may even accomplish it temporarily. But for reasons that are often complicated and sometimes mysterious, you fall back into your old ways. You start smoking again, stop going to the health club, have another bitter argument with your parents (and swear hell will freeze over before you talk to them again), or get another call from the credit company because you once more exceeded your limit. You are right back where you started, and the prospect of beginning again is decidedly unappealing.

"When I'm stuck, I'm an emotional mess and hell to live with," Karen summarizes. "I look at thin people and resent them for being thin. When I see a thin person eating an ice cream cone or a huge Italian dinner while I'm munching on a dinner salad, I want to scream at them. I just want to scream. It's so unfair

"I feel sorry for myself all the time. Poor old Karen, she doesn't deserve this. I go crazy if anyone says anything about my weight. Anyone who tries to help me is a cruel, insensitive know-it-all as far as I'm concerned. Sometimes I get very down on myself and hole up in my house for days. Other times I tell myself being overweight doesn't bother me, but I'm not very convincing. What's the matter with me? In a word—I'm miserable."

In a word, being stuck can make you feel miserable. Being stuck someplace you have been before exaggerates the feelings and often makes getting unstuck even more difficult.

You may be stuck again at square one, wondering if you have the strength to try again. Or you may have postponed and procrastinated, letting something you want slip further and further from your grasp. Or you may be contemplating new or unexpected turns of events you do not know how to manage. Regardless of your unique and personal situation, being stuck feels lousy. It always does.

STUCK IS . . .

. . . feeling helpless, hopeless, worthless, frustrated, angry, trapped, or out of control.

. . . resenting people who possess what you want (but have not attained) and rejecting anyone who happens to notice or might inadvertently hit one of your sore spots.

. . . turning into a screaming meanie when anyone has the audacity to suggest you change, anyone you can conceivably blame for your present circumstances or whoever happens to be in the vicinity when you explode.

. . . becoming a relentless self-critic, hating and berating yourself for every flaw or failure, and convincing yourself you do not have what you want because you do not deserve it.

---

## STUCK IS COMING UP WITH AN INFINITE NUMBER OF "PERFECTLY GOOD REASONS" NOT TO CHANGE

"Basically, we stay together for the kids," says Len, a forty-year-old restaurateur. "I know you've probably heard that a million times before, but in our case it's true. My wife and I make a good parenting team. It's the one part of our marriage that works. We form a united front when it comes to the kids. We talk about their problems and go to school conferences together and show up at their football games. We both love our kids and they deserve to be raised by two parents."

But what does Len deserve? He is stuck in a loveless marriage with Anna. They sleep in separate beds. They talk to one another only when one of the children has a problem. Otherwise, their communication is restricted to bitter arguments—about money, household chores, Len's cigarette smoking, or Anna's latest affair. Arguments are followed by the silent treatment until some trouble with one of the kids forces them to face each other. It comes as no surprise that Len and Anna's children get into a lot of trouble.

Len and Anna married one week after Anna left school. According to Len, they were madly in love. According to Anna, marriage was her ticket out of her parents' home and she "might as well get it over with." She saw Len as "a nice enough guy with plenty of ambition for someone with only a high school education."

He was working as a chef's assistant at the restaurant where Anna waitressed, but he dreamed about opening a restaurant of his own one day. It would be their restaurant, a shared venture, and they had it planned right down to the shape of the menu, the silver pattern, and the decor. Len saw a bright future ahead of them.

"But all that got put on hold when Anna got pregnant," he explains. "We ended up having three children one right after the other. I worked two jobs and Anna stayed home with the kids."

They spent little time together. Most nights Len got home exhausted at two A.M. and fell into bed. To make it to his day job on time, Len left the house at six in the morning.

Anna felt trapped. She told Len she did not appreciate having no one to talk to but three toddlers. Thinking she would be happier if she could get out of the house more, Len bought Anna a car. She used it to go shopping. The balances on their credit cards reached their limits. Len worked harder.

"I couldn't figure out what she wanted from me," he says. "I was working flat out to pay our bills. I'd come home dead tired and she'd want to talk or have friends over for gourmet dinners. Of course, she expected me to cook. Or she'd want to go dancing. I wanted to spend my days off sleeping late, tinkering in the yard, and hanging out with the kids."

As he had done when Anna complained about being without a car, Len dealt with each marital crisis in a concrete manner. He realized Anna was bored and paid for her to take courses at a community college. But that wasn't enough. Anna had an affair, and Len left home briefly to live with his brother. Finally they sought the help of a marriage counsellor. During a session Anna asked what had happened to Len's ambition. Why hadn't they opened that restaurant? Len borrowed money from his parents and drained his savings to buy a small cafe in the seaside town where he had spent his summers as a boy. Going into therapy and opening the restaurant made sense to Len, but neither of these things improved his relationship with his wife.

"Your own restaurant eats up ten times as much of your time. The first year it was a headache twenty-four hours a day. In the beginning Anna was right there working with me. But after a while she lost interest. I guess I should have known she would."

Finally Len ran out of tangible measures to please Anna and resigned himself to his fate. Three years have passed since Len and Anna opened the restaurant. Little has changed. Len works long hours. Anna still has affairs. They've got used to their life. Len does not like it, but he sees no way to improve matters. He often wants to leave, but he always has plenty of reasons not to go.

"I guess an outsider can't understand why we stay

together, but we have our reasons," Len explains. "The kids are one big reason, and then there's the restaurant. On paper we're partners in the business, which means all kinds of messy legal ties. And we're up to our eyeballs in debt. We couldn't afford lawyers, let alone separate houses. If we split, she might as well forget about getting child support. You can't squeeze blood from a stone. Besides, I wouldn't want to lose the kids. Anna would probably move way with them and I'd never see them again. And it's not like we're the only unhappy couple around. After a while you get used to it. You find ways to get by."

Perhaps you are not deeply mired in a loveless marriage the way Len is. Maybe you are just teetering on the brink of a decision about changing careers or wondering if you should move to a bigger house. Len's problems seem so much bigger, but being stuck is *not* restricted to people in dire circumstances. Anytime you want or need to make a change—no matter how small—and can come up with a limitless supply of perfectly good reasons not to change, you can get stuck. Rarely do you come right out and say you do not *want* to change. Instead, you offer a perfectly logical, reasonable, legitimate argument for why you *cannot* change. Human beings have a remarkable talent for this type of circular, negative thinking, and it is one of the most obvious symptoms of being stuck.

STUCK IS . . .

. . . NEGATIVE THINKING. Your thoughts and conversations are overpopulated with phrases such as: I can't; it will never work; that won't make a difference; or I have no choice.

. . . UNDERESTIMATING YOURSELF. You believe you are not smart enough, pretty enough, strong enough, successful, powerful, rich, creative, or worthy enough to get what you really want.

. . . MINIMIZING YOUR SITUATION. You console yourself (and convince yourself not to change) with such half-hearted reassurances as: things are not so bad; other people have it worse; I should be grateful for what I have—I'll get by.

... MAGICAL THINKING. Magical thoughts are excuses in disguise. They usually begin with the phrase—"All my problems would be solved if only" ... if only you could win the lottery; if only your mother wasn't in a nursing home; if only your father had never abused you; if only you had not married so young and so on.

... ONE-TRACK THINKING. When you are stuck, an enormous amount of your time and energy is devoted to worrying about the problem. You put it under a microscope for closer, even narrower inspection. You go over with a fine-tooth comb every single thing you have ever done or said about this problem. You desperately try to find the reason for your present condition.

All variations of "stuck" thinking conspire to keep you stalemated. Rarely do you look up long enough to see solutions. So caught up in these thought patterns, you have little will or energy to change. If you're not careful, stuck can become a way of life.

---

### IF LIFE IS A JOURNEY, STUCK IS A DETOUR

Life is often compared to a journey, a road travelled from the day of your birth until the moment of your death. You set out on your journey intending to reach your destination. The road twists and turns, sometimes by choice, sometimes because unforeseen obstacles impede your progress. Occasionally you lose your way altogether. Everyone does.

You may get all packed and ready to go but never take the trip. You may set out hopefully but turn back at the first sign of stormy weather or get halfway to your destination and panic. Fear brings you to a standstill and you wonder if you truly want to continue the journey. You do not know exactly what lies ahead of you and worry that getting to where you are going might not make you happier. So you turn back or stay where you are. No matter which detour you take, you arrive at the same outcome. You find yourself someplace you did not plan and do not want to be—and you do not know how to get back on track. You are stuck.

How do you get off the track in the first place? Why do you turn off the main road? If life is a journey and your intention is to get to a particular place, how do you end up somewhere else?

Everyone who gets stuck does so because at least one, usually several, and sometimes all of the following eight barriers cause them to reroute, postpone, or abandon their journey. By the time you finish this book you will come to recognize each of the eight barriers. You will have the opportunity to confront them and you will be given the tools to overcome them. You will be able to change if that is what you choose to do.

**1.** LOW SELF-ESTEEM: Negative criticism, perceived failures, and trying to measure up to other people's standards damage your sense of self-worth and lead you to believe you do not deserve better or more than you have.

**2.** NOT SEEING ALTERNATIVES: Without options you have no place to go. Without the decision-making skills to choose options and follow through with a plan, you spin your wheels or slide back to square one.

**3.** NOT KNOWING WHAT YOU REALLY WANT: Confused by conflicting messages about what you should do and be, you let parents, preachers, High Street advertisers, or "The Joneses" set priorities for you. Without a clear sense of what *you* value, you lack the vision to accomplish your goals.

**4.** DEFENDING THE STATUS QUO: You fritter away the energy you have. You use much of it to defend your current position. Instead of setting a goal, plotting a course, and following a plan, you find perfectly good reasons *not* to change.

**5.** FEAR: The prospect of changing frightens you. Change

brings with it the possibility of failure, rejection, disappointment, and pain as well as the chance that getting what you *think* you want will not solve your problems after all. Fear causes you to sacrifice probable gain so you can avoid possible pain.

6. LACK OF CO-OPERATION: You stoically try to go it alone because you do not know where to look for help or you are reluctant to ask for the support of people who love you.

7. PERFECTIONISM: You want a guarantee. You want a perfect solution and a perfect unobstructed road to your goal (which also must yield perfect results). For you it's perfection or nothing. With that ultimatum, you can never achieve what you want.

8. LACK OF WILL: You cannot act on your desires or summon the energy needed to get you going and keep you moving all the way to your destination.

## GETTING BACK ON TRACK

If you are stuck now and particularly if you have been stuck for a while, you may not believe the ideas in this book, or for that matter, that any other ideas will help you get unstuck or lead the kind of life you want and deserve. Nothing anyone can say will convince you there is a light at the end of your tunnel.

Carol, Karen, Len, and other people whose personal experiences are included in other parts of this book were sceptical too. However, they agreed to set aside their doubts and defences so they could try to get unstuck. You will read about the progress they make. In a sense, they are on this journey with you.

If, at this moment, you cannot believe a light will appear at the end of your tunnel, I ask you to pretend it might. Try to remain open to the words you read. Work through the strategies for getting unstuck. If you become confused or sceptical or feel I am asking you to look at parts of yourself you'd rather not see, take a breather. Reread this chapter. Ask yourself if stuck is really what you want to be. Then try again. The brightness of that light, when it finally appears, may just surprise you.

When you are stuck, you tend to look at other people's lives with envy. You come to believe they have some special, magical, unattainable quality that allows them to get what they want out of life. You may think *they* can get unstuck, but *you* cannot. YOU CAN.

It is true that you may never sing as well as Tina Turner or be admired as much as Betty Ford. You may never be an international sports star, the chief executive officer of Chrysler Corporation, or as wealthy as John Paul Getty. You cannot have someone else's life, but you *can* have your life and you can make it different, more and better than it has ever been before. As Richard Bach writes in his book *Illusions,* "You are never given a wish without also being given the power to make it true. You may have to work for it, however."

You did not get stuck overnight. Life was not perfect one day and a horrible, ugly mess the next. You took your first detour a while ago, and it will take some time to wind your way back to the turning point that will take you to the road you want to travel. You may encounter your share of potholes, washed-out bridges, and fallen trees along the way, but you will be on your road and going where you want to go. You can get beyond those obstacles if you work at dismantling them. Be patient. Be resolute. Remember what stuck feels, looks, and sounds like. Ask yourself if stuck is where you want to stay.

# 2

# *Why Change?*

Change. If you made a list of words easier said than done, "change" would top it. One syllable, six letters, meaning *to alter, vary, or make different,* the word "change" elicits a broad spectrum of conflicting emotions from anyone who hears it. What happens to you when you think about change? What are the first words or images that come to mind?

Several years ago, an educator at Kent State University posed that very question to a group of teacher-training students. She asked them to jot down their immediate, uncensored reactions to the idea of change and then collected the folded slips of paper bearing their anonymous responses. She unfolded one slip of paper, then another, then another. The word she saw most gave her quite a shock. A full seventy-five percent of her students thought of death when they heard the word "change."

Why so many students associated change with something as final and frightening as death was never explained to the educator's satisfaction. However, she did learn her students believed change did happen *to them,* and that it was rarely, if ever, *chosen* by them. They adapted because they *had* to, not because they *wanted* to. In most cases change seemed to have been forced upon them, and they most frequently made changes when there was a tangible reward for their action or a punishment to avoid. All agreed that even when the result was positive, change itself was painful, and they probably would have chosen not to change if they could have got away with it.

These young adults viewed change dimly. I must admit at various times in my life I shared their perspective. People of all ages and from all walks of life whom I have taught, counselled, or engaged in casual conversation, almost universally believe change is difficult at best, and certainly well worth postponing or preventing if at all possible.

At first glance, change may seem to be a reasonable proposition. What could be better than abandoning unhealthy habits, altering an unfulfilling relationship, deviating from the same dull routines, accepting new challenges or work to improve the quality of your life? The results of change can only leave us better off than we were before. So why do we dread change? What is our problem with it? How did change get such a bad reputation?

We can learn something about our aversion to change by looking at what motivates people to finally change. I spoke to several friends and colleagues who had successfully changed their lives or altered specific habits and patterns. I asked them why they changed. Here are their responses:

"I cleaned up my act the day I got out of the hospital," explains Jacob, the owner of a small, specialized publishing company. At the age of thirty-seven he had a heart attack.

"My heart attack was one heck of an eye-opener. When the pain started, I thought for sure I was about to die, and it scared the hell out of me. I swore, if I lived, I'd change my ways and I did. No more cigarettes. No more wolfing down fried chicken or bologna sandwiches with extra mayonnaise. I don't work every weekend any more or get angry at every little thing that goes wrong. Hell, I'm downright mellow these days. All because of that heart attack. You might say it scared me right onto the straight and narrow."

"Looking back now, it's pretty obvious my life wasn't working," Cindy, a thirty-year-old public relations director, recalls. "Actually, I didn't have much of a life at all. I worked sixty hours a week. If I wasn't holed up in a mouldy subbasement office listening to the people who shared it scream at each other, I was baby-sitting clients and recuperating from the latest crisis. Everyone was dumping on me: co-workers, friends, my family. My love life was the pits. You name it and it was going wrong. But it never occurred to me to *do* anything about any of it.

"Then, out of nowhere—or so I thought—I started having these attacks, panic attacks I guess you'd call them. I would hyperventilate and cry and feel like my head was going to explode. I thought I was going crazy and I was willing to do *anything* to stop feeling that way."

"Anger. Anger and frustration *made* me change," Lisa claims. "It was straight out of the movie *Network*. I was mad as hell and I wasn't going to take it anymore."

Lisa worked as a sales representative for an office supply company. Constantly given the most difficult territories to cover, she received no recognition for work well done. She was promised rises she never received. She was not considered for promotions.

"They brought in a guy who didn't know the first thing about office supplies and paid him twice what I was making. He would make messes and I would clean them up. He'd cover up his mistakes by lying and saying I had done things I not only didn't do, but didn't even know about. When I went over his head to complain, the sales manager made me look like the bad guy."

Lisa put up with the situation for over a year. It got worse and worse. She got angrier and angrier.

"God, I drove my husband crazy," she sighs. "Then one day something happened—something that wasn't even that big a deal—and I lost it. I quit on the spot. It was not the most rational, intelligent way to handle things. I was unemployed, didn't have a clue about where I would go or what I would do. The next six months were a nightmare, but eventually I got it together."

Nina and Terry are a married couple—she is a therapist and he is the executive director of a professional organization. They are expecting their first child. Everyone who knows them thinks theirs is the ideal relationship. Life was not always so idyllic, however.

"We came very, very close to having no relationship at all," says Nina. "We'd been living together for seven years and Terry wanted to get married. I still wasn't sure. We talked about going into therapy together, but I kept putting it off. I thought I wanted things too stay the way they were. Terry didn't think the way things were was good enough. I literally did not hear what he was trying to tell me until he said he didn't see any point in staying in the relationship if it wasn't going anywhere. If I wasn't willing to work on the relationship, and if I still wanted an easy escape route, he figured we might as well end it right then and there. The possibility of losing Terry suddenly became very real to me. The scales tipped. The idea of not being in a relationship with Terry seemed a whole lot worse than making the changes that really did need to be made.

▉///////

"I *had* to change. I had no choice but to change," says Marilyn, a forty-year-old divorced registered nurse. "At the time I thought of it as 'coping.' "

When Marilyn's husband announced he was leaving her, she was taken by surprise. She was completely unprepared to go on living without him.

"I didn't have any idea of what he was up to. I didn't see it coming. I thought I'd be this happily married housewife forever. But there I was. No husband. Three children growing like weeds and eating like horses and the child-support cheques coming in whenever my ex-husband felt like sending them—which needless to say was not on a regular basis. I was a mess.

"I'd been out of the work force for twelve years. Nursing had changed drastically since the last time I set foot in a hospital. But I couldn't sit around the house and mope forever, although I did do that for a while. There were bills to pay and my kids were depending on me, so I got up off my duff and put my life back together again. It wasn't easy and it wasn't fun. Things are pretty good now. But I didn't get here because I wanted to. Like I said, I had no choice. I did what I had to do."

## COMMON METHODS FOR CHANGE

The experiences that Jacob, Cindy, Lisa, Nina and Terry, and Marilyn had represent some of the most common reasons people change. While their approaches to change work, they may not be the most healthy ways of accomplishing it. Their lives are, however, better than they were before they changed. They abandoned old habits, resolved longstanding problems, improved relationships, expanded their horizons, and regained their balance after experiencing various setbacks.

Other than the benefits they experienced, the reasons

they gave for changing have several other elements in common. In fact, when most of us deal with change, we're likely to approach it in one or more of these ways:

### Scared Straight

When Jacob had his heart attack, he took the scared straight route to change. He was shocked into altering his work habits and lifestyle by a life-threatening experience.

When you change for this reason, you generally do so after years of self-defeating behaviour and repeated warnings from doctors, friends, and family members—pleas and threats that fall upon deaf ears. To be scared straight is to come within an inch of losing your life, home, family, job, sanity, or freedom. The crisis—in whatever form it takes—is so big, so obvious, so painful, and so frightening, you are thrust forward from a dead stop and compelled to change.

### Crying "Enough"

It was not one event, but the cumulative effect of stress, overwork, and underappreciation that led to Cindy's panic attacks—she experienced physical clues that told her she needed to change, clues that caused much pain and discomfort. She reached her limit and became willing to change. Her body simply "cried enough."

We all cry "enough" eventually. We change our lives, behaviours, and attitudes because we can no longer endure the feelings or pay the physical and emotional price of staying the way we are or have always been.

### The Straw That Breaks the Camel's Back

Like crying "enough", this approach to change resembles Chinese water torture. For Lisa, one unappreciated success after another filled a bucket full of anger until it overflowed. One last relatively minor upset with the sales manager triggered a chain reaction. The change Lisa avoided for so long was made impulsively and was followed by a painful period of putting back together the pieces of her life.

When you change in a burst of anger because you've experienced the proverbial straw that breaks the camel's back, you initially regret your decision—if it really was a decision rather than simply a reaction. You suffer through self-recrimination and wonder what you could have done differently before finally looking forward and improving your life.

### Dreading the Alternative

Nina summarized this approach well when she said, "The scales tipped." They tipped in the direction of change because the alternative, losing Terry, was so unappealing.

This reason to change comes into play whenever you've trapped yourself into a corner, your back against the wall. You can no longer postpone, avoid, or resist change because the very real consequence of staying the same will cause more distress than the imagined cost of conducting your life differently. You change to avoid the dreaded alternative.

### Disaster Relief, or Life Is Too Short

Marilyn said she changed because she had no other choice. When her husband left her, she saw herself as a victim of circumstance who had to cope with an event she could neither anticipate nor control. She literally was forced to change.

Perhaps you have found yourself in a similar situation. Job layoffs, natural disasters, divorces, ageing parents who come to live with you, prolonged illness, car accidents—life is full of unforeseen, unprepared-for events. You rarely have any choice but to cope with the aftermath.

The students described at the beginning of this chapter immediately identified disaster relief as the reason to change. This method works, though it also is one of the most painful approaches to change.

Sometimes people change because of a disaster or loss experienced by someone other than themselves.

Let's say "good old Joe" has a heart attack, gets a divorce, loses a loved one, or gets a serious illness. Sympathy for "good old Joe" gives way to realizing that similar misfortune could as easily descend upon you. "Life is too short," you think, and you take action to make the positive changes you were putting off for another day.

All of these approaches to change are effective. They are the reasons most of us finally get around to improving our lives. Unfortunately, they also involve:

POSTPONING, RESISTING, AND AVOIDING CHANGE FOR AS LONG AS YOU POSSIBLY CAN. You wait to change until *not* changing is intolerable. In the interim, considerable damage is done to yourself, other people, and your relationships.

A PRECIPITATING EVENT. A tragedy, trauma, confrontation, or disaster must happen to you before you change. Your life improves, but you believe change was not *your* choice. It was an inescapable reaction to circumstances beyond your control.

PAIN AND SUFFERING. These generally—and mistakenly—are assumed to be absolutely necessary anytime a change occurs.

## THE MYTH OF CHANGE

I am sure at some time in your life you have heard someone say, "You have to hit bottom before you can climb back up to the top." This widely accepted misconception implies you have to grovel, suffer, and lose all hope before you will be able to change to improve yourself and your life. The myth convinces you to wait until a situation is awful and intolerable before you do anything to make it better. And because we have such negative reactions to change, we often convince ourselves that "things really are not so bad." We create our own ready-made excuse not to change.

I have a pleasant surprise for you. Nowhere is it written that you must suffer terribly before you change. In many instances you need not suffer at all, and you certainly do *not* have to endure prolonged pain, frustration, or uncertainty.

Hitting bottom is what *you* make it. The bottom does not have to be the gutter or the coronary care unit. It need not be a welfare line or a psychiatric ward. Bottom is the place and the moment *you* decide you want to be happier, healthier, more creative, successful, or fulfilled than you already are. When you want to get unstuck and move forward, you have to hit your own bottom line and be prepared to rise above it. You can choose to *choose* to change, and you can begin *whenever* you please.

## SO . . . WHY WAIT?

Before you picked up this book, you probably had changed many times over. Perhaps you've been through a job or career change or had to readjust your life at home to the presence of your new baby. However you have experienced change, you know what it feels like. You may not have enjoyed it while you were going through it, but after it was over, you'd successfully altered your life—didn't you feel terrific? Didn't you feel a wonderful sense of satisfaction, pleasure, and pride? From your new perspective, didn't all that avoidance and resistance seem utterly ridiculous?

After I accomplish what I set out to do, I always ask myself why on earth I fought change. Why did I think I could not change? Why did I wait so long?

I tell myself, "Next time I won't wait as long." I'll find a reason to change *before* disaster strikes or my feelings become unbearable or I'm backed into a corner and think I have no choice but to change. To do that, I need some new answers to the question—"Why change?"

---

## A LOOK AT THE REST OF YOUR LIFE

One new answer to the question "Why change?" can be found in the following values clarification strategy.

On a blank sheet of paper, draw a horizontal line from one edge of the paper to the other like this:

---

This line represents your life. To signify when your life began, place an X on the left end of the line and write the year of your birth underneath it.

Now let me ask you a rather threatening question. How long do you plan to live? To age seventy-five or one hundred or even older? Maybe living to the age of fifty or sixty is all you can imagine.

Whatever you decide, place an X on the right end of the line, and beneath it, write the year you plan to die.

It is not a random, casual choice of words to use the phrase "plan to die," because at some subtle level we do indeed plan our deaths—by the way we plan our living.

Now, at the appropriate spot on the line, place an X to represent the present, and underneath it, write the present year. My lifeline looks like this:

X                         X                         X
───────────────────────────────────────────────────
**1927**                  1987                      **?**

This book was written in 1987 when I was sixty years old and had lived over half my years, so you can see where I placed 1987 on my lifeline. Your X for the present may be at a different point on the line depending on how long you have already lived and how much longer you plan to live.

Draw a deep arc below the line between the present and the year you plan to die.

X                         X                         X
───────────────────────────────────────────────────
**1927**                  1987                      **?**

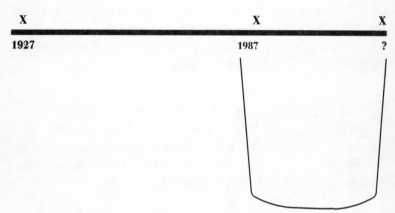

This arc is like a basket or net representing the years you have left to live. It can be filled with all the opportunities, challenges, joys, and experiences still ahead of you. Ask yourself the following questions and list your answers in your lifeline net. Use any other space on the page if you need it.

- What do I want to do with the life I have left to live?

- What do I want to experience?

- What do I want to witness?

- What do I want to learn?

- What do I want to be part of?

- What do I want to change, shape, leave better than I found it?

- In short, what do I want to do for the rest of my life?

I love to watch people in my workshops fill in the rest of their lives. Some have few things they can say they want to do, experience, or become. Others have many visions for the future. However they choose to fill in their lifeline baskets, I simply enjoy watching them discover or rediscover things about themselves that may eventually provide them with the impetus to change. With the lifeline net you can begin to create your own "bottom line."

When Janet, a therapist, completed the lifeline strategy, she found her net overflowing with fun, playful, and wonderous activities, many of which she felt she'd missed out on during her childhood and the years she spent being a wife, mother, and full-time member of the work force.

"I started working when I was fifteen," Janet explains. "I thought feeling good came from keeping busy. Those times I wasn't working, when I was home with babies or towards the end of a pregnancy, I always felt sort of empty."

As the years passed and her children grew older and more self-sufficient, Janet filled her life with work and more work. She went back to school to get a master's degree in counselling while taking care of her family. She did not quit her full-time job until her private therapy practice could sustain her. Afraid she would not have enough work, she led workshops and taught courses at the local YMCA and several community colleges. Before she knew it, every minute from seven in the morning until eleven at night was scheduled and consumed by work.

"I was surprised by what I found in my lifeline net," she recalls. "Everything I wrote down had to do with fun and leisure and having space and time for myself. I wanted to laugh and play and dance and sing. I wanted to have fun and do all sorts of childlike things I'd never let myself do before. It dawned on me that working so much had less to do with feeling good than with not having time to feel anything at all. I had become a workaholic."

To experience the things in her net, Janet would have to let go of other things to make room for what she wanted to do. She decided to change her life so she could work less and play more. This would involve using her time more efficiently and saying no to work she felt obligated to do, but which neither payed well nor fulfilled her. She would have to stop seeing clients on Saturday, regardless of the loss of income, and get up the nerve to ask people to accompany her to places her stay-at-home husband would not go.

"It's never too late to have a happy childhood," she decided, and she took the first step on a journey to create the life she truly wanted to live.

Regardless of what or how much you put into your lifeline net, those hopes, dreams, and plans will help you discover the answer to the question, "Why change?"

You'll want to change so you can have and do all those things you put in your net, so—from this day forward—you can live your life the way you really want to live it.

---

## OVERALL WELLNESS

To move closer to a state of being known as overall wellness is another relatively painless reason to change.

Overall wellness is more than physical or even mental

health. It is an active process, a style of living that promotes physical, intellectual, emotional, and spiritual well-being and satisfaction. Overall wellness speaks to the *quality* of life and also to a *passion* for living.

When you work towards overall wellness, you:

1. Get enough TIME ALONE—time to meditate, relax, reflect, daydream, or be still. You manage to "stop the world" for a little while and get some distance from its frantic pace.

2. Exercise and are conscious of good NUTRITION, controlling what you consume, ingest, or inhale.

3. Have at least one GOOD LISTENER in your life. Whether a professional counsellor or a close friend, this person hears what you have to say and helps you gain an objective view of the world and make decisions. A good listener offers comfort, compassion, alternatives, or a gentle push in the right direction when you are stuck.

4. EXERCISE on a regular basis.

5. Participate in a solid SUPPORT GROUP. The purpose of the support group can be professional or personal. It can meet formally and on a regular basis or casually and occasionally. A support group lets you know there are other people whose concerns are similar to your own and gives you the benefit of other people's viewpoints and experiences.

6. Have a satisfying INTIMATE RELATIONSHIP built on mutual respect and understanding.

7. Employ effective TIME MANAGEMENT techniques to avoid feeling overwhelmed and to make time for the things you want to do as well as the things you have to do.

8. Maintain a sense of PRODUCTIVITY and accomplishment by pursuing challenging work, hobbies, and/or interests.

**9.** Take RISKS and stretch your limits physically, intellectually, and emotionally.

**10.** COMMUNICATE your wants and needs as well as say no to what you do not want or need.

To determine where you stand in terms of overall wellness, take a personal inventory.

On a blank sheet of paper, draw a grid similar to the one shown on page 34 and write in the ten wellness dimensions as I have done.

In the first column, check off the items you have in your life right now.

In the second column, give yourself a rating on a one-to-ten scale (ten is high) based on the amount or quality of each item as it is included in your life right now (e.g., if you have a great deal of high-quality time alone, give that item an eight, nine, or ten. If you rarely get time alone and don't know how to use it when you have it, time alone would get a much lower rating).

In the third column, put a capital *M* beside the items you would like to have more of in your life; a lower-case *m* beside those you would like to increase slightly or improve a little; and an *S* beside those you would like to stay the same. Try not to labour over each of the points for a long time—the important thing is to be honest.

In the fourth column, rank in order all ten dimensions according to how important each item is to your feelings of overall wellness. The number one would go to the most important dimension, the number two to the next most important, and so on down to ten.

In the fifth column, choose the dimensions you would most like to change or improve. Then rank your choices—putting the letter *A* beside the area you would like to work on first, the letter *B* beside the item you would work on next, and so on until each dimension you wish to change or improve has a priority.

| | | | | |
|---|---|---|---|---|
| 1. Time Alone | | | | |
| 2. Nutrition | | | | |
| 3. A Good Listener | | | | |
| 4. Exercise | | | | |
| 5. Support Group | | | | |
| 6. Intimate Relationship | | | | |
| 7. Time Management | | | | |
| 8. Productivity | | | | |
| 9. Risks | | | | |
| 10. Communication | | | | |

Harry, a freelance photographer, is no stranger to change. Five years ago he sold his thriving printing and graphic design business. He packed his van and spent ten months travelling, ultimately settling along the coast where he bought a house and fitted it with a darkroom and studio. He creates photo-art and sells his wares during the spring and summer at art and craft festivals. Frequently, corporate officers and wealthy home-owners hire him to create dozens of pieces to decorate their offices or homes.

At the time he completed his overall wellness strategy, Harry was satisfied and comfortable with his life. He loved his work, enjoyed where he was living, and looked forward to each new day. He felt no pressing urge or painful need to change, but he did the inventory anyway.

"I must say I learned a thing or two about myself," Harry reflected afterward. "Even though I was pretty happy with the way things were going, there was still room for improvement. I saw I could be even happier if I worked on some of the areas on the inventory."

Nutrition and exercise got low rankings in terms of the amount and quality of each in Harry's life. At first glance he didn't think they were very important to his feelings of overall wellness.

"But I thought about it and realized I didn't think they were important because if I did, I would have to do something about them. I had a feeling I'd feel better physically if I quit smoking and cut down on my beer drinking and got those lazy muscles toned up again. When it came around to deciding what I wanted to change, I gave those things a high priority. I was pretty confident I could change those areas of my life."

He was less confident when it came to doing something about the dimension he rated most important to his overall wellness and most lacking in his present life—an intimate relationship. It was the area he most wanted to change.

"I didn't see it as a problem, exactly," Harry explains. "I still don't. I mean, I'm not going to die or anything if I don't meet someone tomorrow. I have women friends and I date. But I don't have what you'd call a real love relationship with anyone. I used to say I was waiting for the right girl to come along. But I don't know exactly what I mean by 'the right girl.'

"Whoever she is, she sure isn't going to come knocking on my door. I have to get out more for one thing, meet more people, do something to get to know the women I'm attracted to instead of waiting to get hit by a bolt of lightning or something."

No dire circumstance forced Harry to change. His life was okay the way it was. However, he saw how life could be better and decided he wanted to make it that way.

By now you should have a clearer picture of what the "good life" looks like. With the overall wellness inventory you pinpointed the areas in which you can change your life for the better. Plus you've found another answer to the question "Why change?"—to enhance the quality of your life and increase your passion for living.

## OVERCOMING CONFLICT AND CONFUSION

Yet another answer to the question "Why change?" is found in the conflicts and confusions that arise in your life. Areas of conflict and confusion are varied and numerous—in fact, any aspect of daily living can be puzzling, uncomfortable, or frustrating at times. Some common areas where conflict and confusion are experienced include:

| | |
|---|---|
| family | finances |
| work | child rearing |
| marriage | diet |
| dependencies | aging |

| | |
|---|---|
| education | sexuality |
| love | friendship |
| race | gender |

Anything posing questions with few easy answers and having the potential to produce stress and dissatisfaction is an area of conflict and confusion.

Lorraine looked up from her duties as superwife and mother and saw her fortieth birthday approaching. Her three children were in school and getting more self-sufficient with each passing day. In a couple of years the oldest would be leaving the nest to attend college. Lorraine's husband had just started a new business—a venture that she was neither equipped for nor interested in pursuing herself.

"I was anticipating a mid-life crisis," Lorraine concludes. "I had one identity. I was wife and mummy. But my children were growing up. They didn't need a full-time mummy anymore. Pretty soon that identity was going to be obsolete all together. Indeed something else. I needed to decide who I was and what I was."

Actually, Lorraine did more than stay at home with the kids. She was a volunteer counsellor at a mental health centre and a certified Parent Effectiveness Training (PET) instructor. These roles caused her conflict and confusion as well.

"I was limited because I didn't have a college degree," she explains. "I saw people who didn't know as much as I did doing work I knew I could do. But they got the jobs and I didn't because they had degrees. I really went along with that mentality. I started believing I wasn't good enough because I didn't have an education or a piece of paper to prove I wasn't stupid."

Before her conflict and confusion about losing her comfortable identity as a mother and being limited by her lack of education reached crisis proportions, Lorraine decided to work on both issues by going back to school—to get a master's degree in social work and start a private counselling practice.

When one area of your life isn't working as well as it could—whether you realize that you're more out of shape than you thought you were or feel that you aren't communicating as well as you could with your family—you *can* take action to fix it. If you're experiencing conflict and confusion, you can act to cure what ails you. You can locate and understand the source of your discomfort and relieve that discomfort before it becomes intolerable pain, before the situation backs you into a corner and forces you to change.

Whether the reason to change is found by completing a lifeline strategy, taking an overall wellness inventory, or examining the areas of conflict and confusion in your life, you can freely choose to change and begin *now* to improve your life. You can, after considering your alternatives and their consequences, choose to do whatever is necessary to live a happier, healthier, less stressful, and more fulfilling life. You can make that choice today.

## OKAY . . . THEN WHAT?

Janet, Harry, and Lorraine chose to change. They made their decisions *before* fear, pain, anger, dreaded alternatives, or unforeseen and unpleasant events compelled them to change. Because desperation did not colour their choices when they embarked upon the road to a better life, they were one step ahead of those people who didn't recognize that change was essential.

This one-step advantage made their journey a little bit easier. However, they by no means experienced fair weather and smooth sailing on their voyage to change.

If making one decision was all it took to create a better life, you would never get stuck. This would be a very short book and you would not be reading it. Deciding to change, what to change, and when to change is a step in the right direction, but only the first step. You know this from past experience. Maybe you've already realized on some level that you want to change an aspect of your life, but when it comes right down to it, you can't seem to follow through.

Having made a decision, you embark upon the road to change only to find it a veritable obstacle course. Signs flash warnings of danger ahead. You begin to doubt the choice you made. Faceless monsters lurk in the shadows and tell you to turn back. Huge solid barriers block your path.

The obstacles, barriers, and monsters are of your own making. Years and years of believing change to be horribly painful and extremely difficult taught you some ingenious methods for resisting, avoiding, and blocking change. You constructed elaborate barriers to protect yourself from the suffering you believed change would bring you. You are not a bad person because you protected yourself from possible pain, and you are not the only one with self-made obstacles blocking change. Everyone has them.

However, now that you have decided to change and want to improve your life, you must push through the blocks to change. You cannot allow them to impede your progress.

The eight most common blocks to change are the focus of the remainder of this book. They are tricky and complicated obstacles, but they are not insurmountable. The most important thing to remember is that "impossible" is *not* part of the vocabulary of this book. If you think carefully about each of the barriers and determine that you can change, you'll be well on your way to a more rewarding and fulfilling life. In fact, you've already taken the first step.

# 3

# Change and Self-esteem

When introduced in the previous chapter, Harry, a freelance photographer, had completed an Overall Wellness inventory and decided he wanted a satisfying love relationship. Hoping ultimately to marry and raise a family, Harry wants to meet a woman he can "trust, talk to, and be myself with. Someone I'm attracted to sexually and feel comfortable with a lot of the time." He seeks intimacy and a partner with whom to share his triumphs and tragedies.

Steven, a thirty-one-year-old plumbing contractor, also wants to find someone to love and to love him. He too hopes to marry and have children, although he expresses his desire differently than Harry does.

"I'm not very good at relationships," he says after reviewing his own Overall Wellness inventory. "My friends say I get involved with the wrong women who play on my guilt and are 'on at me' all the time about everything I say or do. But I'm as much to blame. I think I hold back. I'm moody and I do spend a lot of time with my friends and my family and working on my business. If I was a different man, I'd be married by now or at least living with someone."

Both Harry and Steven want satisfying relationships. Does one have a better chance of getting what he wants? A closer look at each man reveals the answer and the effect of the first barrier—BELIEVING YOU DO NOT DESERVE BETTER.

---

## HARRY

When asked to describe himself, Harry lists many positive attributes. Among other things, he believes himself to be an intelligent conversationalist, a compassionate friend, a good photographer, a socially conscious person, an avid reader, and "someone who can deal with the weirdness of freelance work—where no two days are the same. You have to discipline yourself to get the job done because no one is looking over your shoulder to make sure you produce." Additionally, Harry believes he has a good, if somewhat offbeat, sense of humour, the right amount of ambition, talent, healthy curiosity, a sense of adventure, and "a good idea of what I can accomplish and guts enough to try."

"I'm not perfect by any stretch of the imagination," he says, laughing. "I'm stuck with this short, sort of flabby body and I'm losing my hair. I get very absentminded when I'm working on a big photo assignment, and housekeeping isn't one of my strong points. Get me going on a topic I care about, and I'll talk your ear off, especially if I've had a few drinks. But even with my faults, most mornings I look in the mirror and like what I see."

There are changes Harry wants to make and ways he wants to improve himself. He wants to exercise more often, cut down on his drinking, and of course, have a satisfying, mutually supportive love relationship. He does not think less

of himself for what he does not have or has not done yet.
He believes he is capable of change and worthy of the best
life can offer.

"I'm the guy who sold his thriving business and lived
on the road in my van for ten months, remember?" Harry
points out. "If I could take that risk and come out better than
I was before, I reckon I can do plenty of other things when I
set my mind to it. No doubt about it, these changes are going
to take some work, but they're doable and I owe it to myself
to try."

## STEVEN

To a casual observer Steven seems the more stable and
successful of the two men and the better candidate for a
long-term love relationship.

A tall, handsome, sensitive man, he has many close, loyal
friends and owns a comfortable fifty-year-old home that he
has equipped with many luxury items. He impresses others
as being reasonably ambitious, levelheaded, and thoughtful—
a man who has achieved financial success and personal stability at a relatively early age.

Steven sees himself differently, however, and in a far less
positive light.

"I'm still waiting for the day when I'll feel like I'm good
enough," Steven claims. "I'm always trying to make up for
what I lack and running to catch up with myself. I've felt that
way all my life. I was never as smart as my older sister. I wasn't
as outgoing as my younger sister or as sure of myself as all
my friends seemed to be. I did dumb things without thinking
and got caught every time I messed up.

"As far back as I can remember, I either thought everything I did was wrong or felt like I was missing something. I
never measured up."

In Steven's mind, his business success is overshadowed
by the opportunities he believes he missed and the mistakes

he thinks he made. No matter how good things are, they could have been better if only he were more organized, efficient, decisive, or disciplined. He points to several friends who are millionaires at age thirty. He tends to forget they inherited wealth or holdings in existing companies.

Steven derives little pleasure from his achievements and often feels guilty about the good things that happen to him. When things go wrong, however, he is quick to accept the blame. There is always something he should have seen coming or done differently. He is not sure why people like him as much as they do.

"I guess I try harder to be a nice guy and do whatever they want me to," he says. "That way they put up with my moods and wishy-washiness."

Holding such a low opinion of himself, Steven is rarely content and suffers bouts of severe depression. Doubting his capabilities and questioning his self-worth, he sees every glass as half empty rather than half full, and he unwittingly creates situations that verify his doubts. His past relationships are a good example.

In the past Steven became involved with women who were needy, demanding, and whose self-esteem was even lower than his own. They wanted him to change. They wanted him to stop everything and fill the empty spaces in their own lives. They harped and nagged and told him that he wasn't good enough. As a result, Steven felt guilty. He felt more inadequate and unlovable. Yet he prolonged those relationships even though all he got from them was more evidence of his unworthiness.

"I don't know if I've got what it takes to be in a good love relationship," he sums things up. "I know exactly what kind of woman I'm looking for, but I can't believe that that kind would want me."

Both Harry and Steven want the same thing. They both have a great deal to offer another human being. Harry, however, sees himself as lovable. Steven does not. Harry thinks he can find and build a love relationship. Steven does not. Harry believes he deserves better. Steven does not.

Although Steven is more physically attractive, more settled, and more financially secure than Harry, Harry has a far
better chance of finding the relationship he wants and changing in any way he chooses. Because Steven believes he does
not deserve a terrific love relationship and that he is incapable
of having one, it is likely that he will continue to make poor
choices (when he chooses at all). He will sabotage his own happiness by seeing only what he is missing instead of what he
has or could have. It is highly unlikely he will get what he wants.

Steven is stuck. To get unstuck he must deal with barrier
number one—believing you do not deserve better.

---

## BARRIER NUMBER ONE

Believing you do not deserve better is the bottom-line
block to change. More debilitating than the pain and confusion of your present circumstances might be, it stands in
the way of even your most sincere desire to change. It prevents you from clearing other obstacles from your path. No
matter what you say you want, you will not get unstuck
unless you *believe* you deserve a better life and are capable
of change.

Like The Little Engine That Could in the timeless children's story of the same name, to reach any destination you
must chug along chanting "I think I can, I think I can, I *know*
I can." If barrier number one has a hold on you, you do not
approach life or change with such positive thinking.

Barrier number one has a voice of its own. It loudly and
persistently shouts a different kind of message. It insists, "No
you can't. You are not good enough, smart enough, strong
enough, pretty enough. You simply *are not enough.* You had
better take what you can get."

That nasty little voice may sound like a parent, a teacher,
a former lover, or your ex-husband or ex-wife. They were
the critics who first implied you did not and would never

measure up. Nowadays the voice is your own. You have come to believe you are unworthy, unlovable, and deserving of the fate life deals you—and nothing more.

This barrier's effect on your life is clearer and easier to see than any other. If you think you cannot change, you will not. If you think you are not worthy of life's riches, you will settle for the crumbs tossed your way. If you do not believe you deserve better, you will find no will, energy, or reason to try for more. By virtue of your self-proclaimed inadequacies, you think you are meant to be stuck and cannot get unstuck.

## HOW THIS BARRIER WORKS

In the past few years you probably have read newspaper or magazine articles, seen movies, or watched television programmes about battered spouses. You may know someone who is in an abusive relationship or have personal experience in this area.

More often than not, the battered spouse (wife *or* husband) puts up with mind-boggling physical violence and humiliation and stays with the abuser for years and years after the abuse begins. In many instances the victim never gets out of the relationship and takes no significant action to stop the attacks. Why? Often, the victim's poor economic situation will keep him or her stuck. Social scientists have many other theories, as well. But when all is said and done, it boils down to one very powerful reason. In addition to inflicting physical injury, domestic violence destroys its victim's sense of self-worth. The self-esteem of a battered spouse is so low, she comes to believe she deserves what is happening to her.

Believing you do not deserve better is most clearly seen in what you *do not do.* You do not change, and no outside force can move you to change—not even a physical threat to your survival.

Barrier number one does its dirty work in several dangerous and deceptive ways. Here are the most common outcomes of believing you do not deserve better.

**1.** Underestimating your capabilities and chances for success, *you persuade yourself not to attempt change.*

In the opening chapter of this book, Carol, the social worker spinning her wheels at her job, says, "Maybe I'm not capable of being anything but a little bureaucrat." For so long a cog in the bureaucractic machinery, Carol downplays her talent as a therapist and forgets her past success working with children and families. Defeated and undermined by "the system," she accepts her fate as inevitable. Each time she considers a career change, her heart races with fear. Assuming she will drown if she attempts to move through unfamiliar waters, she stands still—and stuck.

Barrier number one warps your perception of yourself and steals your self-confidence. By viewing yourself in this barrier's mirrors—which reflect only flaws and inadequacies—you become a lousy judge of your own ability. Stuck and disliking yourself for being stuck, you minimize or forget every past success while magnifying every failure, as though it had just happened. To avoid another possible failure you unwittingly sacrifice probable success.

**2.** Fearing others will see you the way you see yourself, *you overcompensate for your perceived inadequacies,* producing stress and stress-related illnesses.

As described in Chapter Two, Cindy, a public relations director, attempted to change her life only after she was plagued by mysterious panic attacks. A five-foot-two-inch bundle of energy, Cindy was rarely seen without a smile on her face and never uttered an unkind word about anyone. Mixing an unflappable sense of humour with perfect comic timing, Cindy won people over with her charm and wit. Creative, efficient, and hardworking, she entered the public relations field as a novice and in two years time, became the consummate professional, one highly respected by famous and powerful members of the entertainment industry. At twenty-five she bought her own home.

As far as Cindy was concerned, however, her success was a cheat. Underneath those smiles, behind all that hard work and upbeat energy, she believed there lived a certifiable nothing. She was petrified people would discover she was not at all nice or creative or funny or competent.

"I worked twice as hard so no one would find out I was only half as good," she explains. "I was always cute, funny, and amusing so no one would see I wasn't particularly bright or interesting. I forced myself to be outgoing. But I was really so shy and scared of rejection that I became physically sick before press parties or show openings."

Seeking from others the approval she would not grant herself, Cindy put up with depressed, argumentative, and hypercritical colleagues who repeatedly imposed upon her, a boyfriend who took her for granted and saw her only when he felt like it, friends who dumped on her, and family members who used her as a scapegoat.

"Until I got into therapy, I never expressed a negative emotion. I never got angry. I never seriously thought anyone was treating me unfairly. I denied it all. I was just grateful to have got so far with the little I thought I had going for me."

The more she achieved, as the gap grew wider between how she saw herself and how other people saw Cindy, her fear of being uncovered as the fraud she believed herself to be reached overwhelming proportions. She worked twelve-to sixteen-hour days. She came home, took the phone off the hook, and stared glassy-eyed at the TV until sleep overtook her. She successfully denied how she felt until, without warning, the stress broke loose in terrifying anxiety attacks complete with hyperventilation, heart palpitations, headaches, dizzyness, and fearful thoughts about dying.

Outward success is not always an indication of inner

confidence or contentment. Many of the movers, shakers, and high achievers in business, finance, entertainment, and many other fields got so far so fast by overcompensating for feelings of inadequacy and unworthiness. Like Steven, they have obtained all the trappings of the American dream but may feel something is still missing. Happiness eludes them. Like Cindy, they cannot take pride in their accomplishments because they fear they will be unmasked as the charlatans and frauds they believe they are. So, they work harder. They smile wider. They polish and perfect the self they show the world in order to protect the "real" self they know to be flawed and inadequate.

You, too, may be a great pretender. You may feel empty in spite of your apparent success. Your efforts to cope may have turned you into a workaholic, ruined more than one relationship, or caught up with you in any number of other ways. Perhaps the stress of overcompensating and over-achieving has become overwhelming, and you have anxiety attacks, migraine headaches, ulcers, or have become dependent on addictive substances. To make matters worse, you are now stuck with these new problems as well as the old ones. You are sure you brought them on yourself, and change seems more difficult and unlikely than ever.

**3.** *You create and live out self-fulfilling prophecies.*

Human beings predict outcomes based on their perceptions of their own ability or worth and act accordingly.

"There's no way I'll pass this test," says the college student. So, instead of studying, he parties with his friends, and his prophecy comes true when he fails the test.

"I'll never get that rise," says the secretary. "My stingy bear of a boss wouldn't part with an extra penny if his life depended on it. Why should I work my tail off for nothing?" Her attitude shows and defeats her. She decides to meet only the minimum requirements of her job, shows no initiative, refuses to work a minute of overtime, and makes sure to use every sick day as soon as she earns it. When her job performance is reviewed, she barely makes the grade and is not offered a rise. This does not surprise her. She knew she couldn't squeeze more mcney from her employer.

Karen begins yet another diet she assumes will fail. Her theory is that "if I had the willpower to diet and was meant to be thin, I would be by now." She sticks to the diet at first. Then, on an exceptionally busy day, her hectic schedule prevents her from eating properly. Famished by late afternoon, she wolfs down a burger and fries. This small deviation from her diet is all the proof of weakness she needs. When she gets home at ten, she orders a pizza. This opens the gates to a three-week binge. Afterward Karen looks at herself in a mirror and says, "Let's face it. I just don't have what it takes to stick to a diet."

In countless ways, each and every day you live up to your self-image. If that image is negative, you consciously or unconsciously reinforce it. You predict failure and fulfill your own prophecy.

**4.** Trying desperately to boost your confidence or block painful feelings, *you develop self-defeating habits and dangerous addictions.*

People addicted to drugs or alcohol, those who are compulsive overeaters, gamblers, and money spenders, as well as those who seek solace through numerous shallow sexual encounters, have low opinions of themselves. They had low self-esteem, however, long before they lost control of their lives, dependencies, and obsessions.

Drugs, alcohol, and the short-lived adrenaline high of winning in a gambling casino offer a false sense of power, confidence, and well-being. Yet they are so appealing that you substitute the artificially induced feelings for the high sense of worth you have not been able to achieve naturally.

Steven, the plumbing contractor, first tried cocaine while attending college. The attraction was immediate. Cocaine produced every feeling he had never been able to feel on his own. Energy surged through his body. He had an edge he never had before. While high on cocaine, he thought he was capable of anything. He hated to come down.

A dozen years later, Steven still uses the drug—heavily on weekends and occasionally during the week. He feels guilty about using cocaine and berates himself for not quitting. "I don't even get what I want from coke anymore," he says. "But I can't seem to stop. I try, but then I get this urge and call a friend who has some. I swear I won't touch the stuff. Then I see it at a party and go for it. I hate myself the next morning, but obviously not enough to say no to coke the next time."

In other instances, drugs, alcohol, food, sex, and spending excessive amounts of money are used not to produce feelings but to deaden them, to mask insecurity, to slow down a world that spins too fast, or to avoid facing real or imagined problems. Regardless of the reason for adopting them, these habits and dependencies inevitably lead to greater feelings of weakness and inadequacy.

Trying to fill your empty spaces with what you find in the medicine chest, drinks cabinet, gambling casino, or refrigerator may appear to work for a while. You cannot fool yourself for long, however. Instead of feeling better or liking yourself more, you are left with one more change to make, one more seemingly impossible mission to accomplish, one more place to be stuck.

5. *You get trapped in an endless cycle,* a spiral descending downward to despair.

The less you like yourself, the more you hurt yourself. The more you hurt yourself, the less you like yourself. If unbroken, this vicious cycle leaves you stuck while the good life goes on without you. You add new items to the list of things you wish you had done, but didn't. You observe your life dimly instead of living it fully. Dreams and goals for yourself fade to black. Perhaps you never even had any dreams or made any goals. Doubts and self-criticism mushroom to enormous proportions.

Are you hungry for a better life but cannot find your way to the banquet table? Do you accept only life's leftovers? If you do, you are under the spell of the most common and insidious of barriers. It grabs you and shakes the will to change out of you. It kicks you when you are down. This barrier goes to work on you when you are already suffering the effects of low self-esteem.

---

## SELF-ESTEEM

Self-esteem is both the image of yourself you carry with you at all times and your opinion of it. Your image of yourself and your evaluation of your worth influences everything you do or do not do. Self-esteem is built on what you feel about yourself, and to some extent, how you *think* others feel about you.

How do *you* feel about yourself? What do you like about what you are? What do you think you lack? What do you do well? What do you wish you did better? Are you competent, lovable, intelligent, funny, pretty, creative, socially adept, unique, fun, friendly, kind, responsible, or talented? Or are you inadequate, dumb, boring, clumsy, average, incapable, unlovable, shy, awkward, or apt to fail? Are other people likely to accept you, like you, respect you, admire you, converse with you, or be there for you when you need them? Or are they more likely to reject you, ignore you, laugh at you, hurt you, abandon you, or see through your facade? How many positive personal qualities can you list? On the other hand, how many sentences beginning with "I'm not very . . ." can you finish?

Your answers to such questions make up your own personal, highly subjective measure of what you think you are worth—to yourself, to the people you love, to the people you look up to, and sometimes to the world at large. Those answers shape your beliefs about what you *can* do and your chances for success in any area of life. When your self-esteem is high, you usually predict good fortune and go after the best possible results. You are more motivated, more positive, and more open to change. You are less self-destructive because the more you like yourself, the less likely you are to hurt yourself.

Low self-esteem has the exact opposite effect. It has been linked to poor school performance; overeating, alcoholism, and other addictions; aggressive and criminal behaviour; promiscuity; and depression and suicide. It plays a powerful part in getting and keeping people stuck.

Yet self-esteem is not static. It changes. You see, everyone is born with high self-esteem. Infants are the positive centre of their own universes, and toddlers believe themselves to be the brightest stars in the galaxy, until somehow, a little bit at a time, they learn to view themselves differently.

## SELF-ESTEEM WRECKING BALLS

Since you were born with high self-esteem, how did you lose it and come to believe you deserve far less than you desire?

Picture your self-esteem as a building under construction. Based on the blueprints drawn up for you at birth, you were promised a wonderful lifelong home. Each time someone demonstrated his love or acceptance of you, the building's foundation was made stronger. Each success you experienced and each task you mastered—no matter how small—was another brick added to your building. Each risk you took, and every ounce of recognition and support you received, reinforced the idea that you were lovable and capable and made your building more liveable. At the same time, each bit of negative criticism, every hurtful name, derogatory label, and exam paper returned with red-pencil corrections on every page hurled a wrecking ball at your building. Unmet expectations, failed love affairs, being dropped from the basketball team, rejected for a job, beaten up by the neighbourhood bully, or embarrassed in any way knocked out another wall or window.

Sometimes there has been enough construction to overcome the destruction and maintain high self-esteem. Sometimes the wrecking balls strike frequent powerful blows and building blocks cannot be put into place fast enough. Then, the building's foundation begins to tremble. It's tough to find safety, security, or success when your self-esteem has been demolished.

Who propelled those wrecking balls at your brick building? The original demolition crew were people you loved and respected. Parents may have plied you with negative criticism. In moments of anger they called you hurtful names. Sometimes they wished aloud that you were different or did not exist at all. Teachers found fault in your best efforts. They compared, you unfavourably to students who were smarter, stronger, or better behaved. They rapped you on the knuckles when you did not conform to their standards and gave you labels such as "slow learner," "behaviour problem," "unmotivated," or "not living up to potential."

Preachers swore you would burn in hell. Bullies pummelled you and stole your lunch money. Peers laughed at you, made fun of your clothes, or picked you last for the relay-race team. Fashion magazines presented images of beauty you could not attain. You saw your home life was not like they showed on the TV ads.

An even greater price was payed when abuse, domestic violence, or alcoholic parents were part of your childhood. It was harder still to be a member of a racial or ethnic minority group, to be poor or to be disabled in any way. All this took its toll on your self-esteem.

Steven recalls, "When I was eight or nine years old, Dad would take out a dictionary after dinner and pick words at random for my sister and me to spell. My sister, the genius, could spell anything. But I was a lousy speller and my dad knew it. I don't blame my sister, but she'd sit there waiting for me to screw up so she could spell the word right and hear Dad say how wonderful she was. Meanwhile Dad would yell at me, 'Sound out the word for Christ's sake.' Eventually I'd get so nervous I'd start to cry and he called me a sissy. So I wasn't just dumb, I was a weak little crybaby. To this day, every time I make any kind of mistake I hear my father saying, 'Come on, dummy. Think. You're not trying hard enough.' "

Steven is thirty-one years old, yet he still thinks of himself as that very sensitive young boy who could not measure up to his father's expectations and often acted impulsively with disastrous results. His father does not have to criticize him anymore. He has taken over that job himself—just as you may have.

By now you may have become your own demolition crew, able to aim and release your own wrecking balls. From well-meaning but critical role models, you learned the art of put-downs. By now you have become a brutal and unyielding judge of your own character defects. Where parents, teachers, preachers, and peers left off, you have taken up the slack with a vengeance. You can't help it, for self-criticism has become the way you talk to yourself.

Few of us see ourselves as total failures, thank goodness. Most of us reserve our most scathing self-criticism and painful self-doubts for specific areas in which we never thought we measured up. Sarah's sore spot is her physical appearance and appeal to men.

While Sarah was growing up, she often heard herself described as the "smart one," while her sisters were called the "pretty ones." She knew she had unruly brown hair and unremarkable features. She wore glasses and carried a few extra pounds around her hips and thighs. Conversely, her sisters were slender blondes, considered very attractive by their peers. They dated often and went out with the most popular and handsome boys. Sarah had steady boyfriends of the "nerd" variety in between long dateless stretches.

Sarah knew she had other strengths, however, and she managed to fend off the wrecking balls until a remark intended as a joke she was not meant to hear demolished a big chunk of self-esteem. Sarah was nineteen at the time and working at a summer camp for handicapped children. Her parents and two sisters came to visit and take her and a friend out for dinner. They arrived during the camp carnival, and Danny, the drama counsellor, was in full clown-face makeup when Sarah first introduced him to her family. Later they were able to see he was an exceptionally attractive blond, blue-eyed man and appeared to be quite taken with Sarah.

As the group walked toward the restaurant with Sarah and Danny several yards ahead, one sister whispered, "God, he's *gorgeous*!"

"I know," sister number two agreed. "How'd she get him to go out with her? Bribe him with dinner?"

Both Sarah's sisters and her parents had a good long laugh about that one.

"That was the clincher," says Sarah. "They were only kidding and I wasn't supposed to hear what they said, but it was a big deal for me."

Now twenty-eight years old and a special education teacher working on her Ph.D., Sarah remembers the moment "as if it were yesterday. When I meet a good-looking guy and he seems attracted to me, I say, 'No, he couldn't be. What could he possibly find attractive about me? Do I have to bribe him with dinner?'"

We all withstand more than our fair share of put-downs, embarrassing moments, and seemingly devastating disappointments. Some we take to heart. Some we do not. Some are countered by equally persuasive successes, compliments, and triumphs. Sometimes it is not the criticism or failure that damages our self-esteem, but the feeling we are not recognized and do not belong.

Cindy's younger brother, born with a heart problem, was sick throughout his short life, required constant care, and died when Cindy was twelve years old. Cindy was shuttled from relative to relative, and when she was living at home, she might as well have been invisible. She always had to be quiet and on her best behaviour, never voicing her needs and complaints. After all, she was lucky to be healthy. As a result, Cindy put on her happy face and came to believe anything she thought or felt was unimportant. She felt that her role was to please people by being cute and funny.

Cindy still had to walk on eggshells after her brother's death. Her mother was understandably despondent. Cindy tried to second-guess what her mother wanted so as not to upset her. She guessed wrong—a lot. And Cindy began to feel that her own ideas and feelings could not be trusted. This belief was reinforced when Cindy began dating the high school football hero. Everyone greatly admired him, but secretly he physically and emotionally abused her. Cindy did nothing to end the relationship, however, reasoning she had done something wrong to deserve such treatment, since everyone kept telling her how she lucky she was to date such a wonderful guy.

"By the time I reached adulthood," Cindy says, "I was convinced nothing I felt was valid and nothing I did was quite right. I tried to please everyone I met and never, *ever* asserted myself."

Sometimes the self-esteem demolition derby begins later in life. The picture of yourself that you have accepted and come to like, as well as your vision of your life going on indefinitely in a certain manner, can be turned upside down by unanticipated events. For example, when Marilyn's husband left her, she temporarily lost all sense of herself and her value. The role of devoted wife and mother no longer fitted her, and it would be some time before she redefined herself as a working woman and a single parent. Before she reached that point she criticized herself for not seeing the crisis coming, blamed herself for the failure of her marriage, and examined her life intensively to see what she had done wrong and in which areas she had not been good enough.

Similarly, real accumulating problems at home, work, or in relationships can eat away at self-esteem. Lisa experienced major wrecking balls for the first time when she began working as a sales rep for an office supply company. Previously she had rarely doubted her competence and professionalism while successfully selling at another firm.

"I started working in sales straight from school," she explains. "I worked hard and was good at my job. I moved up quickly to higher and higher levels of responsibility." Therefore, Lisa was surprised when the sales manager who interviewed her made a big deal about her lack of a college education. It put the first of many doubts in her mind. Maybe she wasn't educated or sophisticated enough to be included in planning meetings or asked for opinions or considered for promotions, she thought. In the past she had never considered her gender a disability, but as the only woman in the sales department, now she was often told she was being too emotional or acting "just like a woman." Thinking her colleagues and superiors might be right, she kept her feelings to herself. The ways in which she had always been good enough did not seem to be good enough anymore.

"These were successful professionals," Lisa comments. "They worked for the number one company in the market and were incredibly successful. They had their college degrees. How could they *not* be right? I *had* to be the one who wasn't playing the game the way it was supposed to be played. I was the one who didn't measure up."

We all experience unexpected events, life crises, and stressful situations that create self-doubt and lower self-esteem. If for the most part our basic self-image has been positive, we can bounce back and rebuild rather quickly, as both Marilyn and Lisa were able to do. Low self-esteem carried like excess baggage since childhood, as well as the damage done by being stuck in an abusive or degrading situation for many years, is more difficult to rebuild or repair. It is not impossible however.

Low self-esteem is *not* a curse, your lot in life, or an irreversible condition. Believing you do not deserve better is a barrier. Like all barriers, it can be dismantled. Consider—pretend if you must—that there is at least a remote possibility you deserve better and are capable of learning how to get it. If this is hard, pretend it is possible for a good friend of yours, someone you admire, care about, or like a great deal. Then read on. Familiarize yourself with the following self-esteem building blocks and how to use them to create a positive self-image.

## DISMANTLING BARRIER #1: BUILDING SELF-ESTEEM

I do not intend to mislead you or paint a rosy, unrealistic picture of what lies ahead. This barrier is difficult to dismantle. A lifetime of experience created and fortified it, and within its walls are every belief and idea about who you are and what you can do. These images may be unproductive and unhealthy, but because they are familiar and belong to you, you may feel tense and defensive at the mere thought of altering them. If you think you are not good enough, you probably also think you don't stand a chance to become more or better. Such thinking causes pain or sadness, and so you build barricades to protect yourself from those feelings. Many of those defences become new barriers, ones that you will read about later. But you have to deal with the problem of self-esteem first. Without raising self-esteem and starting to believe you deserve a better life, you will have no motivation to dismantle the other barrier or try to change in any way. All roads start with and lead back to self-esteem. Difficult to get rid of or not, this barrier has got to go.

This barrier is at work in your life because you believe what it tells you about yourself. As you try to dismantle it, it will talk louder, stir up more self-doubt, and cast more smoke screens. Of course all that noise and clutter occurs only in your own mind and imagination. In fact, you are in control here. You really are. It is your own voice you hear and you can have it say whatever you want.

So I ask you now to try to drum up some faith. In spite of churning stomachs, sweaty palms, and little voices crying, "No way. Not me. I can't," open your mind to the *possibility* that you might be more or better than you think you are and that what I suggest may work for you the way it has for thousands of other people.

I offer no magical formula to bring about a magnificent overnight transformation. I simply propose two logical methods for increasing positive self-esteem. The first is to add bricks to your building, and the second is to ward off the wrecking balls before they can do more damage. Both ends are achieved by accumulating self-esteem building blocks and cementing them to the foundation of your self-image.

### Self-esteem Building Blocks

I have explained and given examples of self-esteem wrecking balls. Unfortunately you probably already knew a lot about them. You may not be as familiar with self-esteem building blocks. What are they? How can you get more and use them to fortify your self-image?

From my own experiences as a teacher/counsellor and based on the ideas found in *Self-esteem* by Harris Clemes and Reynold Bean and *101 Ways to Enhance Self-esteem* by Jack Canfield and Harold Wells, I have chosen seven self-esteem building blocks and offer strategies to help you incorporate each into your life.

Before I get down to specifics, let me mention that your present negative self-image and low level of self-esteem may be the result of traumatic events or ongoing degradation you have blocked from your mind and are unable to consciously recall. Even with these memory gaps, the building blocks I describe will help you like yourself more and believe you deserve better. However, to fully dismantle this barrier you may want to unravel the mysteries of your past, come to terms with it, and learn how it influences your present circumstances and behaviour. Professional counselling in the form of individual and/or group therapy will help you achieve that understanding.

---

## MENTORS AND MODELS

Part of your self-image and some of your beliefs about being "good enough" came from observing the people around you. Mentors and models can be parents, older brothers and sisters, teachers, favourite aunts and uncles, the supervisor who took you under his wing on your first job, or people you admire but do not know personally. Their lives or specific actions inspire you, encourage you, and give you hope to be more or better. They have something you want. You try to learn from them to enhance self-esteem. But you should not try to *be* your mentor or model. You may lose self-esteem if you draw comparisons or imitate a model/mentor so completely that you lose yourself, becoming a second-rate copy of him or her instead of a first-rate original you.

Harry found and learned from a self-esteem model/mentor named Pat whom he met during his cross-country travels. "Pat was travelling too—by herself in a van," Harry relates. "She was older than me by at least a dozen years, and she was incredibly serene, which was downright amazing when you found out what she'd been through."

Once so poor she did not know how she would feed her children, Pat's life had been full of ups and downs. A pilot and flight instructor, she'd flown in several transcontinental air races. When Harry met her, she was forty-five. Her children, whom she had raised alone, were grown. She went where she wanted to go, camped out under the stars whenever she could, wrote poetry, studied psychology, and worked on her dissertation while she was on the road. All this, even though she had cancer.

Harry continues, "Pat wasn't going to live to be one hundred. She might not even make it to forty-six. But that didn't stop her from wanting to learn and do new things. She taught me things I'll never forget, not that she ever thought she was teaching me anything. We'd just talk. The main thing was that she thought life was a gift and that her mission was to make the most of it, to make every day worth something and never stop getting better."

Pat's words stuck with Harry, and she turned out to be a perfect self-esteem model for him. He glows as he recalls the time he spent with her. "That lady touched my life. She's the reason I try not to look backwards or dwell on what I haven't done or don't have yet. Because of her I try to get a little bit better at something every day."

Harry's model/mentor helped him be more and believe in himself. Your models and mentors can do the same for you. They can inspire and instruct, and you can build positive self-esteem when you use that inspiration and instruction to enhance *your own* strengths and attributes.

**Mentor/Model Strategy**

Take out a blank sheet of paper and draw five circles. Scatter the circles over the page, leaving ample spaces between them like this:

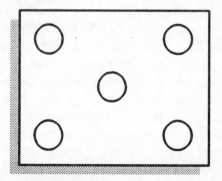

Now, think of five people whom you believe have high self-esteem, people who like themselves and have a positive opinion of their own worth. They can be people you know well or casually or people you simply know of, such as celebrities and political or religious leaders. Write each person's name in a separate circle.

Think carefully about these people.

- How do they show their self-esteem?

- How can you tell they like themselves?

- How does their self-esteem work for them?

For each way in which these mentor/models exhibit their self-esteem, attach a daisy petal to their circle and write a characteristic of their self-esteem in it, as in the diagram:

There is no set number of petals per person. Several or all people can have some of the same qualities written in their petals. Some of those common characteristics will turn out to be standard self-esteem building blocks. After you complete the daisy petals, create a daisy for yourself, with your qualities in the petals. It is often harder to do this for ourselves, but I urge you to try. One of the reasons it is hard is that we become intimidated by thoughts of all those people we know who have more petals than we do. Next list the qualities you would like to have and the ways that these high self-esteem people might serve as models and mentors for you.

Models and mentors show you how to be more, believe you deserve better, and go after what you want. They built their self-esteem with the same building blocks you will use. As I describe the remaining building blocks, think about how your models and mentors used them, as well as how you have or will fit them into your own life.

## RISK

To build self-esteem, take more risks.

Take intellectual risks. Read books. Take courses. Engage in stimulating—even infuriating—conversations. Try to see the world from other points of view. Expand your horizons by gaining appreciation, skill, and understanding of art, music, theatre, films, computers, or gourmet cooking. Challenge yourself to know more than you know now.

Take physical risks. Rock climb. Water-ski. Ride a dirt bike. Camp out. Take beginning aerobics, then intermediate, then advanced. Train for a five mile run, enter a race, and finish it. Push your limits of strength and endurance, and even live on the edge occasionally, but intelligently. Develop skill, practice safety, play by the rules, and then learn to hang glide, parachute, ride a hot-air balloon, or ski down the advanced slopes.

Take emotional risks. Visit new places. Meet new people. Start conversations. Return a smile. Join a singles' group. Accept a blind date. Ask for a rise. Express your ideas. Assert yourself. Disagree. Be the first one to say "I love you."

Are your hands shaking, your lips quivering, your mind reeling? Are you thinking, "This man is nuts. I can't do those things"? Are you asking—"What if I fail? What if I look stupid, embarrass myself, injure myself?" Are you predicting you will be rejected, disappointed, criticized, fired, or ignored? Fear and conquering fear are what risk taking is all about. By definition, risks bring with them the possibility of failure. But what is failure anyway?

Linda Gottlieb, the author (with Carole Hyatt) of *When Smart People Fail*, describes failure as merely "a judgment about an event. Not a condemnation of character . . . not a permanent condition . . . not a contagious social disease. You lose your job, your show closes, you don't pass a crucial test. Those are events, facts. *Everything* after that is your interpretation of those events. . . . Failure makes us feel powerless and casts us into the status of victim, but it does not have to."

Instead, failure can be seen as a reason to re-examine strengths and weaknesses and an opportunity to take on new challenges. Risks offer more than chances to fail. They bring potential gain, success, pleasure, pride, and increased self-confidence. Risks embody the true meaning of "nothing ventured, nothing gained." You lose only when you do not take them.

People with high self-esteem take risks. Each risk teaches them something. If they risk and lose, they learn to risk differently in the future. If they risk and win, they learn to trust and like themselves more. A risk, well chosen and intelligently taken, stretches your limits. It makes you *more*—more agile, more informed, more sympathetic, more confident, and more sure you are lovable and capable.

A risk, carefully considered and conscientiously executed, delivers a truckload of bricks for your self-image building. Risks give you successes to savour. They give you another item to add to the list of what you *can* do. You have taken millions of risks in your lifetime already and you have succeeded. You stopped crawling and learned to walk. You left mummy and went to school. You played a tree in the kindergarten Christmas show.

The stakes got higher, but you continued to risk. You went out on your first date. You walked the balance beam in gym class. You tried out for the church choir, went away to summer camp, learned to drive a car. You earned degrees, applies for jobs, got married, raised children. Of course I have not mentioned the times taking those risks ended in doom, disaster, or disappointment. You can recall those risks without my help and use them as reasons not to risk again. But you *must* continue to take risks nonetheless. The risks you take are the scale on which you measure the ways you *are* lovable and capable. If you accept no challenges, you will become a spectator in your own life instead of the active player you could be.

### Risk Strategy

Risk taking is explored in more detail in the chapter on barrier #5, cold, raw fear. However, now is a good time to prepare yourself for future risk taking. This strategy will help you do that.

You came into this world helpless and totally dependent on your caregivers. On your own you could perform only the most basic bodily functions. No matter how rotten you feel about yourself today, you are more now than you were then. You know more. You can do more.

How much more? To find out, I want you to list *everything* you once could not do which you *can* do now. Start with the very basics and keep building from there, and don't worry about someone else's doing anything on your list better than you do. You'll find you have accomplished a lot in your life. For instance, once you could not walk, but now you can. Once you could not run, talk, read, write, tie your shoes, or name the pictures in your alphabet book. Once you could not drive a car, travel alone by plane or train or taxi cab. Once you couldn't cook, make a bed, iron a shirt, or open a savings account. You get my drift. There are many, many, many things you once could not do that you can do now, and each new task required a risk. You could have failed, but you took the risk and you are more today because of it.

Make a long, long list and come back to it once a day

for a week or two and add more successes to it. When you are done—temporarily, for the list will grow as you do—put your list somewhere you can find it easily. Tack it to a bulletin board or tape it to your refrigerator. Keep it in your handbag, stash it in your top desk drawer, or fold it up and stick it in your wallet. Look at your list often, especially when you are considering whether a risk is worth taking. It will remind you that you have taken risks before—not once but thousands of times—and your *can* take risks again.

## EMOTIONAL SUPPORT

To build self-esteem you need "a little help from your friends." As much as you might value independence, as determined as you may be to take care of yourself, as thoroughly as you may believe that needing other people is a sign of weakness or inadequacy, you will not like yourself more by isolating yourself or stand much of a chance to get unstuck by "going it alone." The absence of emotional support when you needed it in the past contributed to your present low level of self-esteem. You sought approval but received criticism. You longed for acceptance but experienced rejection. You needed sympathy but were called a crybaby. You stopped hoping to find the emotional support you needed, and so you stopped looking for it. You convinced yourself you didn't need anyone.

At her lowest point before the panic attacks began, Cindy used to say, "My life would be perfect if there were no people in it." She was tired of trying to please other people. She wanted to move into an isolated mountain cabin that had no telephone. She was also sure that no one she knew or might meet could or would do anything to help her.

Yet Cindy got back on her feet and started liking herself *because* of the emotional support she received. Her mother, who had seemed so insensitive and uncaring during Cindy's childhood, knew exactly what to do when Cindy's anxiety attacks struck. A counsellor helped her understand the reasons for the attacks and taught her new ways to look at herself and behave, while her father and an old friend made her laugh. For an hour or more every night, another friend talked with Cindy on the telephone, assuring her she was not crazy and helping her relax. Then, a caring, compassionate man fell in love with her and helped her finally believe she could be herself without being rejected or abandoned.

Had Cindy remained alone with her ailing self-image and those nasty negative voices judging, criticizing, and picking at her, she might never have felt better about herself. Neither can you. Blinded by your imagined shortcomings, you may have lost your perspective. Too busy putting yourself down to build yourself up, you will need emotional support in any of the many forms it can take in order to get past this barrier.

Emotional support reminds you that you are lovable and capable and encourages you to move onward and upward. It cuddles and fusses over you when you are down and gives you a kick in the pants when you have wallowed in self-pity long enough. Emotional support shows you that you have people in your corner. Like a boxer's trainers, they can't fight the round for you, but they can cheer you on and tell you they believe in you. Emotional support can be objective advice, appreciation of your accomplishments, or respect and affection regardless of your achievements. It is knowing someone will push you to be your best and that someone will be there for you when you are at your worst.

"Oh, please!" you cry. "I don't have that and I never will. You must live in a dream world, mister. Even if I thought I needed emotional support, how am I supposed to find it? The people I know don't give a damn."

Not true. Not true at all. You think emotionally supportive people do not exist because you haven't found them yet. But they are out there. Sometimes they are right under your nose, but right now you just can't see what they have to offer.

"If you had asked me beforehand, I would have sworn I had no supportive or caring people in my life," Cindy explains. "I would have told you all counsellors were idiots and I'd die before I would go to one. Nobody I knew gave a damn about me as far as I was concerned, and I never in my wildest dreams thought I'd find a man who really loved me."

The people in Cindy's life surprised her. "They were there all the time," she marvels. "Only I didn't look for them. I didn't see they cared. I never asked for their help."

### Emotional Support Strategy

How to find, ask for, and receive the cooperation and emotional support you need is the subject of Chapter Eight. However, you can begin now by learning how to recognize sources of emotional support, people who are part of your life today or whom you can seek and find in the future.

The most common and deceptive mistake you can make when seeking emotional support is expecting one person to have *all* the supportive qualities you need. When you seek that kind of total support from one person, you will often be disappointed and end up overlooking what he or she *does* have to offer.

"My mother was the world's worst when it came to dealing with my feelings," claimed Lisa, the sales representative. "She actually told me *not* to feel the way I felt, as if I could turn off my emotions like a tap."

On the other hand, Lisa's mother turned out to be a great validator. She constantly expresses her pride, appreciation, respect, love, and admiration of Lisa and her accomplishments. She brags about her children to anyone who will listen, is ready and willing to come through with financial assistance, and when Lisa was looking for a new job, she called everyone she knew to inquire about available positions. If Lisa had gone to her mother seeking solace, empathy, and a shoulder to cry on, she would have been very disappointed. But when Lisa asked her mother for the kinds of support she was capable of giving, she received more than she expected.

Cindy's mother downplayed her daughter's achievements but gave Cindy the sympathy she needed during times of crisis. Her father, on the other hand, had no concept of the stress inherent in Cindy's public relations work and could not understand Cindy's anxiety attacks. Yet he made her laugh and told her tales of times he was down as low as he thought he could get but rose above his problems, giving her hope of doing the same. Cindy found still a different type of support from her best friend. She refused to feel sorry for Cindy, but she did listen and offer wisdom and new direction.

No one person can give you all you need in the way of emotional support, and so such unrealistic expectations invariably lead you to disappointment. However, you may be surprised to find that almost everyone you know has something of a supportive nature to offer. The key is to identify the types of emotional support you want and seek that support from the people who are capable of giving it.

Below I list several types of emotional support people. Read each description and try to think of people you know who fit the description. They need not be perfect at giving that particular type of emotional support, as long as they can give you at least a little bit of what you need in that particular area. Some people will fit in several categories.

After you read each description, jot down the names of people you know who could give you that kind of support the next time you need it.

*CHICKEN SOUP PEOPLE.* These are people who comfort you when you feel down, saying things such as, "Poor baby. What a rotten day you had. No wonder you feel so blue." They coddle and pamper and are just what the doctor ordered when you need to wallow for a while.

*COMIC-RELIEF GIVERS.* These are the zany, offbeat people in your life. No matter how low you go, they can make you laugh or at least smile. They point out life's absurdities, bring over their entire collection of Three Stooges' video-tapes and watch them with you, and do hysterical "If you think you've got problems" monologues. When humour will help, these are the people you should call.

*THE GREAT DISTRACTORS.* Similar to comic-relief givers, these folks take your mind off your troubles. You should call them when you want to get out of the house or away from yourself for a while. They'll go with you to the movies, take you to ball games or concerts, or play gin rummy until dawn, offering you distance and a brief vacation from what ails you.

*THE CRISIS CORPS.* These people may or may not be much help over the long haul, but one thing's for sure, if your world should unexpectedly fall apart on you, they are capable of helping you pick up the pieces. They support you calmly, encouraging you to take control of your own life.

*THE LISTENERS.* They listen. They'll listen to your self-pity, anger, and the same sorry story as many times as you need to tell it. You know you can call them when you need to unload your feelings, bounce around ideas, or get a reality check.

*THE ADVISERS.* Problem solvers by nature, these people look objectively at your situation and give suggestions. They think of new alternatives, help you set goals, and point out plans of action that seem unrealistic. You don't have to take their advice, but their type of support gives you options and ideas so you can make your own decisions.

*THE DOOR OPENERS.* These are the helping-hand people. They may not have the answers, but they usually know where you can find them. They will connect you with people you want to know, refer you to a decent therapist, call when they hear about a job opening, co-sign for bank loans, or write reference letters. They hold the key to doors you cannot open yourself.

*I'VE BEEN DOWN AND DIRTY A FEW TIMES MYSELF PEOPLE.* These are people who once had or now have problems similar to your own. As a result, they are capable of accepting you without judging you. Those further along in their recovery can become models for your own improvement efforts.

(If you do not know people like these, look for self-help groups such as Alcoholics, Overeaters, or Gamblers Anonymous, or support groups for abused women, women in transition, single parents, or other similar groups. Call your local advice centre for a list or look in the telephone book.)

*UNCONDITIONAL ACCEPTERS.* If you had more of these people in your life, your self-esteem would already be relatively high. You'll find more imperfect support givers in this category than any other. Flawed though they may be, however, these people forgive you, loving you even when they do not like you very much.

*PROFESSIONAL HELPERS.* These people are trained and paid to give you exactly the emotional support you need. They fit into almost every other category, but you rarely think of putting them there since therapy is seen as a treatment rather than a form of support. At one time or another, professionals helped many of the people described in this book, including me. Professional help is available in every corner and crossroad of the country. You can look in any telephone book, but you improve your chances of finding good professional help by asking people who have found it themselves. Your door openers can help you here.

Perhaps you can think of other kinds of emotional supporters. If you can, list those types too and try to match them with people you know or can locate. Then, hang on to your list so that when you are ready to attempt a change or dislodge an obstacle to change, you will know whom to call.

---

## POWER

Powerlessness is a breeding ground for low self-esteem. Victims of abuse and people who view themselves as victims of circumstance usually do not like themselves and do not believe they deserve better. Low self-esteem is found in people who readily submit to peer pressure and routinely go along with the crowd. Self-esteem is also lost when people keep quiet although they have something to say, allowing others to take advantage of them or avoiding making decisions.

You could see the effect of powerlessness on Lisa, whose superiors and co-workers disregarded her feelings and opinions. Because they were more educated and experienced than she, Lisa assumed they knew what was best. The personal power that was not taken from her, she willingly gave away. She was not included in decisions that affected her and did not ask to be, and she quickly stopped expressing her opinions. She did not protest unfair treatment or even question why she did not receive the pay rise she had been promised. Instead, she swallowed her feelings and went along with other people's plans although she often did not like or agree with them. As her self-esteem plummeted, she saw herself first as a hapless pawn and ultimately as a mindless victim.

On the other hand, people with high self-esteem exercise a great deal of personal power. They don't have to be royalty or heads of state or chief executive officers in multinational corporations to do this. But they do believe they have control over their lives and use it to get more of what they want. They also believe in their ability to change. If they have no other tangible power, they always have the power to choose.

You *get* personal power by making decisions based on your personal values and desires. You *give up* that power when you allow and/or ask other people to decide for you.

When you increase personal power, you build self-esteem by claiming your choices as your own, feeling proud of your achievements and regaining control over aspects of daily living. You get personal power by asserting yourself, asking for what you need and expressing your ideas or feelings about matters that directly affect you.

You give up this power when you convince yourself other people are better, more qualified, more articulate, or need more and know more than you do. You give them the power to ignore or dismiss your ideas, take advantage of you, have their needs met at your expense, or otherwise abuse you. As Lisa discovered, not exercising personal power unleashes very dangerous wrecking balls.

You *reclaim* personal power when you say yes more often to life's challenges and possibilities and say no more often to unreasonable demands and self-defeating pursuits. You *exercise* personal power when you set a goal, make a plan, and stick to it. You increase personal power by changing bad eating patterns, breaking detrimental habits, spending money only within your budget, bringing your credit card balances down, and asking that tasks not included in your job description stop being assigned to you without your okay.

**Personal Power Strategy**

When you are stuck or see yourself as a victim, you cannot use personal power to build self-esteem because you do not know you have it. To increase personal power you must first identify ways to be decisive and assertive. Then you must practise, starting small and moving upward. Here are eleven ways to practise using personal power:

1. Take an assertiveness training course.
2. Stop at a service station and ask for directions.
3. Return a gift that does not suit you to the department store where it was purchased.
4. Tell a particularly verbal friend you want to end a telephone conversation. Offer to call her back later, but do not make excuses about why you want to get off the phone.

**5.** Tell a teenage child you will drive him to a school event, but he must find someone else to drive him home.

**6.** Choose *not* to cook dinner one day of the week. Ask someone else to take responsibility for that meal.

**7.** Suggest a work-related improvement to your supervisor.

**8.** Do not eat the dessert that comes with your meal the next time you travel on an airline.

**9.** Ask the waiter for a different table than the one where he is about to seat you.

**10.** The next time anyone asks you what you want to do and you are tempted to say, "I don't know," think about what *you* really do want and answer accordingly.

**11.** Say no if you mean no when your co-workers pass around the doughnuts, your colleague encourages you to have a lunchtime martini, a salesperson tries to sell you an accessory, or cocaine is available at a party.

To get a clearer picture of how you personally exercise or abdicate your power, think about the week that just passed. Think of twenty instances during that week when you could have exercised personal power, made a decision, expressed ideas or opinions, asserted yourself, made a request, or said no. Write your power points on a scrap of paper.

Of those twenty opportunities to exercise personal power, how many did you actually use? In contrast, how many times did you let someone else decide, hold back your opinion or say yes when you really wanted to say no? Now, think about the rest of today and all of tomorrow. Based on what you know of your schedule and routine, list at least five ways you can use your personal power. Write these as affirmations, positive statements recognizing the power you do have and confirming exactly what you will do, (i.e., "I have personal power and will use it tomorrow by driving right past the doughnut shop without stopping on my way to work.") Read your affirmations before you fall asleep tonight and again tomorrow morning, then follow through and accomplish what you have written.

---

## UNIQUENESS

What a miracle it is that there exists no other person on this earth who is exactly like you are. Not even your twin— if you had one—would look, sound, think, and relate to the world the very same way you do all of the time. You are unique.

You may not think being unique is such a big deal, especially if being unique means you believe you are uniquely inadequate, unlovable, and unworthy. You may spend a great deal of your time trying to look more like a cover-girl model or a world-class weight lifter. You may dress for success, laugh at jokes you think are not funny, practise witty repartee in the mirror, and compare your bank account to your peers'. Perhaps you pore over the dictionary and pepper your speech with polysyllabic words so you seem more intelligent, or you force yourself to swallow more wine coolers then you should in order to be sociable at parties. Maybe you fabricate or embellish details of your job, home, love life, and sexual conquests to make them all sound more exciting than they really are. But each time you try to be like someone other than yourself, you really end up hurting yourself by relinquishing your uniqueness. You think you are not good enough the way you are, and this erodes your self-esteem. To paraphrase a point made by Dr. Leo Buscaglia in his best-selling book *Love,* if you are a plum, no matter how you try, you will never be anything but a second-rate banana. What's more, in a vain attempt to be a banana, you lose your sense of plumness.

Instead of trying to be who you are not, why not put your time and energy into being a better you? You can be a first-rate you. Such an effort enhances self-esteem, magnifying your strengths and helping you overcome your limitations.

This does not mean you can't try to change for the better. If you want for yourself the abilities or qualities you see in someone, go after them because they will make you a better you, not because they might somehow earn you someone else's life. Make them part of your life and express them as only you can.

## Uniqueness Strategy

What exactly is unique about you? That's an easy question, right? You believe you are uniquely unattached, unattractive, and unimportant, the only one in the world with fat thighs, without a college education, and apt to stick your foot in your mouth every time you open it.

Stop. Let me rephrase the question. What assets, abilities, and positive attributes make you unique? That's harder to answer, isn't it, but I think you can manage a response if you try.

On a sheet of paper, I want you to write forty positive characteristics that are uniquely your own. Yes, forty of them. Break them down into three categories: twenty things you are able to do (you do not have to do them perfectly or even as well as the guy next door); ten interesting or positive physical attributes (yours—not Jane Fonda's or Arnold Scwarzenegger's) or personality traits; and ten interests or beliefs you have. Do not give up until the list is complete. If you must, call a friend or two and ask them for help.

Remember, you are not trying to better or measure up to anyone else. This is not the time to wish you were better or different. You are simply taking stock of the assets you have—and believe me, there are many more than forty. A year from now when you have long since got unstuck and raised your level of self-esteem, you will be able to list forty more without trouble. But for now, spend some time coming up with the first forty and save your list. You will refer to it again while working on other self-esteem and barrier dismantling strategies, and it certainly would not hurt to consult it the next time you try to tell yourself you are not good enough.

## BELONGING AND RECOGNITION

Earlier in this chapter, while discussing self-esteem wrecking balls, I mentioned that Cindy's self-esteem suffered because she did not feel as if she belonged in her family or in the fast-paced, high-pressure world of entertainment public relations. In addition, she did not believe her feelings, needs, or point of view were recognized or appreciated.

Feeling that you belong and are connected to other people, as well as having your actions and emotions recognized, builds self-esteem and validates your existence, your place in the world and your worth. Without belonging and recognition you will naturally feel isolated, unappreciated, and unlovable. You may come to the point where you mistrust your own perceptions because you have no way to test them or check them against other people's views of reality.

The quest for belonging and recognition is a lifelong project. You first sought it from your family. "Who am I?" you wanted to know. "How do I fit in? What do I do that is acceptable and likely to be rewarded in some way?" You found your answers in your relationships with family members, and those relationships had a huge impact on your self-image—for better or worse. Then you looked again for belonging and recognition when you went to school where you worked for gold stars, A grades, and nods of approval. Do you remember knowing an answer and waving your arm frantically, thinking, "Me. Me. Call on me. Look at me." If you were noticed and rewarded, you felt capable and ready to take on the next challenge. If your uniqueness and value went unrecognized for long enough, you decided you were not good enough, and sometimes you stopped trying to be more.

Your quest for belonging, connection, and recognition eventually may have led you to intimate love relationships where much of what you found depended on what you had previously learned about belonging. You may have found that nothing had ever been as close as the intimacy of a love relationship. Your experience, good or bad, shaped your image of yourself and your ability to belong.

You cannot go back and change what has already occurred. You cannot make your parents love you more than they did at the time. You cannot take back the dumb remark that caused the girls in the "in" group to laugh at you. You cannot make your ex-spouse love you again in a better way. You *can* look at how not belonging and not being recognized in the past affects your self-esteem today, and then you can move forward.

A good way to start is to look for new ways and places to belong. This time, instead of compromising who you are in order to fit in, build on your uniqueness. Look for the people, places, and activities that fit who you already are.

If you are a single parent, join a single parents' group. If you are interested in art or music or gourmet cooking, join a club or take a course. If you are a freelance professional, own your own business, or work in a particular field, become part of a network or professional association. If you like bowling, join a league. The resources for belonging and recognition are limited only by your imagination and vision.

### Belonging Strategy

Using your list of unique assets as a reference and paying particular attention to your interests and activities, list groups, clubs, courses, or meeting places that complement your interests and assets. List as many as you can think of.

Then do some additional research. Check the telephone book, new neighbour's guide, or community calendar section of your local newspaper.

When you are ready to increase your supply of belonging and recognition building blocks, consult your list, choose three resources, and make a plan. Your plan can include finding the appropriate telephone number, calling for information, registering (if necessary), asking a friend to go with you (if you need moral support), and attending your first class, group meeting, or making your first connection. Be sure to set a date for each step in your plan and use affirmation statements to convince yourself you *can* belong and be recognized.

## PRODUCTIVITY

When asked about people who feel they're losers and can't move on with their lives, Linda Gottlieb, co-author of *When Smart People Fail,* suggests, "Do something in which you can succeed, accomplish something. One man built a tree house. Another person learned to swim. It really doesn't matter *what* you do. Just do something."

Her advice is well suited for people with low self-esteem. To be productive in some way—any way—is an essential self-esteem building block. Nine times out of ten, when you are asked to describe yourself, you probably start by describing something you do. This is because your self-esteem depends heavily on what you think and feel about what you achieve, accomplish, or produce. It drops noticeably when you stand still or feel stuck.

Often you can see the relationship between productivity and self-esteem in an older adult who retires from the work force. He walks out of the workplace with a gold watch in his pocket and a huge part of himself missing. If he whiles away the hours watching TV and snoozing in a retirement home, he deteriorates quickly, feeling he has little to live for and little proof he is lovable or capable anymore. Millions of senior citizens waste away from lack of productivity.

Dan could have, and he did for a time after selling the large family restaurant he had owned and operated. For the first time since he was twelve, he found himself with no job to do. He had money enough to meet his needs, a loving wife, friends, but no way to feel productive. Fortunately he blundered into a way to contribute to society and be productive by turning a charitable organization's warehouse full of donated merchandise into a thriving thrift shop. Now he earns money for a worthy cause and feels useful and rewarded. As a result, Dan's self-esteem is just fine these days.

Invariably the times you have liked yourself most were also times you have felt productive, active, busy, and creative. You can find that feeling of productivity from working, completing a course or passing a test, building a model airplane, cleaning out the garage, collecting newspapers and aluminum cans for recycling, lining the linen closet shelves, or organizing pictures in a photograph album. Choosing a task, starting it, and finishing it is the quickest and easiest way to accumulate self-esteem building blocks.

## PLAN AHEAD FOR A HIGH SELF-ESTEEM YEAR

Now that you are familiar with the seven self-esteem building blocks, how will *you* use them and in what order or combination? How will *your* self-esteem urban renewal project repair the damage done by old wrecking balls?

While your unique experiences have created unique gaps in your self-esteem, your strengths are also yours alone, and you will build self-esteem differently than anyone else. However, you must take an active role in your own rebuilding project. Take an inventory, create a vision, and devise a plan to enhance your self-esteem.

Taking an Inventory

On a blank sheet of paper draw two vertical lines and two horizontal lines so the page looks like this:

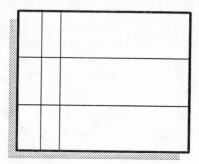

The three horizontal sections each represent a high self-esteem year in your life. Identify those years when your self-esteem was high, your outlook positive, and when you liked yourself the most. In the left-hand column of each horizontal section, write the approximate dates of your high self-esteem years. In the second column, use the numbers one, two, and three to rank in order those years, with the number one indicating the year of highest self-esteem.

Starting with the year you ranked as number one, write notes to yourself about that year in the wide third column. Then ask yourself, what went on during that year? What were you doing? Who were the important people in your life? Why do you think you liked yourself then? Think about these questions and make comments for all three high self-esteem years. Then review your self-esteem inventory and notice which self-esteem building blocks you had on hand during the years you most liked yourself.

Cindy had never seen herself as much of a risk taker, yet when she did this inventory, she immediately noticed that all three of her self-esteem years included major challenges. During each, she began a new job and turned it into more than it started out to be, learning and doing things she had never done before. Belonging played a big part, too.

Cindy says, "I was really hooked into being productive, too. I was working hard and accomplishing a lot at work. I moved into my own apartment one year, and bought my house during another year and handled repairs and renovations myself. And last year, when I was publicizing theatrical road shows all over the United States and in Japan, people were always telling me what a great job I was doing."

Compare how you felt and what you did during your high self-esteem years with how you feel and what you do now. If you plan to reach that high level of self-esteem again, what will you need to do, learn, or become? Then, for each self-esteem building block (mentors/models, risks, emotional support, power, uniqueness, belonging/recognition, and productivity) list at least one way you can get more of each.

### Creating a Vision of High Self-esteem

Negative self-fulfilling prophecies were described earlier in this chapter. When you predict failure, you get it. Fortunately, you can predict success as well. To improve your chance of getting high self-esteem, visualize yourself having it already. Now think about and describe another year in your life. This time the year should not be one you have lived already, but a year you are going to live, the next year of your life.

Write a letter to the year ahead. Think of next year as a close friend and in your letter tell that friend about the success you anticipate, the risks you hope to take, the tasks you want to accomplish, and all your other goals.

Cindy wrote such a letter and allowed me to reprint it here:

Dear 1988,
I think one of the scripts Sue and I wrote will be sold this year. I know that is out of my hands, but I think we

do good work and I'd like to do more. I'd like to learn more about filmmaking too, especially the production/business end of it. I think I'll also take some college courses and get back to work on my degree. I wonder if filmmaking and psychology mix, because I'm also interested in what makes people tick.

I'll move closer to New York City. My relationship with Joe is too close and important to keep it a long distance one. Besides, the train fare is killing me! And speaking of finances, while I'm waiting to become a rich and famous screenwriter, I'd better find more freelance work or sign on with a PR agency—in New York preferably. I have some job leads already. This time around, though, I'm going to hold out for work I really want. I get by on my freelance projects. I don't have to jump on the first offer I get. I'm good enough at what I do now and have enough of a track record to pick and choose.

I'm going to travel more. I can't believe I spent so many years in a small town. Now that I've tasted travel and adventure I want more. Joe and I will take that trip to Europe. I have big plans for this year, don't I?

I will meet new, exciting people. I will make my relationship even better than it is. I might even mention the word "marriage" again—talk about risk taking! I will pay off my loans and credit card balances and get started on the children's book I've been meaning to write. Most of all, I will trust my feelings and my intuition. I'll open up and trust more, not just to Joe and Sue. Of course, I don't want to go overboard either. I'll just say what I'm thinking. Sue's not the only one who can be assertive in a business meeting. If I've learned anything, it's that people will not run the other way when I'm being something other than cute, funny, and amusing.

These exercises have helped me see all I can do. I went through a rough time financially last year, but it helped me see I am more than just an extension of my work. I used to feel lousy because I hadn't travelled much and wasn't very sophisticated, but I learned it is never too late to start. I learned to trust and open up to more people, that I can take as well as give. I definitely figured out that things *never* turn out as badly as I think they will when I let my imagination run away with me, and that I'll survive without everyone's liking me all of the time. I peeked at the rough draft of this chapter and I agree with Pat. Life really is a gift and I'd better make it count. That's exactly what I plan to do next year.

## The Self-esteem Plan

How will you make next year happen the way you described it in your letter? What will you do? With your vision of a high self-esteem year in mind, once again look at each building block and determine how you will use each one to have the year you want. List at least one goal for each building block. Phrase your goal as an affirmation, positively stating what you believe will occur. Lisa wrote: "I will take intellectual risks by signing up for two college courses, completing them, learning from them, and passing them with flying colours!" Lisa sounds as if she believes she can do what she planned. How about you?

You now have the building blocks, vision, and blueprint to enhance your self-esteem. If you follow your own plan, you will soon see how much more you deserve and you will be able to accomplish the life changes that previously blocked you. You will be better equipped and more motivated to remove other obstacles from your path. You can begin this task immediately, by learning about barrier number two—not seeing your alternatives.

# 4

███ █ █ ██ ███ ██████████████████████

# *Change and Options*

---

Read the following statements carefully, many of which
will sound quite familiar to you. You may have had
similar thoughts or feelings the last time you were stuck
in an uncomfortable, unhealthy situation or the last time
you wanted to change in any way. Perhaps you feel that
way right now.

After each statement you will find three comments.
Circle the one that is most true for you.

" Look, there is absolutely nothing I can do about this
situation. I have no choice—unless you can come up
with a magic wand or a miracle, that is."

I OFTEN              I SOMETIMES          I NEVER

FEEL THIS WAY        FEEL THIS WAY        FEEL THIS WAY

"I'm caught between a rock and a hard place. The *only* thing I could do would leave me as badly or worse off than I am now."

I OFTEN            I SOMETIMES        I NEVER

FEEL THIS WAY      FEEL THIS WAY      FEEL THIS WAY

"There are alternatives, but they are not *good* alternatives. It's obvious they would never work."

I OFTEN            I SOMETIMES        I NEVER

FEEL THIS WAY      FEEL THIS WAY      FEEL THIS WAY

"I ask people what they would do if they were in my situation, and maybe their ideas would work for them, but none of their suggestions are right for *me*."

I OFTEN            I SOMETIMES        I NEVER

FEEL THIS WAY      FEEL THIS WAY      FEEL THIS WAY

"I have tried everything under the sun, but nothing ever works. I always end up right back where I started."

I OFTEN            I SOMETIMES        I NEVER

FEEL THIS WAY      FEEL THIS WAY      FEEL THIS WAY

"There are plenty of things I could do. The problem is I can't figure out which one I *should* do."

I OFTEN            I SOMETIMES        I NEVER

FEEL THIS WAY      FEEL THIS WAY      FEEL THIS WAY

"I don't want to make the wrong decision. What if I do something and still feel lousy? What if I lose what little I have?"

I OFTEN                I SOMETIMES          I NEVER

FEEL THIS WAY          FEEL THIS WAY        FEEL THIS WAY


"Ask me to make a decision on the job, ask me what to
do about *your* problem, and I'm terrific. But when it
comes to my own life and my own problems . . . forget
it!"


I OFTEN                I SOMETIMES          I NEVER

FEEL THIS WAY          FEEL THIS WAY        FEEL THIS WAY


If you have ever harboured thoughts or feelings similar to
those just listed, then you have experienced the effects of
the second barrier to change–NOT SEEING
ALTERNATIVES. If you circled "I often feel this way"
after many of the statements, it is quite likely this barrier
now obstructs your path.

In a scene from the 1954 Academy Award winning
motion picture, *Marty,* the title character and his friend
try to decide how to spend an evening. Their dialogue
goes like this:

"What do you want to do tonight, Marty?"

"I don't know. What do you want to do, Ange?"

"I don't know. What do *you* want to do?"

In this understated film about a somewhat limited
man stuck in his somewhat limited world, that short
scene brilliantly captures Marty's dilemma. For Marty
and his friends, Saturday nights and their entire lives
were full of possibilities and alternatives, but they simply
could not see them.

The conversation between Marty and Ange rings true
because we play the same scene over and over again in
our lives. When faced with choices, too often we ask
ourselves what to do, only to ultimately answer, as Marty
did, "I don't know."

## BARRIER #2: NOT SEEING THE ALTERNATIVES

Without realizing you have alternatives, you have no vision to guide you when a choice must be made. Without all your options, you have no destination to move toward and no *reason* to alter your course. You stay where you are because you simply cannot determine any new direction.

The following story was told to me by a suicide prevention hotline worker. It is a true story about a conversation he had with a suicidal teenager.

Jeff was working an overnight shift at a crisis centre in Ohio. The night had been quiet and Jeff passed the time by studying for a graduate course final exam and listening to the radio. "Every half hour or so, the DJ would read the weather report," Jeff relates. "It was going to be a beautiful day and he must have said a dozen times how much he was looking forward to it. I started looking forward to it too and figured if it was still quiet at dawn, I'd go out onto the fire escape and watch the sun come up.

"Around four-thirty I got a call from a girl who couldn't have been more than fifteen or sixteen years old. She didn't waste time on small talk. If I couldn't give her one good reason to live, she told me, she was going to hang up and kill herself. I tried to get her to talk about why or even how she wanted to commit suicide, but she wasn't buying. She just repeated her ultimatum—'Give me a reason to live or I'm going to kill myself.'

"Let me tell you, those are the kinds of calls nightmares are made of. But I wasn't dreaming. I was wide-awake and up against the wall. My mind was racing, trying to think of what to say. Finally I remembered the DJ and the weather report and told the caller if she killed herself she would miss seeing the sunrise.

"It wasn't a great intervention and she told me so. In fact, she said it was the stupidest thing she ever heard. I asked her to think about it anyway, and while she was at it, to think about all the other things she'd never see or do again if she killed herself. We made a list. At first she came up with all the lousy stuff in her life and all the reasons suicide was the answer to all her problems. But with a little pushing from me, she began to see the good things she'd miss and that the list got pretty long. Once I could tell she was starting to see the method behind my madness, I asked her if there wasn't something else she could do besides killing herself—seeing as she'd have to give up all this good stuff forever if she did that.

"Her first reaction was to say no. She *knew* there were no alternatives. 'Oh, you've already looked at all the options, then?' I asked. But she hadn't looked at all. She had decided right off the bat that her situation was hopeless and there couldn't possibly be anything to do about it except kill herself. As soon as she made that decision, she stopped looking for other solutions. All she had thought about for the past two weeks was suicide. She had backed herself into a corner, when, as it turned out, there were lots of other things she could do."

Jeff helped the caller see the alternatives and she agreed to try them. I'm happy to report that several of her options worked out well, and two years later the caller is alive and thinking about answering phones at the crisis centre. Of course, Jeff was thrilled with the outcome, but he went on to say: "That story isn't the least bit unusual. Most of the people I talk to haven't considered their alternatives. Hell, they don't even see there are alternatives."

Perhaps your job seems dull, routine, and unfulfilling, or your relationship with your children or your parents is strained and unsatisfying, or you are overwhelmed by the demands of your overflowing schedule and wish there were more hours in the day. Maybe you are constantly at odds with your supervisor or your spouse. You may spend every Saturday night at the same bar, hoping you will meet someone special—but you don't. You ask yourself what you could do differently. You wonder how to improve the situation or get out of it or how to give up a habit that is hurting you, and you come up empty-handed.

And then that helpless, hopeless, claustrophobic feeling overtakes you. You sigh, complain, pour yourself another drink, pick a fight with your spouse, or spend money at the shopping precinct. You pull covers up over your head, praying to wake up and find all your troubles magically erased. In short, you get stuck and see no alternative to being stuck.

This barrier works as well as it does because you assume that just because you can't see your options, there *are* no options. You believe you are stuck because you have no alternatives, when in fact you are stuck because you do not know how to look for alternatives. You believe you have no choices, when what actually gets you stuck is not knowing how to make choices effectively.

This block to change can be a bit tricky because it presents itself in several different forms. You may have encountered them all at one time or another, or you may have experienced only one familiar version. All work in their own ways to keep you from getting unstuck.

### Alternatives Blindness

The teenager who called the suicide prevention hotline was suffering from alternatives blindness. She honestly believed she had *no* options. Her world was dark. She did not realize that all around her were switches she could flip to turn on the lights. This psychological tunnel vision can overcome you when you feel cornered, blocked, or powerless. That's when it's easy to focus all of your attention and energy on the problem and the pain. Staring so single-mindedly at the closed door, you do not notice the open ones, and convinced your situation will last forever, you are sure there is absolutely nothing you can do to change it.

Alternatives blindness is most likely to strike when an ongoing problem reaches overwhelming proportions or when a sudden, unexpected life crisis occurs. Down so low as a result of abuse, illness, or chronic depression, or thrown off balance by a death, a financial loss, job layoff or a divorce, you may lose your perspective and your ability to think clearly. As a result, you cannot see anything *but* the way things are at the moment.

### Between a Rock and a Hard Place

Slightly different from alternatives blindness, although no more helpful to getting unstuck, is seeing only *one* alternative, one which is just as or more distasteful than the way things are now. Carol, the burned-out social worker described in Chapter One, has been thwarted by this version of the second barrier to change. From her perspective the only alternative to staying in a job she hates is to have no job at all. Of course, choosing this alternative usually has all sorts of negative consequences. She imagines going on welfare, losing her home, custody of her kids, and ultimately becoming a bag lady. With such a mindset, being stuck and unhappy in a job that provides a steady income seems the preferable option. Even though there are dozens of other avenues open to her, Carol does not see them.

You know this version of the barrier is operating in your life when alternatives seem to be black and white, when choices seem to be either/or. *Either* stay in an abusive relationship *or* be desperately alone. *Either* go to the bar on Saturday night *or* become a couch potato who sits by herself on the sofa eating junk food and watching TV. *Either* put up with your mother's constant criticism *or* never speak to her again.

Of course, when the only course of action you can visualize taking will leave you as unhappy, unhealthy, and unfulfilled as you already are, there truly is no sense in pursuing it. But what about the rest of the spectrum, the other, less catastrophic options? They are there, but that one disastrous option on your mind is so unappealing it may distract you from the search. If that happens, you may stop looking, and you'll probably stay stuck.

### Focusing on the Fatal Flaw

You can get stuck and sabotage your efforts to get un- stuck by recognizing alternatives to your present situation, but rejecting them one by one. You can generate a long list of possibilities, all right. The problem is that you are struck instantly by the fatal flaw in each one. Without taking the time to pursue it, you eliminate the option because you think an imperfect alternative is a useless alternative.

Julie is an absolute genius when it comes to finding those fatal flaws. She can reject alternatives faster than any- one can suggest them. For example, Julie is firm in her belief that all forms of therapy are useless because she's been to see therapists before and they did not help her. She has also made up her mind that taking art courses is out of the ques- tion because she's too tired after a full day of work and all art students are weird anyway. Bars are meat markets popu- lated by psychopaths. Getting to know men through work is impossible because her co-workers gossip and meddle. Self- help books are all the same. Personal ads, singles groups, and blind dates are for only desperate people and losers. She has a "Yeah, but" comeback for every suggestion, and what she honestly believes is a perfectly good reason not to pursue any option—not one is flawless.

Focusing on fatal flaws is the most common form of this barrier. If you are so inclined, you will always be able to find legitimate reasons why an alternative plan of action might not work for you. But you must keep in mind that while the flaw you have discovered may be real enough, it often is far from fatal. Look at the alternatives closely. It is possible that you have not looked for the potential good in the option. When you are stuck, you may not notice that the probable positive outcome of changing your situation far outweighs the possible negative consequences. When you are stuck, the flaws are all you see. As a result, you may pass up reasonable avenues for getting unstuck because smooth sailing and a direct, uninterrupted road to complete happiness cannot be guaranteed.

### Grasping at Straws

Grasping at straws is the flip side of finding fatal flaws. In both instances you can see the possible alternatives to your present situation, but you do not thoroughly and conscientiously consider their true potential for getting you unstuck or weigh the potential negative *and* positive consequences. When you are grasping at straws, however, you try an alternative before you reject it. In fact, you jump on any and every alternative as soon as you find it, hoping it to be the quick fix you think you need. Invariably, however, you are disappointed when immediate, dramatic, all-encompassing results are not forthcoming, and this causes you to abandon the effort and move on to a new, equally impulsive course of action.

Len, desperately searching for solutions to his marital problems, repeatedly tried quick fixes. He bought his wife a car, paid for her college courses, saw a marriage counsellor, and even went deeply into debt buying a restaurant in hopes of rekindling the dream he and his wife had shared at the beginning of their marriage. He never looked below the surface. He just knew that he had to do *something* and went for the first solution that came to mind. He did see the alternatives. He did try them. But he did *not* achieve his goal. If anything, his marital problems got worse.

Because being stuck often causes desperation, you may be willing to try *anything* to relieve the pain and solve the problem. You may solicit advice from every imaginable source and lunge for every possible "out," like a drowning man clinging to a life preserver. That's what Jack did.

A high-level accountant for a large company, Jack feared

he was racing full steam ahead to a nervous breakdown because the stress in his life was so great and so constant. He shared his concerns with everyone he knew, hoping they would suggest a surefire remedy. His brother told him a chiropractor could relieve his stress-related aches and pains. After his first session, however, he felt worse instead of better and he stopped seeing the chiropractor. His assistant told him to meditate. He tried, but during his meditation time, he found himself obsessively worrying about work. He stopped meditating. His ex-girlfriend made an appointment for him with her psychiatrist, who prescribed medication that made Jack dizzy and lethargic. He stopped taking the medication and no longer sees the psychiatrist. He joined a health club but stopped going regularly because he got too nervous about finding time to work out. He delegated job responsibilities, but worried that they wouldn't be accomplished to his satisfaction, he took them back. He took vacations, drank strange teas, and consulted a hypnotist.

What Jack really needed was an overall stress reduction plan and the patience to follow it. Instead, he tried one "sure cure" after another, abandoning each when his stress did not disappear instantly. Consequently, he is still heading straight for a breakdown.

If this version of the second barrier to change is working its wily ways on you, you blindly pursue alternatives without thinking clearly about them. You never ask yourself if the "cure" has any connection with the "disease." Instead, you go off on a wild-goose chase only to return to square one. What's more, by trying alternatives impulsively and rejecting them before they have a chance to really work, you eliminate those that could succeed in time or under the proper conditions.

## Overwhelmed by Alternatives

On any given Saturday night you could go to a play, a movie, a bar, a party, an art auction, a concert, or stay at home. You could have a romantic dinner for two, meet friends at a restaurant, invite guests to a gourmet meal in your home, barbecue in the backyard, or have pizza or Chinese food delivered and rent a videotape, play charades, Trivial Pursuit, or have a sing-along. You could forgo socializing and work, pay bills, supervise your daughter's slumber party, read a Gothic novel, or give yourself a pedicure. With so many choices, how do you choose?

How *do* you choose? Unfortunately, you can have plenty of options and still get stuck. All of them may, at first glance, appear to be equal, and choosing one means not choosing another. But what if you want them all? What if you make the wrong choice? It's true that you could make the wrong choice, but becoming paralysed in your decision-making process is even worse. All your options are rendered useless if you are unable to evaluate them, prioritize them, and make a decision.

When Margaret, the public relations coordinator for a large health services organization, learned her position would be eliminated, she was stunned and confused. She loved her job. It was exactly the type of work she wanted to do. The people she worked with, the pay she received, and the creativity and freedom she was allowed met her needs perfectly. The situation upset her terribly at first, and while she was reacting to the unexpected news, she temporarily believed she had no choices. The next thing she knew, however, she was presented with more alternatives than she could handle.

"First of all, I was offered a different position with the same company," she says. "Then a friend called to tell me a position like the one I was leaving was available at her company. Another friend, who was self-employed as a publicist, had more work than she could handle and asked me to become a partner in her business. A hospital offered me some freelance public relations work, and a local newspaper asked if I would write some freelance feature stories, which got me thinking about starting my own business. The college where I got my degree was looking for an associate professor. And my husband, who makes enough money to support us, suggested it might be the right time to have a baby, which, of course, put all the other possibilities into a new light."

While you might envy Margaret because she has so many places to turn, those very viable options did her little good. They all were reasonable. They all were available. But which alternative was the right one for her? Although in the workplace Margaret made countless decisions every day, when it came to her own life and deciding on a specific course of action that could affect her for years to come, she did not know how to choose. Most of the choices were very, very appealing. She ran over each alternative in her mind, considering each from every conceivable angle, afraid she would make the wrong choice. But the more she reviewed her options, the more confused she became.

With all those doors open to her, Margaret nonetheless was frozen in her tracks. What's more, while she spun her wheels, some of the doors closed. She didn't realize that not choosing is a choice in itself. If you postpone a decision for long enough, you will be left with only one path to take, and it will not necessarily be the best path. Margaret finally decided to freelance and try to get pregnant. Although she does not regret her decision, she still wonders if it was the right one.

As a rule, the more alternatives you have, the better, *only if* you can also evaluate them, assign a priority to each, and select one. Having options without knowing what to do with them is as debilitating as seeing no options. If you cannot choose, you cannot move.

Barrier #2 takes on many disguises and cunningly keeps you from getting what you want for your life. It is a two-sided barrier—one side blinds or distracts you from seeing the alternatives, while the other keeps you from choosing an alternative to pursue. So, you stay exactly where you are—and you know where that is—stuck.

## DISMANTLING THE BARRIER: HOW TO SEARCH FOR ALTERNATIVES AND MAKE EFFECTIVE DECISIONS

Alternatives *do* exist. You just get stuck when you do not know how to recognize them. You feel trapped because you have not found viable options—*yet.* But you can learn how to look for them. And you will find them. Of all the barriers to change, this one is the easiest to dismantle.

Why? Because alternatives *do* exist. There is always at least one option, and usually many more than one. There is always *something* you can do (or stop doing). Merely realizing alternatives do exist relieves stress and counteracts that desperate feeling you get whenever you believe you are trapped in a corner with nowhere to go.

The alternatives you find may not be perfect. They may not show results immediately or completely or magically alter your existence. And alternatives are not *all* you need to get unstuck or achieve your goals. However, learning to recognize all your options is a step. A step is movement, movement that can bring you closer to your chosen destination.

This barrier is also easier to tackle than most because specific, reliable tools and techniques can be used to search for alternatives, increase options, evaluate and prioritize them, and decide upon the best route to take. These tools and techniques have a proven positive track record. They are used every day by teachers and therapists. They work. You can make them work for you.

### An Option for All Seasons

No matter where or why you are stuck, you always have *one* alternative. You can *ask for help.*

"No man is an island" is a phrase I'm sure you have heard. It is particularly true when applied to the *no alternatives* barrier. Ultimately you make your own choices and follow the path that is right for you. However, you do not have to grapple with each decision by yourself, nor do you have to travel your path alone. You can ask for help when you need it.

Unfortunately, people who are stuck and feeling lousy tend to isolate themselves. Think about Karen, who was described in Chapter One. She cannot maintain her weight loss. She thinks people judge her negatively because she is overweight and holes up in her house when her eating is out of control. She does not want to hear any advice, which she interprets as criticism. She wants to be left alone. So do alcoholics. So do abuse victims (and their abusers). So do people getting divorced, ending a relationship, or experiencing a great deal of stress. Just when they most need support, they push people away from them. They think they must solve their own problems and make decisions all by themselves. Yet what they need to do is ask for help.

Asking for help will not rob you of your dignity. It will not take away your independence or demonstrate that you are weak-willed or incompetent. Indeed, seeking advice prior to making a decision is a sign of levelheadedness and wisdom. Contrary to what you think when you are stuck and hurting, you are not the only person who has ever experienced that particular conflict, found yourself in a certain situation or decided to change without knowing where to begin. The fallacies in this line of thinking have been shown again and again.

Help comes in many forms. It can be professional, such as the help offered by a suicide prevention hotline or any other crisis intervention service listed in the telephone book. You can get into counselling with a trained psychiatrist, psychologist, or social worker, or find help by talking to friends, relatives, colleagues, or supervisors. Sometimes help can be found in books such as this one, inspirational tracts, or even biographies of people who have overcome adversity. Some of the very best help is offered by self-help groups (also listed in the phone book or "community calendar" sections of the newspaper). Groups such as Alcoholics Anonymous, Over-eaters Anonymous, and Al-Anon are the most well-known, but groups are available in almost every community for al-most any concern you can imagine.

You can ask for help at any time for any reason. How-ever, seeking help is particularly beneficial when you cannot see available alternatives or make decisions about the op-tions you do see. Searching for alternatives and evaluating options is easier with someone else's assistance and support. The "helper" may not always or immediately suggest alter-natives you like. However, they do have some distance from your problem and can be more objective about it. They will see the merits and drawbacks of an option before you do and may be able to shed light when all you see is darkness. At the very least, asking for help (and remaining open to the advice offered) points you in new directions and stimulates more productive thinking.

Begin to increase your alternatives by asking people what *they* would do or what *they* did when they faced similar conflicts. Read profiles of people you admire. You do not *have* to take anyone's advice. You do not *have* to follow in the footsteps of Elizabeth Taylor, Eric Clapton, Shirley Mac-Laine, or anyone else. All you have to do is ask, read, listen, hear—and you will discover new options.

---

## BRAINSTORMING

"The typical eye overlooks the ninety percent *good* in any idea because of the ten percent *bad* that the conventional eye never fails to see."

—*Charles Kettering*

Charles Kettering's statement reminds me of every com-mittee ever assembled to tackle a problem or plan an activity. Without fail, dozens of ideas are proposed and immediately eliminated because someone instantaneously spots a flaw.

It never matters that the flaw is small and easy to correct. Conclusions are drawn prematurely and great ideas are passed over, leaving only mediocre ones.

On the other hand, you increase your alternatives when you suspend judgment during the idea-gathering stage, accumulate options, and evaluate them later. This process is called *brainstorming*.

People whose jobs require them to solve problems, make group decisions, plan for the future, or be creative are familiar with the brainstorming technique. Advertising teams commonly use it to generate ad campaign ideas. It can be seen at work in union/management meetings when ideas are needed to prevent a strike or in corporate board rooms when sales need to be increased. Therapists brainstorm with their clients; teachers brainstorm with their students; supervisors with their employees; generals with their staffs. Yet I am constantly amazed at how few people apply this proven technique to their own lives. There is no better way to increase alternatives.

To brainstorm, you turn down the volume on your inner critic and let the creative juices flow, freeing you to seek out any and all possibilities. Brainstorming asks you to identify, without evaluation, every conceivable alternative—no matter how wacky, wild, or improbable that alternative appears to be at first glance. Brainstorming can be employed to generate alternatives to any situation.

You can brainstorm:

- things to do on a Saturday night

- ways to make your job more exciting

- ways to better manage your time

- how to spend your holiday

- ways to improve a relationship

- ways to save money

- how to celebrate Christmas

- things you want to accomplish in your life

- risks you want to take

- ways to make sure you stick to a diet or exercise programme

- how family members can share household chores

Anytime you feel stuck and need alternatives—BRAIN-STORM!

Brainstorming can be done alone, but often it works best with other people. It is generally done in one sitting. However, if there is no time limit for resolving a problem, I like to spread my brainstorms over several sessions. Then I can take advantage of those brilliant ideas I get in between sessions while driving my car or taking a shower.

Brainstorming begins by clearly phrasing the problem or question at hand. Here are three examples:

"We have two weeks in August set aside for vacation. I want it to be a fun and worthwhile vacation for everyone. How can we have a vacation like that? Let's see how many vacation ideas we can come up with."

"All Rita and I do anymore is fight. It's getting so bad that I've been staying at work later and finding reasons to go places without her. I do love Rita and I want our relationship to work. I just don't know what to do anymore. What are my options?"

"My job is making me crazy. I am physically sick and emotionally drained because of it. I can't just quit, because I need the income. What other alternatives do I have?"

In all three examples the problem is identified and the task is clear—to discover as many alternatives as possible, *without* focusing on finding the one right and perfect solution. The person phrasing the question asks for a multitude of options, one or a combination of which will *later* be chosen as a step toward getting unstuck.

For brainstorming to work, the following rules *must* be followed:

**1.** NO CRITICISM. Do not judge or evaluate the alternatives at this point. Do not censor yourself in any way. Absolutely anything that comes to mind should be listed.

**2.** ENCOURAGE FREEWHEELING. Let those creative juices flow—the wilder the idea, the better. You can always eliminate the outrageous and trim your ideas down to size later on.

**3.** GO FOR QUANTITY. Make a long, long, long list. By generating lots and lots of ideas while brainstorming, you increase the probability of finding good, workable ideas when you go back over your list.

**4.** PIGGYBACK, EXPAND, COMBINE. Modify or spin off new ideas from old ones or combine previously listed options to create other alternatives that work.

---

### GIVE IT A TRY

In Chapter Two you completed an Overall Wellness inventory. You examined ten aspects of daily living which contribute to your physical, emotional, intellectual, and spiritual well-being and identified those elements you personally felt needed improvement. If you are to actually improve those areas of your life, however, you will need alternatives, both as steps toward your ultimate goal and as guideposts for getting unstuck. It is easy enough to say "I'll improve my nutrition by going on a diet," but what sort of diet will you choose? Will it be a short-term low calorie diet for weight loss only, will you eliminate white sugar, processed flour, and fried foods or adopt a lifetime eating plan? How will you begin? How will you make sure you do not cheat? What will you do to keep the pounds from coming back? Will you go it alone?

You can instantly "decide" to exercise, but what form of exercise will you choose? When, where, and how often will you exercise? What can you do to make sure you stick to your programme? What are your options?

If you want to better manage your time, how will you go about it? Are you aware of the many time-management tools and techniques? Have you considered which best fit your lifestyle?

Unless you ask those sorts of questions, you cannot *choose* the options that are right for you. To improve, increase, or change an aspect of overall wellness, you must first look for and list as many alternatives as possible. You must brainstorm.

To begin brainstorming:

**1.** CHOOSE an overall wellness area you have identified as a priority for change.

**2.** ASK YOURSELF—*How* can I change it? *What* can I do to have more, less, or something better in this area? *What* are my options?

**3.** Take out a sheet of paper, get a pencil, and ANSWER those questions by BRAINSTORMING alternatives.

**4.** REMEMBER— Anything goes. Be playful, zany, sarcastic, creative, or whatever it takes to make a long, long list. Go for QUANTITY not quality.

**5.** Try not to interrupt the flow of ideas by going back through the list to see if you already wrote down an idea or one like it. You can eliminate duplications later and variations are considered as separate options.

**6.** Ask for help if you need it. Explain the exercise to a friend, relative, co-worker, your spouse, or your therapist. Ask them to help you generate alternatives. (Don't forget to explain the rules of brainstorming to them).

## Harry's List

In Chapter Two, I introduced Harry, the freelance photographer who completed the Overall Wellness inventory and selected several areas for improvement. One of his priorities was to find and nurture a love relationship. He knew that simply *wanting* a relationship was not enough to have one. He also knew that the first thing he had to do was stop isolating himself and start meeting women. This is his brainstorm list.

To meet a woman to have a relationship with I could:

- go to singles bars
- take some adult education courses
- join a singles group
- place personal ads
- answer personal ads
- sign up with a dating service
- ask friends to introduce me to single women
- ask relatives to introduce me to single women
- ask customers to introduce me to single women
- smile and say hello to women I see
- strike up conversations in the grocery store
- at the post office
- at the dry cleaners
- on the beach
- join a health club (since I need to exercise anyway)
- wear a sign saying I'm looking for a relationship

- write my number on restroom walls
- hang a "WANTED: A Relationship" poster around town
- join clubs/groups in areas that interest me
- get to know women who display things at craft shows
- be friendlier to women who stop to look at my photos
- go out more in general
- cut my hair
- tone up my body
- stop looking at the pavement when I walk places
- go on blind dates
- make a list of what I want in a woman (so I know her when I find her)
- go to workshops
- learn how to overcome shyness
- woo away my best friend's wife
- give up and become a monk
- talk to that lady I always see at the laundrette
- same for the woman who works at the bakery
- get to know other women I've noticed but never approached

Harry's list is something to behold. It is all the more impressive if you know that immediately prior to his brainstorming session, he had thought that "what I could do to meet women was limited to hanging out at singles bars or putting a classified ad in the personals section of the newspaper. Neither idea appealed to me. I never considered that some of the things I wanted to do anyway could also be social opportunities. The other thing I hadn't figured on was that I already knew women casually whom I could get to know better.

"You know it was a real relief to see the situation wasn't as hopeless as I thought," he continues. "I thought brainstorming was going to be a real pain too, like pulling teeth, but it wasn't. Actually, it was sort of fun."

Brainstorming *can* be fun. Very often you get a few good laughs about a situation you had previously seen as excruciatingly painful and completely hopeless. Brainstorming opens a door and lets ideas rush in. Brainstorming works. It is a surefire way to increase alternatives.

All options are not created equal, however. As Margaret, the woman who was overwhelmed by options when her job was eliminated, can tell you, having a plentiful supply of options is not enough to get you unstuck. Jack, who grasped at straws hoping to miraculously and immediately eliminate stress from his life, would agree that trying options just because you see them does not work either. Each option must be clearly and consciously evaluated or you will chase your tail trying to make a decision as Margaret did or waste a great deal of time and energy the way Jack did. To make your alternatives work for you, you must . . .

### Narrow the Field

Use a combination of logic, gut feelings, and value judgments to evaluate and choose options from those you listed while brainstorming. As you can see from Harry's list and from your own, brainstorming leaves you with more alternatives than you can comfortably analyze in depth. You have to narrow the field.

To trim your brainstorm list to a manageable number of alternatives, you should rely primarily on "gut" instincts, using your intuition to weed out the options that just don't feel right for you. Therefore, immediately after brainstorming, prioritize each item on your list. This can be based on *general appeal* (what you most *want* to pursue); *practicality* (those options that are most doable); *immediacy* (options you could, with little difficulty, begin to pursue right away); or a combination of these criteria. Give each item on your brainstorm list an A, B, or C priority. Assign an A to items that have *high* appeal, practicality, and/or immediacy. Give a C to those that are low priority and B's to those that fall somewhere in the middle.

When you are stuck, unhappy, or unsure of yourself, it is all too easy to be indecisive, even after setting your priorities. To avoid this, try to assign *an equal number* of A, B, and C priorities. Thus, if there are twenty-four items on your list, eight should get A priority, eight should get B priority, and eight should get C priority. It may be a struggle to achieve such parity, but doing so is essential. So, take some time now to go over your brainstorm list and narrow the field by assigning A, B, and C priorities.

## Carol's "A" List

"The brainstorming was really hard for me," says Carol about her attempt to find alternatives for her unsatisfying work situation. "In fact, other people came up with most of the ideas on my list. I was still being very negative when I tried to narrow the field. If I hadn't been forced to come up with A priorities, I wouldn't have any. Nothing would have got more than a B."

Reluctantly, Carol identified five very disparate A items from her list of fifteen alternatives. They were:

- quit my job immediately (worry later)
- take on more clients until I can afford to quit
- get a job with another agency

- pick a date to quit my job, take steps to advertise my practice, and line up consulting jobs in the meantime

- stick it out here until I can take early retirement

Now, having narrowed the field, you (and Carol) are ready to take a closer look at your A priorities. It is from these that you will choose an eventual course of action.

## Evaluating Options

Although emotions and intuition come into play throughout your decision-making efforts, the evaluation of A priority alternatives requires the application of logic. Many variables can be considered when choices must be made. However, most logical analysis boils down to weighing the *positive* that can result from pursuing an option against the *negative* consequences it might produce.

Take out a separate sheet of paper for each of your A priority alternatives. Then, write the alternative across the top of the page and draw a line down the centre. The left-hand column will be for POSSIBLE POSITIVE OUTCOMES and the right-hand column will be for POSSIBLE NEGATIVE CONSEQUENCES. Think of as many good results as you can and write them in the left-hand column. Do the same for negative consequences.

Julie stumbled and fell at this point in the decision-making process. She was so skilled and accustomed to finding fatal flaws that she drew a complete blank when asked to think of possible positive outcomes. She also countered other people's positive suggestions with matching negatives and ended up by throwing her pencil down in despair. "I told you there was nothing I could do," she moaned. "Maybe this stuff works for other people, but it isn't working for me."

I hope you do not allow yourself to fall into the same trap. Human beings *are* prone to negativity. As the earlier comment from Charles Kettering affirms, most of us zero in on what won't work and overlook what will. The tendency to find fatal flaws and reasons not to pursue perfectly good alternatives increases when self-esteem is low and being stuck has drained you mentally and emotionally. If you honestly want to get unstuck, push yourself to identify the positives. Take some time to make your own plus and minus list for each alternative. If you get stuck, call on an objective outside party to help add items to your plus column.

### One of Carol's Options

"I did the pluses and minuses by myself first." Carol explains. "After that, I knew that my negative attitude was colouring my decisions, so I asked my therapist for some ideas, and then I went to a friend who had left the agency where I work and started her own business. Both women came up with good ideas, and I even came up with a few more pluses on my own once I got the hang of it."

Her analysis of the option to set a date to leave the agency and take steps to increase her private practice looked like this:

### PLUSES

I would know there was an end in sight.

I would be forced to find referral sources, line up consulting jobs, get a brochure, business cards, etc., and come up with a budget for myself, (i.e., I could stop procrastinating).

If I did all those things, I wouldn't worry so much.

I would stop wasting so much time (and hating myself because of it).

My kids and my friends would stop rolling their eyes and walking away from me because of my constant complaining.

My private practice would benefit.

I wouldn't have to stay here forever.

I would feel more secure.

I would have a steady paycheque for a few more months.

## MINUSES

I would have to put up with this job for a while more.

I still wouldn't know if my private practice would support me.

I'd have to give up the paycheque eventually.

Could I really work without the bureaucracy's telling me what to do?

What about health insurance and my retirement fund?

Might feel trapped if the date to quit came and I still wasn't comfortable with leaving.

Is this fair to my kids?

Carol took several weeks to complete her plus and minus lists. She asked for other people's opinions. Then she moved on to the next step:

### Weighing the Consequences

The number of items in a column can be deceiving. Like alternatives, all consequences are not created equal. Some mean more to you than others, some will have a greater impact on your life than others, and some are just plain scarier than others. In essence, each consequence has its own weight or value. The next step you should take is to consciously, thoughtfully, assign weights to each consequence.

To do this, give each positive and negative consequence a numerical weight. I like to use a scale of numbers between one and five with fives assigned to consequences that matter the most. Really think hard before you assign a number. Ask yourself how much each item *really* matters and make sure fear and self-doubt are not getting in your way. Sometimes it helps to pretend there is nothing else to consider but that one consequence. If all other conditions were good, how much would that one factor influence you?

After each consequence has been given a numerical weight, review your entire list for each alternative. Cross off your list items that seem to cancel each other out. You can even add up the numbers in each column and divide by the number of items to derive total positive and negative values for each alternative. You will rarely need to go that far, however. By the time you rank consequences and eliminate items that cancel each other out, you will have a relatively clear picture of the viability of your alternative.

Carol's weighing of consequences looked like this:

## PLUSES

I would know there was an end in sight. *5*

I would be forced to find referral sources, line up consulting jobs, get a brochure, business cards, etc., and come up with a budget for myself, (i.e., I could stop procrastinating). *4*

If I did all those things, I wouldn't worry so much. *1* (I'd worry anyway)

I would stop wasting so much time (and hating myself because of it). *5*

My kids and my friends would stop rolling their eyes and walking away from me because of my constant complaining. *5*

My private practice would benefit. *4*

I wouldn't have to stay here forever. *5*

I would feel more secure. *2* (no, I wouldn't)

I would have a steady paycheque for a few more months. *3*

## MINUSES

I would have to put up with this job for a while more. *2*

I still wouldn't know if my private practice would support me. *4*

I'd have to give up the paycheque eventually. *5*

Could I really work without the bureaucracy's telling me what to do? *2* (this is my low self-esteem talking)

What about health insurance and my retirement fund? *5*

Might feel trapped if the date to quit came and I still wasn't comfortable with leaving. *2* (fear, just as good a chance I'll be thrilled!)

Is this fair to my kids? *1* (it isn't fair now)

Much to Carol's surprise, the possible positive outcomes of this alternative far outweighed the feared negative consequences. Such was not the case for other A priority options, such as hanging on at the agency until she could take early retirement or looking for a job with another agency. By listing and evaluating positive and negative consequences, Carol began to see a direction she could go. If you have been taking the steps described here, you too should see at least one alternative to the way things are, and at least one path clear for travel toward your goals and aspirations. Now, it is time to:

## Make a Choice

Ah, the moment of truth has arrived. Even though you have searched for alternatives, used your instincts to narrow the field, racked your brain (and other people's too) to find the negative and positive consequences, weighed and measured and put a great deal of careful, clear thinking into the decision-making effort, you are once again possessed by the fear of choosing. Your hands shake. Your lower lip quivers. Your mouth is dry. Your heart pounds and your blood pressure rises. What if you make the wrong choice? Worse yet, no matter what you choose you are going to lose that good old fallback line—"I have no choice. There is nothing I can do." You might have to *do* something. What if what you choose to do does not work?

I'll deal with that last question in a moment. First, summon up some courage and rank each of your options. The most acceptable alternative should get a number one. Give the next most acceptable a two, and so on until you have given each option a different descending rank. By ordering each option rather than choosing one and discarding the rest, you leave yourself some breathing room. The number one ranked option will be the one you choose to pursue *at this time*. Yet, keep in mind that the other options remain available to you. You are not losing anything—except your unwanted "stuck" status.

You see, no decision has to be final. It is exactly this thought of finality that brings up all that anxiety and fear. If you make a choice, give it a chance to work. If it doesn't, you can always try the next option on your list or make another choice. The first alternative you choose may not turn out to be the one and only perfect answer. After all, there is more than one route to any destination.

What's more, for most of us one alternative is not all we will need. Our journey to the lives we desire and deserve will require many steps and many decisions. The choice you make now is merely the first step in the right direction. But don't forget, if you are stuck, any step in the right direction is a milestone.

Carol, who chose to set a date to quit her job and to spend the interim time preparing for a successful private practice, will still have to choose to actually quit her job when the target date arrives. She will have to decide whether to use her retirement fund to tide her over during the first months of self-employment or leave it in the bank to accrue interest. She will have to make choices about cutting living expenses, what to charge clients, how to use her time when she is her own boss, and how long to wait before deciding whether self-employment works for her or not. Yet, even with all these uncertainties ahead of her, Carol feels better because she has made that first choice and taken that first step.

"Just to know there's *something* I can do makes me feel

better," she says. "Things don't look so bleak. I have a goal to work for. I'm not just getting by. I'm going for something. I'm still scared and I'm still worried about making ends meet, but I don't feel as helpless or as trapped."

Jack, the accountant with the stress problem, practically had to be tied to a chair and forced to work through these strategies. But when he did, he discovered that many of the options he had already tried would have to be tried again, this time in some sort of logical order. He also realized that he should not expect that his stress would disappear overnight, and that he must give the option he had chosen time to work. "I'm going to have to run through all my A alternatives eventually," he says. "But I can do them one step at a time. And I'm going to think about them before I do them this time, too."

Searching for all their alternatives and taking the decision-making steps described in this chapter worked well for Carol, Jack, and Harry, and they were able to make healthy choices from viable options. You also now have the opportunity to generate alternatives and make choices. Will you?

If your answer is YES, then you can see the light at the end of the tunnel and begin to map your route toward your goals and aspirations. You may still have trouble getting started on that journey, and you will certainly encounter other barriers along your way. The following chapters describe those barriers, which I'll help you recognize and dismantle. But keep in mind that if you have begun to dismantle the NO ALTERNATIVES barrier, you have already taken a giant step toward getting unstuck.

If your answer is NO, if somewhere along the line you become queasy and confused, if you are unable to list alternatives or evaluate them, chances are you have come upon another barrier already. Perhaps it's that old low self-esteem throwing up a smoke screen in front of you, or one of the other barriers stands in your way. It might be barrier number three—the subject of the next chapter—NOT KNOWING WHAT YOU REALLY WANT.

# 5

## Change and Values

The other day I spent a pleasant afternoon with Mary, Peter, and Laura. When dinnertime rolled around, we decided to order pizza. Mary went into the kitchen to boil water for tea and find the telephone number of a nearby pizza parlour.

By the time she returned, I was engrossed in Peter's stories and snapshots of last summer's trip abroad, and Laura was reading a magazine article and working on a self-test from the magazine to determine if her boyfriend is as romantic as she is. Mary asked us what toppings we wanted on the pizza. Distracted, we answered quickly and barely looked up from the photo albums and magazine.

Peter said, "Don't ask me. I eat anything."

Enthralled by a breathtaking photograph of a scenic castle, I absentmindedly agreed, "I don't know. Whatever everybody else wants, I guess."

Laura, too, claimed to have no preference. "Doesn't matter to me," she mumbled. "You decide."

We all went back to what we were doing. Left to her

**115**

own resources and knowing exactly what she likes on a pizza, Mary ordered two large pies with extra cheese, peppers, mushrooms, and sausage. Ravenously hungry when the pizzas finally arrived, we opened the boxes the moment Mary set them on the table. Mouths watering, we grabbed slices of piping hot pizza only to have our delight turn to disappointment.

Laura, a vegetarian, scorched her fingers while removing bits of sausage from each slice before eating it. Concerned about cholesterol, I was dismayed to see all that extra cheese oozing grease. And it turned out that Peter hates mushrooms and peppers.

Because Peter, Laura, and I did not consider, choose, or communicate what we actually wanted on our pizza, we got stuck with a pizza we did not like. We ate it anyway. Normally, pizza toppings are of no great significance. They certainly won't alter the course of our lives. Yet this simple story makes a powerful point.

UNLESS YOU THINK ABOUT, CHOOSE, SAY, AND DO WHAT YOU *REALLY* WANT, YOU RISK GETTING STUCK WITH A LIFE OR CIRCUMSTANCES YOU DO NOT DESIRE.

Not knowing what you *really* want is the third barrier to change. It obstructs your path whenever you:

**1.** make decisions without giving careful consideration to your options and their possible short- and long-term consequences.

**2.** make choices based on what "everybody" does, what you assume you *should* do, or because you feel guilty or inadequate.

**3.** give other people's preferences priority over your own or believe you do not deserve to get what you want and therefore fail to communicate your needs or speak up for yourself.

**4.** behave impulsively, indecisively, rebelliously, or waver back and forth.

## HOW THIS BARRIER GOT YOU
## STUCK IN THE FIRST PLACE

Many of the people described earlier in this book got stuck because they did not know what they really wanted. They chose the easiest, quickest, most obvious route, and it took them somewhere other than where they wanted to be.

Remember the burned-out social worker, Carol? She is stuck working for a social service agency she cannot wait to leave. She had originally signed on with the agency because they were the first to offer her part-time work with children. She asked no further questions and immediately stopped exploring other options.

When Carol wanted to advance professionally and financially, she once again jumped the gun. Instead of identifying the various means to the end she desired, she automatically chose to become a supervisor within the same agency. She did not *really* want to stop working directly with children or get buried under mountains of paperwork, but that is what happened.

"At the time, it seemed like the way to go," Carol says today. "If I knew then what I know now, I would have done things differently. But to tell you the truth, I didn't give it much thought at all."

Neither did Janet, the workaholic therapist whose lifeline net in Chapter Two revealed that her days are overflowing with activities she believed she *had* to do. She describes herself as overworked and overwhelmed. She is drowning, with no time for the fun, leisure activities or the relaxation she truly desires and deserves.

"I just said yes to everything that came my way," Janet explains. "I assumed that more was better, that busy was happy, that successful people worked at success twenty-four hours a day. Those were the ideas I was raised with and I never questioned them. I honestly thought that if I slowed down, I would lose everything. You can see where those ideas got me. I'm so overcommitted that I can't get a moment's peace."

Lisa, the office supply sales representative introduced in Chapter Two, says, "I wanted to be a team player and I thought that meant going along with the programme even if I didn't like it. If I was unhappy, it was my own fault. I should try harder to please people. If they brought in someone else to be sales manager, then I must not have been good enough. Who was I to question my superiors? If my opinion was worth anything, they would have asked for it."

Thinking along these lines, Lisa put up with whatever happened in the company. She did not think she was good enough to make her own decisions and thus drastically reduced her chances of getting anything she *really* wanted.

You are stuck today because of decisions you made in the past without careful consideration, and by neglecting to use your power to say and act upon what *you* really wanted. Like Carol, you may look back now and wish you had done things differently or made different choices. Like Lisa, you may have gone along with the crowd. Now you may hardly remember why or when you first got on this roller coaster ride. Like Janet, today you are paying the price for yesterday's choices. Yet, if you reviewed those choices with an open mind, you would see they had little to do with what you genuinely wanted and a great deal to do with what you thought you ought to do "under the circumstances."

Perhaps you were busy with other activities and the demands of daily living and did not take the time to consider your alternatives. It was more expedient to let someone else decide or simpler to latch onto the first available option (perhaps one that someone else suggested). At the time, you did not think that particular decision would make much difference over the long haul. Or the situation seemed so overwhelming that you gratefully headed for any port in the storm. Perhaps you can see that this barrier is also a symptom of barrier number two—the inability to recognize the alternatives available to you.

Maybe you made choices when your self-esteem was low. Already believing you did not deserve much in this life, you were more than willing to go along with the crowd. You reasoned that choices made by someone you saw as smarter, more creative, more assertive, or more powerful than you had to be better than the ones you could make. And because of that same low self-esteem, you believed that what someone else wanted had to be more important than what you wanted. But denying your own desires can only make you feel even more miserable and powerless. Not knowing what you want becomes a more difficult barrier to dismantle when combined with low self-esteem.

In the poem "The Road Not Taken," Robert Frost describes two roads that "diverge in a yellow wood." Frost took the road less travelled. Many of you took the other road, turning onto it automatically. You never wondered if it was the right road for you. After all, if so many other people had walked that way before you, it must be the way you too should go.

Sometimes the main thoroughfare ridden by the nameless, faceless majority took you where you did indeed want to go. More often, however, it led to another fork in the road where, once again, you went the way everyone else was going or in the direction you somehow came to believe you should go. If you are stuck now, chances are you took a few turns too many based on someone else's values instead of your own.

---

## HOW NOT KNOWING WHAT YOU REALLY WANT SABOTAGES CHANGE EFFORTS

In today's rapidly and constantly changing world, not considering, choosing, or doing what you definitely want is a malady shared by most people.

Consider the case of the Cabbage Patch doll. Recently, many Christmas shoppers worked themselves into a frenzy in pursuit of a bundle of cloth-covered foam stuffing. At five in the morning, parents, grandparents, aunts, and uncles stood on line in front of department stores that would not open their doors until ten A.M. Once inside, they literally clawed their way through crowds of hysterical and equally determined consumers who had to get their hands on one of a limited supply of Cabbage Patch dolls. Fights broke out. People fell to the floor, and other people stepped over and sometimes on top of them. As they left the stores empty-handed, those unable to grab a doll for their children shed tears of despair.

Was this really how people wanted to spend their time and money during a holiday season intended to foster joy and goodwill? Did a doll reflect their true feelings and beliefs about Christmas? Would a doll actually tell their children how much they were loved and cherished? Did anyone stop to ask these questions? Or was the great Cabbage Patch caper the result of too little thought and too many media and High Street messages telling people that the dolls were the hot item for Christmas giving? Had they simply been convinced that children who did not have Cabbage Patch dolls would be ostracized by their peers and traumatized for life?

Cabbage Patch capers, Transformer robot search-and-buy missions, and Rambo worship, as well as other rapidly passing and largely interchangeable passions, are relatively modern phenomena. We have become a more mobile population and come into contact with more ideas from more sources in a few years than our ancestors did in a whole lifetime. We are influenced by more people and bombarded by media messages. As a result, there are so many possibilities and so many versions of the good life—so many different ways we are *supposed* to be.

Always trying to live up to the standards put before you by parents, friends, teachers, peers, churches, and the media ultimately blocks change. You simply cannot please all of these people all of the time. When the messages received from various sources conflict—as they often do—you become confused. With so many versions of what you *should* do, how do you decide what you *will* do? All but lost and forgotten is the notion of what you might actually *want* to do.

What happens when you choose your path primarily because others have travelled it before you? What happens when you attempt to change primarily because someone else insists you should? To start with, you will not get what *you* actually want. In most instances, neither will you achieve the goal "they" convinced you to pursue. Efforts to change undertaken to satisfy someone else, options pursued because you feel obligated or guilty, and goals set so you can "keep up with the Joneses" are those most often and most quickly abandoned.

When Karen was introduced in Chapter One, she was back at square one and facing another tortuous effort to lose weight. Although she was not aware of it yet, the reasons why she chose to lose weight in the past contributed to her going up and down the scale like a yo-yo. She began all previous diets because her parents nagged and berated her, her lovers teased and sometimes humiliated her, pictures of models in fashion magazines frustrated her, or she hoped to impress former classmates at her high school reunion or an ex-boyfriend when she saw him at her cousin's wedding.

Hoping to please herself by pleasing other people did not keep Karen on track. Obesity and weight-loss research shows that dieting and maintenance of a goal weight are less likely to succeed when prompted by anything other than the dieter's sincere, inner desire to change. Karen will not achieve her goal until staying thinner is what *she* genuinely wants for her own happiness and well-being.

Consider, too, the teenage boy who performs poorly in school. He does not complete homework assignments. He daydreams during classes. He is thought to be lazy, unmotivated, and possibly educationally disabled since he has such a short attention span for schoolwork. Yet this same young man spends eight uninterrupted hours each Saturday rebuilding the engine of his car (which he loves dearly and had religiously saved money to buy). When it comes to his car, he reads technical material proficiently, grasps complex ideas, and completely focuses his attention for hours at a stretch. Is this the same lazy, unmotivated, educationally disabled fellow his teachers see each Monday morning? He inhabits the same body. Whether or not his teachers approve, he values engine mechanics more than English literature or ancient history. He accomplishes what he really wants to do.

**With any goal or aspiration you will stick with the programme you personally want to pursue, finding the time, energy, and resources to achieve what you honestly want to achieve. When you've made a personal commitment, you dismantle the barriers you find on the path you sincerely want to travel.**

On the other hand, when you do not know what you clearly want, when those "should" and "ought to" messages obscure your personal vision, and when you easily, quickly choose the path of least resistance or the one everyone else travels, you get lost and you get stuck. You lack staying power. You easily find reasons to abandon the "self-improvement nonsense" that was someone else's idea instead of your own. You dissipate your energy rebelling against know-it-all authorities or scatter yourself by trying to conform to and comply with each new suggestion you are given. Wishy-washy, listless, and confused, you take one detour after another.

---

## HOW NOT KNOWING WHAT YOU REALLY WANT
## KEEPS YOU FROM GETTING UNSTUCK

This barrier does more than get you stuck. It does more than undermine your efforts to change. Abdicating your power to choose and constantly turning to others for the answers to your life's questions robs you of the ability to look for and find what you *really* want.

"All my life, other people came first," says Lorraine, the mother of three who faced the conflict and confusion of no longer being needed as a full-time wife and parent. "When I was a kid, I lived to please my parents. Then I got married and lived to please my husband. Then I had children. Everyone knows a good mother puts her children's needs first, and I was a very good mother."

Then Lorraine's children went off to college, her husband turned his full attention to his new business, and her parents had long since stopped influencing Lorraine's daily living. In her early forties, Lorraine had many years left to do what she really wanted to do only she did not know what that was or how to find out.

"For the first time in my life I had no one to please but myself, and I didn't know how to do that. Everyone tells you what a good daughter should do and a good wife and a good mother. But no one tells you what you're supposed to do once your family doesn't need you anymore. Where was I supposed to go from there? What was I supposed to do with my life?"

Lorraine's dilemma illustrates a particularly dangerous feature of the third barrier to getting unstuck. Having developed a habit of not doing what you really want, the next time you reach a fork in the road or a crisis point in your life, you do not know *how* to choose a new direction for yourself. Like the scarecrow from *The Wizard of Oz,* you dangle from a pole pointing first one way, then another, then back the other way again. All roads lead somewhere. But from your present vantage point all roads look the same.

You feel a need for change, but you do not know how to change. You wonder what you *should* do. You wish someone would tell you what to do. You ask for advice and discover people have plenty to say. Unfortunately, their opinions about what you ought to do conflict and leave you confused, ambivalent, befuddled, frustrated, and depressed. In such a state, is it any wonder you can't get unstuck?

### But I Do Know What I Want

I suspect some of you have been reading this chapter and thinking barrier number three does not apply to you. After all, you do know what you want. You want to be happier or healthier; more successful or more attractive. You want to get out of a rotten marriage or into a better profession. You want to start exercising regularly or stop smoking. Furthermore, you are absolutely, positively sure you know what you want. Everyone I interviewed for this book felt the same way.

Think about Jack, the accountant who wants to reduce the stress in his life and ward off a full-fledged nervous breakdown. He impulsively tries every possible panacea but finds no lasting relief. Never once does he identify the sources of his stress, connect cause, effect, and cure, or evaluate any action's true potential to help him. He is not lying when he says he wants to feel better. But he does not stick to any one effort or get what he wants because he DOES NOT CONSIDER HIS ALTERNATIVES OR THINK ABOUT HIS CHOICES.

Likewise, Karen's every weight-loss effort ends in failure. She wants to lose weight and not gain it back, but why does she want that? She diets to please or impress other people and to avoid nagging and criticism. She frequently resents having to diet and often wishes people could just accept her for the way she is. Pressured to change, her valiant efforts always lead her back to square one. She has NEVER CHOSEN FREELY.

What about Lisa, whose self-esteem plummeted thanks to her sales job and more precisely because she failed to speak up for herself or her beliefs? She never got the respect and responsibility she wanted. In fact, with each passing day

her dissatisfaction grew. Because, she DID NOT COMMU-
NICATE HER DESIRES or protest her unfair treatment.

Finally there is Jacob, the heart attack survivor described in Chapter Two. He wanted to live. It was what he
wanted long before he was admitted to the coronary care
unit. He knew smoking, poor eating habits, and his lifestyle
were dangerous to his health. He knew his alternatives and
the consequences, often said he would change. Yet he did
nothing differently and suffered a heart attack that nearly
killed him. Jacob TOOK NO ACTION.

Jack, Karen, Lisa, and Jacob knew what they wanted,
but only in a general way.

If you truly want something, you:

1. give it careful thought and consideration
2. choose it freely
3. communicate it to other people
4. put it into action

With these criteria in mind, you can see that *saying* you
know what you want is different than *really knowing* what
you want. If you skip a step or rush blindly after the majority,
you get stuck.

### But Does Knowing What I Want Really Change Anything?

After a lecture she attended, one of my colleagues challenged me with the following scenario.

"Let's say I *really* want to sing like Ella Fitzgerald," my
colleague began. "I want to perform in smoky bars and sold-
out concert halls and read reviews about how my voice made
people cry with ecstasy. But I can't carry a tune, never have
been able to carry a tune, and never will be able to carry a
tune. What I really want doesn't make one bit of difference,
does it? If I can't sing, I can't sing, and all the desire in the
world won't change that."

She was absolutely right, of course. Similarly, if you are

a five-foot-four-inch-tall forty-five-year-old, you will never be the star player in an international basketball team—no matter how much you want that. If, at age thirty-two, you have never taken a dance lesson, you will not, in this lifetime, dance the lead in *Swan Lake* for the Royal Ballet. For one thing, each of us has certain tangible and inalterable limitations. Furthermore, simply wanting something does not guarantee you will get it. Still, if you really want to sing, you can sing your little heart out at church services, rock concerts, or in the shower. You can play basketball twice a week at the YMCA. You can learn to dance, then dance at discos and parties and dance-school recitals.

Applying the four criteria for knowing what you truly want eliminates fantasies, wild-goose chases, and efforts doomed to fail. You become realistic as well as clear about what you want. Sometimes that means changing a goal or trimming a fantasy down to size. In my life, however, I have met more people who underestimated themselves than people who aimed too high. The same four criteria may help you discover you actually can do more than you previously believed you could.

---

## BARRIER DISMANTLER #3: CLARIFYING VALUES

### A Question of Values

It is time to discover what *you* really want. When I ask you what you *really* want, I am, in fact, asking what you value.

Values are guides for daily living that influence your thoughts, feelings, words, and deeds. They shape your personality and give direction to what would otherwise be an aimless, purposeless life. Your values are reflected in your goals, hopes, dreams, attitudes, interests, opinions, convictions, and behaviour as well as in your problems and worries.

Traditionally, values are thought of as absolutes. If asked

to name values, you might offer words such as "honesty," "cleanliness," "freedom," "harmony," "thrift," or "brotherly love." You might recite mottos such as "Cleanliness is next to Godliness"; "A penny saved is a penny earned"; or "It is better to give than to receive." The universal principles you embraced as values were considered "good," while those you rejected were labelled "bad" or "evil."

But on a day-to-day basis, values are more difficult to name with a single word or simple saying. Values come into play every minute of every day and every time you make a decision. They are found in your answers to questions about what you *really* want.

Do you really want a hot fudge sundae with a double dip of walnut deluxe delight ice cream? Do you seriously desire higher wages for the work you do? Do you truly want to quit smoking, drinking, gambling, overeating, or compulsively spending? What about going back to school, changing careers, getting married, staying single, having children, or taking two days to a prepare a meal your family will wolf down while watching the Christmas Day TV movie?

When you know what you value, such questions are easier to answer. Your course of action is clearer to you. You are more likely to follow through with plans and persevere until you reach your destination.

## But I Do Have Values!

At this point in any lecture that I give about values, someone in the audience invariably asks, "Are you trying to tell me I don't have values?"

The question may be asked innocently or indignantly. The person may be slightly confused or downright angry. After all, he or she was raised to know right from wrong, and I seem to be attacking that upbringing and belief system. I do not know if you feel similarly attacked, but let me take a moment to clear up any confusion.

EVERYONE HAS VALUES. Some people simply understand their values more clearly than others—they realize values affect all aspects of their lives. Seeing the connection between values and actions, they act consistently and with commitment. This does not mean, however, that they intrinsically are better people.

People who know and live by their values took steps to consciously develop and clarify those values. You can take the same steps and they will pay off in the same ways. You will end up knowing what you *really* want, and you will improve your chances of getting it.

I do not guarantee that clarifying values will get you everything you want or remove every obstacle from the road you travel. However, from personal experience and years of observation, I can honestly say that values clarification will help you make self-enhancing rather than self-defeating decisions, gain a realistic perspective on your life, and shape a vision of the way your life can be in the future. It helps you go one step further to committing yourself to the course of action you have chosen.

## VALUES CLARIFICATION

Clear values—those that make daily living both personally satisfying and socially constructive—are conscientiously and freely chosen; prized and cherished; and acted upon consistently. Choice, pride, and action, the three levels of valuing, are achieved by using seven guidelines for recognizing what you value.

### Choice

All three steps under this heading were discussed in detail already. Earlier, in Chapter Four, I talked about searching for alternatives and considering consequences. And I've already discussed the impact and importance of free choice in the first half of this chapter. The three guidelines for making choices are recapped below.

*You choose what you value from the available alternatives.* Obviously, you cannot know or live by your values if you are blind to your alternatives or trapped by any other form of barrier number two. You must search for and understand your options *before* you make a choice, or you risk running full steam ahead into a brick wall. A valuable choice is made only after you explore all the avenues open to you.

*You choose what you value after considering the consequences.* Simply stated, you make a valuable choice by determining both what you might get and what you might lose by pursuing an alternative. You must also evaluate the true potential of the option to lead you to the life you truly desire and to resolve the conflicts and confusions you are experiencing. It is also time to think about whether a certain course of action could hurt the people around you or get you stuck again in the near future. And of course, at this stage you should also examine your personal strengths and limitations.

*Freely choose what is valuable.* A free choice is made without outside pressure or coercion; it is not based on a reward you expect someone else to give you or a punishment you hope to avoid. What other people might say or do is never a primary concern when you make a free choice. *You* are the one who must live with the choice.

## Pride

Pride, commitment, and communication come into play with the next two valuing steps.

*You prize and cherish what you value.* A valuable choice lets you feel good about yourself and gives you a sense of accomplishment and self-worth. You feel proud of what you *really* want. Values are cherished. You are reluctant to part with them. At times you are willing to give up something else to keep what you truly value.

Unproductive, unfulfilling, or self-destructive pursuits are not prized and cherished. Automatically and habitually undertaking them, you do not feel proud of your behaviour before, during, or after the fact when that behaviour is not valued.

For instance, how do you feel about yourself when you wake up next to someone you met for the first time the night before—someone whose last name you do not know, someone you have no desire to know better? Have you felt this way before? Do you honestly want to feel this way again? Are you making choices you prize and cherish?

What about the toffees you often eat in your car on the way home from work; the overflowing ashtrays and stale cigarette smell that greet you when you awaken each morning; the money you spend on trendy Christmas toys that lie broken and abandoned by New Year's Day? You only prize and cherish what you *really* want. When values are involved, nothing can steer you off your course.

*You publicly affirm what you value.* When you truly value a choice or goal, you are ready and willing to talk about it. You admit your values when asked about them in public and voluntarily share them with family, friends, and acquaintances. You express treasured opinions, communicate important feelings, and proudly acknowledge valued accomplishments.

On the other hand, you are less anxious to speak out about matters you do not honestly value. You feel embarrassed, ashamed, or guilty about them. They are secrets or topics you avoid when conversation turns to them. You are not about to publicly affirm your penchant for eating toffees in your car. In fact, each time you leave your car at the parking garage, you pray the attendant will not notice the wrappers you shoved under the driver's seat.

Sometimes you will loudly defend actions you do not actually value. Defending a practice is not the same as affirming it. When nagged about smoking, you may claim your habit is no more risky than crossing a street where a truck might hit you. While you may offer these excuses to defend yourself, you probably wouldn't come right out and proclaim your loyalty to practices you are not proud of. For example, would you wear a button proclaiming "I smoke and I'm proud of it"? Would you tell a friend, "You should try cigarettes. They're terrific"?

Of course, public affirmations can be overdone—as anyone who encounters the newly reformed or converted can tell you. Consider others' feelings and use discretion when communicating what you value. As much as you may value parenthood, for instance, it is just plain insensitive to flash your baby pictures and gush about the joys of motherhood while dining with a couple who desperately want children but cannot conceive. Shouting your values from a rooftop is not always necessary or appropriate. However, if you feel proud about what you genuinely want and truly value, you will be willing to say so.

## Action

Values must be translated into action and acted upon consistently.

A value prompts you to *take action*. You do something to get and keep what you sincerely desire. The choice you make, the pride you feel, and the words you speak become meaningful when put into action. It is then that you can move beyond fantasy and take steps to get what you want.

When you value parenthood, for example, you choose to have children. Proud of your children, you are more than willing to talk about them. Truly valuing parenthood, you go further. You act upon your value by learning and then doing what effective parents do, and you act in ways that are loving and advocate growth for all concerned. You offer guidance and discipline, encourage communication, and offer a secure, stable home. You make certain sacrifices. Your *behaviour* is visible proof of what you value.

Similarly, if you value health, you take action to get and stay healthy as well as give up behaviours that are detrimental to your health. If you value learning, you continue throughout your life to take courses, read books, attend lectures, have thought-provoking conversations, and so forth. In *doing*, you are able to express and live by your values.

Furthermore, you *act consistently and repeatedly* for something you value. You make a commitment and you persevere. What you do one day, you also do the next. At the first sign of trouble, you do not turn back or give up your value. You rarely slide back to square one. Flitting from one project to another, breaking promises, and abandoning efforts to change soon after you begin are signs of *not* knowing what you actually want.

This last valuing step is the true acid test. If you act upon your beliefs again and again, you indeed will be living the life you honestly want to lead.

### But I'll Never Be Able to Do All That!

By now you must think clarifying and living by your values is an impossibly tall order. It is hard work—and a lifelong process. I have yet to meet anyone who has achieved perfection when it comes to knowing and doing what they *really* want. But then, perfection is not the goal. The goal is to make progress.

You will not *always* know exactly what you want, but using these guidelines can help you know more clearly and more often what is valuable to you. You will never attain perfect clarity or be perfectly consistent, but you can be more decisive than you are now. Your life *can* have more purpose and more zest.

Working to understand and live by your values is a process that never ends. Throughout your life you will have to make choices and live with them. As a wise traveller on life's journey, you likewise will continue to strive to discover what is truly important to you. See the bibliography on page 291 for a recommended list of books that will guide you during your quest for clearer values.

## You Can Start Today

Here are two values clarification strategies to do right now that will help you begin to see what is truly important to you. With a somewhat clearer perspective on your life you will be better able to tackle the remaining barriers to change. The *values grid* puts past and present efforts to change into a valuing framework, while the *planning board* lets you describe and rank what you are actually looking for in various areas of your life.

## THE VALUES GRID

How are the valuing principles really working in your life? The values grid strategy helps you answer that question and identifies ways to ensure that future changes you make will reflect what you *really* want.

On a lined sheet of paper, draw a grid like the one pictured on the next page:

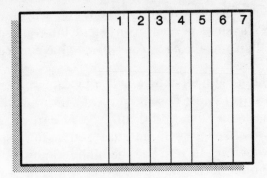

Think of six efforts to change that you have attempted in the past. Any sort of change will do. The change could involve habits you wanted to break such as nail biting or cigarette smoking; problems you tried to solve such as getting out of an abusive relationship or improving communication with your rebellious teenager; self-improvement measures such as exercising regularly or learning to speak a foreign language; or major life changes such as getting married or returning to the work force. *Three of the efforts you choose should be ones that succeeded, and three should be efforts that did not.* List all six in the wide first column of the grid.

Each narrow column has a number that corresponds to a values step listed below. Each step is followed by one or more questions. Think about those questions and answer them as honestly as possible. If your answer to each question is yes, and you did indeed complete that values step during your effort to change, check the appropriate column. If your answer is no and you did not complete the step, leave that column blank. Do this for each step and each change.

**1.** I CHOSE FROM THE AVAILABLE ALTERNATIVES. Did you search for alternatives and look for all open avenues before you chose a course of action?

**2.** I CHOSE AFTER CONSIDERING THE CONSE-QUENCES. Did you list and weigh the potential benefits as well as what, if anything, you stood to lose? Did you ask yourself if the option would get you where you wanted to go without hurting someone or getting you stuck again in the future? Did you take your strengths and limitations into consideration?

**3.** I CHOSE FREELY. Did you choose the route that was best for you? Did you make the choice without feeling pressured or coerced, without expecting a reward or hoping to avoid a punishment? Did you think for yourself?

**4.** I PRIZED AND CHERISHED MY CHOICE. Were you proud of what you did? When challenged, were you willing to fight for the change rather than readily abandon it?

**5.** I PUBLICLY AFFIRMED MY CHOICE. Did you express your feelings about your effort? If you did not have the actual opportunity, would you have been willing to do so?

**6.** I TOOK ACTION. Did you do what you set out to do? Did you translate your choice or goal into action?

**7.** I ACTED CONSISTENTLY AND REPEATEDLY. Did you stick to your plan? Did you persevere despite adversity? Did you take action often enough and with enough regularity to form a pattern? Did you keep going until you reached your destination? Are you still acting upon those values today?

The columns you check will form a noticeable pattern and help you answer the following questions about your past change efforts:

. . . How did your successes differ from your failures?

. . . How did what you really wanted contribute to your past successes?

. . . How did *not* knowing contribute to your past failures?

. . . Which steps seem to give you the most trouble? Why?

. . . Specifically, what will you do differently the next time you try to change?

Janet, the therapist who needs more time for fun and relaxation, made several discoveries. "It came as no surprise that my freely chosen column was completely blank," Janet reveals. "Even my successes weren't my idea. I guess I just followed the right person's advice those times.

"A funny thing happened when I got to the prize and cherish column. I checked it for my successes, but I found I wasn't as proud as I might have been. I wanted to say I was lucky or give someone else the credit for the success. Of course, I wasn't at all proud of my failures. I wanted to forget them and not talk about them.

"The real clinchers were the action steps. I acted when I succeeded and I'm still doing those things. But I didn't follow through on my failures, and I distinctly remember when I gave up that I was feeling pressured and angry because it wasn't what I had wanted in the first place."

Your discoveries may be similar to or different from Janet's. However, you no doubt will see that you completed more and perhaps all of the valuing steps when you succeeded and few if any when you failed. But what about future changes? How can the values grid help you get unstuck this time? Let's look at some of the changes you want to make in the future. Think back to Chapter Two and the lifeline strategy. As part of the strategy, you listed a number of things you want to do in your lifetime. Choose three of these wishes and list them several lines below the other items already on your grid. Now ask and—as honestly as possible—answer the following questions.

1. Do I need to consider more alternatives? Could there be something along the same lines that I might want *more* than the wish I listed? Do I want to give the option more thought?
IF YOU ANSWERED YES, DRAW AN "X" IN COLUMN 1.

2. Do I need to examine more closely the consequences of achieving this wish? Do I need to assess my ability real-

istically to attain this goal? Am I aiming too high or too low?
Have I overlooked anything about this wish?
IF YOU ANSWERED YES, DRAW AN "X" IN COLUMN 2.

3. Do I want this for myself or am I trying to please
someone else? Is this something I think I *should* do, and do
I resent having to do it? Will I be happy about this wish even
if no one else is?
IF YOU DO NOT KNOW, DRAW AN "X" IN COLUMN 3.

4. If I accomplished this, would I feel proud? Would I
be happy about what I'd be doing to reach my goal? Is this
important enough to me to put time, energy, and emotion
into it? Would I fight to do it?
IF YOU ANSWERED NO, DRAW AN "X" IN COLUMN 4.

5. Do I plan to keep what I'm doing a secret? Do I feel
ashamed or embarrassed by my choice? Have I thought about
not saying anything because other people won't understand
or agree with what I'm doing?
IF YOU ANSWERED YES, DRAW AN "X" IN COLUMN 5.

6. Can this desire be translated into action? Will I do
what I set out to do? Am I sure this isn't a pipe dream?
IF YOU ANSWERED NO, DRAW AN "X" IN COLUMN 6.

7. Is this going to be something else I start but do not
finish? Will I lose my resolve if I do not see immediate results? Will I give up if the going gets tough? Could something
else come along to distract me? Will I then abandon this
plan?
IF YOU ANSWERED YES, DRAW AN "X" IN COLUMN 7.

If you are to get what you want, you will have to do some
work on the steps marked with an X. You should be able to
look at your grid and make a list of things to do before
attempting that particular change effort. Ask yourself the

same questions for any goal or aspiration you hope to reach. If you filled out the grid honestly, you will better understand what you really want and act accordingly.

Lisa, the office supply sales representative, always said she wanted to earn a college degree. Her values grid helped her see why she never took the steps necessary to reach her goal. "I don't know if this was what was supposed to happen," she begins, "but I found out I wanted something different than I thought. See, I used to think getting a college degree would get me a better job and make people on the job respect me. It was one of the things I thought could solve all my work problems.

"But when I *really* thought about going back to college, it just turned my stomach. The idea of taking sales and marketing courses so professors could tell me things I had already learned through experience definitely did not appeal to me—so I didn't go, not even when my boss offered to give me time off to attend classes.

"When I did the values grid, it suddenly dawned on me that I really did want to finish college. I just didn't want a degree in marketing. Maybe I'll take communications or business management. I have to look at my options. But I do know, if I go to college, it will be to learn what I want to learn."

Lisa might have reached the same conclusions if she had asked herself which aspects or outcomes of getting her college degree were most important to her personally. That is the question the next values strategy asks about several other areas of conflict and confusion.

## PLANNING BOARD

A favourite values clarification strategy of mine, a planning board is another way to find out what you *really* want.

It can be used to gain a clearer perspective on almost any topic.

A planning board requires two sheets of paper, both the same size. On one sheet, draw a board that looks like this:

| | |
|---|---|
| 1 | 7 |
| 2 | 8 |
| 3 | 9 |
| 4 | 10 |
| 5 | 11 |
| 6 | 12 |

Fold and tear the second sheet so you have twelve slips of paper roughly the same size as the spaces on your planning board.

Anytime you have a decision to make, are thinking about a change, or need to clarify what you actually want from a given situation, write the points to consider on slips of paper and arrange them on the planning board in order of their importance to you.

The number one space always represents the element that is *most* important to you, and number twelve is always the least important. Only one slip of paper can occupy a space. However, while trying to determine your priorities, you can move the slips around as many times as you like.

## Family Relationships Planning Board

Family relationships often are a source of conflict and confusion. Since all of us are involved with families of one sort or another, examining our relationship to our families using values clarification strategies serves as a good example of how to use the planning board effectively.

You may have grown up in the conventional two-parent family that conforms to media stereotypes. Perhaps you got by with one hardworking parent or were raised by your grandmother. You might even have been abused as a child, confused by alcoholic parents, or bounced from foster home to foster home. Whatever your past experience was, today you hold a certain personal perspective of how families are supposed to be.

Your current family—whether it is traditional, single-parent with children, cohabiting adults, or any other type—may or may not live up to your expectations. You may have problems with communication, discipline, or household management. You simply may not feel as close and connected as you wish you could. You take a step toward making your family life more satisfying when you examine what you *really* want from family relationships.

Following are eleven features of family living. Each aspect is described briefly and given a key word—signified by bold capital letters. Read and think about the first item. Write the key word on a slip of paper and place the paper on your planning board. Choose the space that represents that feature's importance to you personally. Remember—number one is most important and number twelve is least important. Each element of family relationships listed below should have its own space on your planning board. Give each element careful thought. You can move a slip of paper you have already placed if its importance changes in relation to other elements.

The first feature of family living to consider is:

- The family household runs in an orderly fashion because all members understand, follow, and have a say about **RULES**.

How important are rules and an orderly household? If they are very important, place your slip of paper at the top of the planning board in the one, two or three space. If they are hardly significant, use the bottom spaces—ten, eleven, or twelve. If they are somewhat important, place the paper somewhere in the middle.

The remaining features to consider and place on the planning board in order of their importance to you are:

- **DISCIPLINE** of children is appropriate and consistent.
- Family members **TRUST** one another and feel free to share their problems and concerns.
- The family shares **RELIGIOUS VALUES** and worships together.
- The family spends **RECREATION** time together.
- **CHORES ARE SHARED** and one family member is not overwhelmed or irritated by household responsibilities.
- Family members effectively **COMMUNICATE**—really listening and allowing everyone to have their say— even when there are disagreements.
- **SAFETY** and mutual support are available along with the sense that mistakes won't lead to rejection by other family members.
- Parents present a **UNITED FRONT** on important matters so children (or anyone else) cannot play one against the other.
- Family members **VALIDATE** each other, expressing what they love, admire, appreciate, and respect about each other.
- Family **HARMONY** exists because the family has a

workable method for resolving conflict and solving problems.
- **WILD CARD**—include any aspect of family living you can think of that I did not list above.

Once you've arranged these elements on the planning board the way you want them, ask yourself about the family life you now have and the family life your planning board suggests and confirms you really want. Are the two the same?

Your planning board will measure your satisfaction or dissatisfaction. If the highest ranked items are what you already have in your family, you may be better off than you thought. Perhaps the source of your unhappiness lies somewhere else. If the highest-ranked features were those you *do not* have, you now know why you feel dissatisfied and can begin to improve the situation—one step at a time.

Your planning board can open lines of communication, particularly if you have all family members complete one. With a clearer idea of what each of you wants, you can work together to improve family relationships.

Sometimes you discover you have been upset about and wasting your energy on matters that are not really very important to you. Doug and Marion discovered that during a family values workshop for foster parents.

"We've been arguing and worrying about discipline and rules for weeks now," says Marion. She and Doug share their home with three teenage foster children. With backgrounds of abuse, neglect, and instability, the youngsters do need rules and discipline, but they need a few other things as well.

"Rules and discipline didn't even make the top eight on either of our boards," Doug chimes in. "Trust and communication and harmony and doing things together were a whole lot more important. Maybe those are the things we should pay more attention to."

Doug and Marion decided to go home and do the planning board strategy with the kids. Then they would try to come up with a plan to give them more of what they all wanted.

Planning boards are excellent jumping-off points for your efforts to change. First, they help you set priorities. Then, often, you can go on to develop goals and plans for action based on the strategy's outcomes.

Family life may not be an area of conflict or confusion for you at the present time. That's why I have included a list of elements for three additional planning boards. In addition, you can always make up planning boards of your own. Simply follow the steps outlined previously to complete planning boards for the following areas of your life.

### Love Relationship Planning Board

What is important to you in a love relationship?

- A partner who has a good sense of humour so that there is lots of **LAUGHTER** in our relationship.
- A good and satisfying **SEX** life.
- **COMMON INTERESTS** and mutual friends.
- Some **INDEPENDENT INTERESTS** and separate friends.
- A partner who is **PHYSICALLY ATTRACTIVE.**
- **COMMUNICATION** that is open and ongoing. We really talk and listen to each other.
- We should be able to **TRUST** each other with feelings and not do anything to hurt the relationship or each other.
- The relationship must include **HONESTY.**
- We should be **OPEN ABOUT OUR FEELINGS.**
- A partner who is **NOT CLINGY** or overly dependent and gives me room to breath.
- A partner who **PUTS ME FIRST** in his or her life.
- **ROMANCE.**

### Job Planning Board

What do I really want from a job?

- **GOOD PAY**.
- A good job will allow me decent and somewhat flexible **HOURS**.
- I will be **CHALLENGED** and asked to use my skills and abilities.
- There will be enough variety in what I do so I feel **STIMULATED** by my job.
- My opinions are taken seriously and I'm asked for **INPUT** on decisions that affect me.
- **RESPECT** from peers and superiors.
- Enough **INDEPENDENCE/AUTONOMY** to get the job done and respect myself.
- Job **SECURITY** so I know the job will be there as long as I want it.
- Room for **ADVANCEMENT**.
- Little or **NO SEXISM** in the workplace.
- Friendly, cooperative **CO-WORKER RELATIONSHIPS**.
- To be **PROUD** of the work I do and have other people be proud of it too.


### Free Time Planning Board

How do you really want to spend your free time?

- **LEARNING** by taking classes, reading books, or completing correspondence courses.
- **SOCIALIZING** with other people.
- **STAYING AT HOME**.
- **GOING SOMEWHERE**.
- With **PHYSICALLY CHALLENGING** activities such as rock climbing, hiking, volleyball, or hang gliding.

- **EXCITEMENT,** adventure, meeting new people, doing things I haven't done before.
- I like to **PLAN IN ADVANCE** what I will do.
- I'd rather be **SPONTANEOUS** and do things that strike my fancy at the last minute.
- To **CATCH UP** on chores and things I don't get to during the work week.
- To **FULFILL COMMITMENTS** such as visiting my parents, taking care of my nieces, or entertaining people to whom I owe invitations.
- **ALONE.**
- It doesn't matter what I do as long as it **KEEPS MY MIND OFF WORK** or other problems.

Like believing you do not deserve better and not seeing alternatives, not knowing what you *really* want is only one barrier to change. It is a powerful one and almost every other barrier gets tangled up with it at one time or another. Still, there is more to getting unstuck than discovering your values and knowing what you truly want.

# 6

███████████████████████████████

# *Change and Letting Go*

Helen is a colleague of mine who conducts stress management and overall wellness training seminars. In her presentations she includes the eight barriers to change. She summarizes barrier number three—not knowing what you *really* want—and introduces barrier number four by expressing the following opinion: "There are hundreds of things we do without asking ourselves *why* or if we really want to. A perfect example is watching the eleven o'clock television news every night before going to bed—a truly pointless, self-defeating practice if there ever was one.

"Think about it," Helen suggests. "The news is almost always negative. You get to see graphic video footage of fires, overturned trailer trucks, murders, and violence—your basic mayhem and madness. Do you *really* want to look at all that nasty stuff right before you go to sleep? Do you rest more comfortably knowing that, yes, indeed, the world is still one fine mess? It will all be there in the morning.

"No matter what you see on the eleven o'clock newscast,

there is NOTHING YOU CAN DO ABOUT IT! You aren't going to get out of bed, rush over to your desk, and whip off a letter to the editor. You are not going to place a telephone call to the family of a murder victim and express your condolences. Even if the news affects you directly—if rumours of massive layoffs at the factory where you work are reported, for instance—WHAT CAN YOU DO ABOUT IT, at eleven P.M., except lie awake half the night worrying? Honestly, watching the late-night TV news has got to be the most mindless, wasteful way anyone could end their day."

How do you feel about Helen's point of view? Do you think she is too darn opinionated or wonder who gave *her* the right to tell *you* what to do? As someone who views late-night newscasts on a regular basis, do you feel personally offended or attacked by Helen's words? Can you think of several perfectly good reasons to watch eleven o'clock news programmes?

Helen's audience can. Her unsolicited opinion leaves them feeling offended, irritated, and argumentative. As soon as she stops talking, a heated debate begins.

"I disagree," says the first person Helen calls on. "I consider myself a well-informed person. I want to know what's going on in the world."

"I admire that," Helen replies. "But what good does it do you to be well-informed while you sleep? You can catch up on the news in the morning."

Another audience member has an answer to that point: "I don't have time to watch the morning news *or* read the morning newspaper if that's what you're going to tell me to do."

"How about listening to an all-news station while you get ready for work or on your car radio?" Helen suggests.

"What about the weather report?" someone else asks. "If it's going to snow, I want to know the night before. I'll need more time to get to work. I can't just wait to look out my window in the morning."

"You're right," Helen agrees. "Storm warnings are a valid reason to watch the late news. But certainly there are not storms pending every single night of the year."

"I watch for the sports report," another audience member claims. "I like to know how my favourite teams did."

"I do too," Helen says. "But the sportscast is at the end of any news show. It isn't worth enduring everything that comes before it, especially when I can get the same information in the morning."

"But there isn't anything else on before the 11.30 game show. I like to watch that. It makes me laugh and forget about all that bad news I just saw."

Helen counters each argument with an equally convincing counterpoint. While she presents her case calmly, her audience becomes increasingly agitated. Finally one man jumps to his feet and loudly condemns her.

"This is a free country," he shouts. "I can watch what I want whenever I want to. What you are proposing is censorship, and as far as I'm concerned, you can take *all* of your ideas and shove them!"

Whether you agree or disagree with Helen's position, how important *is* the eleven o'clock news? If the TV networks discontinued late news broadcasts, would your life be irreparably damaged *or* dramatically improved? Of course not. Yet Helen's audience used a full fifteen minutes of seminar time to defend the practice—ultimately accusing the trainer of being downright unpatriotic and discounting everything else they had already learned from her.

The issue at hand was relatively harmless and insignificant. What was not insignificant is that the audience was confronted with the possibility of change and that they recoiled at the thought. They felt threatened and mobilized their defenses—automatically. Blindly and at full speed they crashed into barrier number four—finding perfectly good reasons *not* to change.

When someone else challenges something you do routinely or habitually, barrier number four is a knee-jerk reaction to what you believe is a personal attack. You immediately focus your attention and emotional resources on defending the way things are—instead of considering how things could be. You shut out all incoming messages and look for perfectly good reasons *not* to change.

Barrier number four also defeats you when you really do know—without anyone else's telling you—that you could change for the better. Yet, with no one to convince but yourself, you still find perfectly good reasons not to change.

Twenty-five years ago Jennifer met George. He was a year ahead of her at college. She knew immediately that he was the man she wanted to marry, and as she puts it, she chased him until he caught her. Twenty years ago (and two weeks after George's college graduation) Jennifer and George got married. Her parents adored George, gave the marriage their blessing, and bought the newlyweds a small house in which to live. Her friends celebrated her good fortune. George was going to be a doctor. "And in those days, you couldn't do better than to marry a doctor," Jennifer explains.

While George attended medical school, Jennifer worked to support them. By the time he had completed his traineeship and qualified, they had three children. George joined a thriving cardiology practice attached to a prestigious city hospital. They bought a huge, luxurious home in the suburbs, sent their children to the best private schools, and became pillars of their community. George's practice flourished, and Jennifer headed charity drives, volunteered at the hospital where George worked, and enjoyed all the privileges accorded a doctor's wife. "I was living out my childhood fantasies," Jennifer says. "My life was exactly what I wanted it to be and exactly how everyone said life should be."

Then, ten years ago, George had his first extramarital affair, with an operating-room nurse. The relationship was common knowledge among the hospital staff, and neither participant tried to cover it up, but Jennifer was truly shocked when another doctor's wife "did her a favour" and told her about the affair.

"I was devastated that George could be unfaithful to me and humiliated that everyone else knew about it before I did," Jennifer recalls. "I felt like a fool. I was hurt and angry. When I wasn't wondering what I did to push him into another woman's arms, I was thinking about packing up and leaving him. But I didn't. The kids were young and they loved their dad. I loved him. I'd loved him since I was fifteen years old and could not picture life without him."

Jennifer confronted George. He cried and begged her forgiveness, promising to end the affair immediately and to never again be unfaithful. "He swore he loved me and the kids more than anything in the world and never wanted to hurt us. I believed him."

She believed him again two years later and again when he had his third affair. She timidly suggested marriage counselling the fourth time he strayed, but he insisted theirs wasn't a marital problem. It was his fault alone. He again promised to stop having affairs. Jennifer did not bother to confront him the next time he was unfaithful and has convinced herself his sixth and current affair is something she can live with.

"I know that sounds crazy," she says, "but I have my reasons. George is a good father and a good provider. He is respected and admired by important people. So am I. I like that. I like what I have. I would lose it all if I got a divorce, and the kids would be devastated. I can't do that to them. When I look at it objectively, my life isn't so bad. Sharing George with his mistress isn't such an awful price to pay. . . ."

Does Jennifer's conclusion seem reasonable or does it appall you? Has she realistically assessed her situation, or is she minimizing her feelings about her husband's repeated affairs and ignoring the impact of his infidelity on the marriage, the children, and her own self-esteem? Is she someone who has learned the art of compromise, or someone who is stuck?

Sometimes you fool yourself into thinking that by *not* changing you are doing what is best for all concerned. But are you really? I think not. When your life clearly could be better but you actively work to convince yourself and others that it is good enough the way it is, you are stuck and blocked by barrier number four.

Barrier number four is there each time you rationalize a self-destructive habit such as smoking, drug use, excessive drinking, overeating, or compulsive spending. It is at work each time you abandon your hopes and dreams by deciding your physical health, your job, your relationship, your social life, or any other situation is "not so bad." It is part of every excuse you make *not* to ask for a rise, assert yourself, see a doctor about the funny-looking mole on your shoulder, start an exercise programme, or sign up for a college course. It keeps you stuck by supplying a steady stream of perfectly good reasons *not* to change.

---

## WHY YOU LOOK FOR REASONS NOT TO CHANGE

Perfectly good reasons not to change are the by-products of defensiveness. When faced with change—whether it is your own idea or someone else's—your first reaction, in almost every instance, is to defend the status quo, to protect yourself from a possible loss of self-esteem, independence, or a familiar aspect of daily living.

Think about the audience's reaction to Helen's opinion about late-night news watching. Before the first complete sentence escaped her lips, people began to feel uncomfortable. They stopped listening to her actual words. They heard instead what they *thought* she was saying about them *personally* and began to build an argument in their own defence. Why did they react this way?

First of all, when Helen claimed watching the eleven o'clock news was dumb, mindless, wasteful, and self-defeating, the audience believed she was implying that *they* were stupid, unthinking, wasteful, and self-destructive people. Her challenge of a specific behaviour was a challenge to who they were as human beings. Their self-image was under attack and they did not like it. They felt threatened, hurt, and angry, and so they defended the practice of TV news watching in order to protect their self-esteem.

Often, admitting a need to change can appear to be the same as admitting you are not good enough the way you are. The premise is false, but you do not think about it logically. *Change threatens your self-esteem, so you defend your behaviour to protect yourself from feelings of worthlessness or inadequacy.*

Tell a cigarette smoker that smoking is bad for his health and he hears that he is a bad person because he smokes. He replies defensively, "Give me a break. I could just as easily die tomorrow because a truck hits me while I'm crossing the street." Or he rejects the alternative: "I tried to quit once. It wasn't worth it. I gained twenty pounds and was hell to live with." Or he denounces the advice-giver: "There's nothing worse than a reformed smoker trying to convert the rest of us."

A teacher suggests to a mother that her son's schoolwork might improve if she spent thirty minutes each evening helping him with his homework. Instead of thinking about how the teacher is trying to help her son, the mother assumes that the teacher is calling her a lousy parent. So she turns the tables, saying, "If you can't do your job in the classroom, don't expect me to do it for you." Or she defends herself: "I'm a single parent and I work full-time. My kids are lucky if they have thirty minutes alone with me in a week." Or she blames the victim: "I help Joey with his homework. He's just a slow learner. He's not as bright as the other kids; never has been."

Each time change is an option, it raises the possibility that you are not good enough the way you are. After all, if you were, you would not need to change. So, you turn things around. To dodge a self-esteem wrecking ball and prove you are good enough, you convince yourself you really do not need to change.

In addition to feeling their self-esteem threatened, Helen's audience did not appreciate her telling them what they *should* do. They reacted with anger to what they believed to be her attempt to assert control over their lives. You too may react defensively and find perfectly good reasons not to change when you *feel your independence or autonomy is threatened or that outside forces are trying to control you.*

Jennifer says, "My friends tell me to leave George and get on with my life. Well, maybe that's what they would do, but they are not me. They don't know what's best for me. I'm the only one who knows that."

The alcoholic defends his drinking and asserts his independence when he says, "I can stop drinking whenever I want to. I just don't want to right now."

The lover who balks at the idea of committing herself to marriage thinks her partner is trying to control and stifle her. She says, "Don't push. I like things the way they are. Besides, I'm not going to get married just so I can impress other people with a piece of paper. It's my life, not theirs."

The rebellious teenager shouts from the bottom of the staircase, "YOU CAN'T MAKE ME DO IT!"

Barrier number four appeals to the rebellious adolescent in each of you. No one can make you change, and you put up one heck of a fight when they try.

Finally, Helen's audience reacted to a feeling that Helen was trying to take something away from them. Watching the eleven o'clock news was a practice to which they had grown accustomed. It was not a practice that actually meant much to them one way or another, but it belonged to them, they were comfortable with it, and they were not about to give it up.

You also find reasons not to change in order to *defend against the possible loss of something you already have.* Jennifer is accustomed to and enjoys the luxuries and status of being a doctor's wife. She will lose them if she divorces George. Or, there is the worker who hates his job, but at least he knows what to expect from it. Dissatisfying as his job may be, if he quits, he gives up familiar surroundings, relationships, and routines.

Self-destructive as their habits might be, the alcoholic does not want to lose the alcohol high or the escape it provides, the overeater does not want to lose the comfort and pleasure of food, the gambler does not want to lose the risk and adrenaline rush of gambling, and the compulsive spender sees an emotional release and thrill being taken away from her.

The fear of losing what you already have is the driving force behind barrier number four. Hanging on to what you have wins out over the possibility of getting something better. No one can *guarantee* change will leave you better off than you were before. And that, my friends, is one of the all-time winners among perfectly good reasons not to change.

Whether you defend the way things are to protect self-esteem, assert your independence, or to keep yourself from losing what you have (regardless of its true value), the result is the same. You look for perfectly good reasons not to change, find them, and use them to justify staying stuck.

## HOW THIS BARRIER WORKS

Barrier number four creates several negative outcomes that get you and keep you stuck.

1. *It decreases and/or eliminates viable alternatives.*

Julie is alone and lonely. She says she wants to change that. She wants to meet a man and have a relationship with him. Yet she offers perfectly good reasons not to pursue any avenue that could lead her to what she wants.

"A friend of mine met her husband in a yoga class," Julie's friend Kate mentions during a telephone conversation that began with Julie claiming she would probably die without ever meeting a man she could love.

"I don't like yoga," says Julie.

"So don't take yoga. Take a course in something you do like."

"I don't have time."

"I thought you just said you have too much time on your hands."

"I meant I wanted something fun to do. Classes aren't fun. They're work."

"Okay, then go out. There are some great clubs down where you live."

"I hate bars. They're all meat markets."

"How about a museum, then? You're right down the street from—"

"Forget it. What am I supposed to do—walk up to some guy and say, 'Nice Picasso. Want to come home with me?' "

Julie goes on to say that only losers join singles groups and only weirdos answer classified ads or sign up for dating services. Her friends and relatives arrange blind dates, but the guys are never her type.

"Julie, you have an excuse for everything," Kate sighs.

"That's because I know the situation is hopeless," Julie concludes.

Julie uses perfectly good reasons to prove her point. By finding fatal flaws in every alternative, she ultimately convinces herself there is indeed no alternative to the way things are.

Barrier number four often leads you back to barrier number two. Like Julie, you have a perfectly good reason *not* to change when you reject every available option and can see no alternative to the way things are. If you have forgotten how debilitating this can be, turn back to Chapter Four.

**2.** *Barrier number four destroys the motivation to change by convincing you "things are not so bad" the way they are.*

In spite of her husband's infidelity and a marriage in name only, Jennifer claims her life is not so bad. She discounts the pain, humiliation, and frustration of sleeping alone most nights, making love with a man who regularly makes love to someone else, the countless petty fights she picks because she chooses not to confront the real problem, and the way her children idolize a man she knows to be far less than what they see. She instead reminds herself of the perks a doctor's wife gets, the luxuries she can afford, and the image she has in the community. By reinforcing the status quo and persuading herself that her life is not so bad, she believes she has no reason to consider marriage counselling, divorce, or any other option that would improve her own life.

Len, as you may recall from Chapter One, is also stuck in a loveless marriage. He defends his stuckness by claiming, "We stay together for the children." He avoids change and defends his avoidance by observing that "plenty of people put up with lousy marriages." He rationalizes that if they can, he can, too. It is what he is used to, and "when you get right down to it, it really is not so bad."

By defending a behaviour, habit, or way of life and conjuring up perfectly good reasons to continue on your present course, you persuade yourself change is not necessary. And when the "things are not so bad" defence develops a few leaks, you turn to the flip side of the same coin and remind yourself that "things could be worse." You defend your current position by painting a more negative and unappealing picture of changing.

You defend your decision to stay in a job you hate. "Things could be worse," you say. "I could be unemployed."

You spend Saturday nights in noisy, crowded bars and have a series of one-night stands. You console yourself, "It's better than sitting home alone, pigging out on junk food, and watching TV."

You put up with an unfaithful lover because at least he does not drink. If he drinks, at least he does not take drugs.

The money he spends on drugs is nothing compared to what
your financial situation would be if he gambled. A gambler
is okay as long as he does not beat you, and if he beats you
once in a while, it is okay because he never lays a hand on
the kids. You can always find at least one way things could
be worse than they are.

In view of how bad things *could* be, you figure you are
lucky to be where you are. You decide to count your blessings
and stop worrying about being stuck. You draw the logical
conclusion—if your life is not so bad and could be worse—
YOU DO NOT NEED TO CHANGE.

**3.** *As you look for one perfectly good reason not to change
after another, you hurt and alienate the people who care about
you.*

You do not get unstuck all by yourself. Emotional support from other people builds the self-esteem you need to
attempt change. Asking for help from other people increases
your alternatives and dismantles barrier number two. A later
chapter in this book will be devoted entirely to the matter
of gaining cooperation from other people as a step toward
getting unstuck. No matter how you look at it, you need
people if you want a change effort to succeed. Yet barrier
number four drives away the people who want to help you.

When you want a reason not to change, you may reject
the person who presents the possibility of change or offers
you advice. In your defensive mode you may play a hard
game of "get the helper." Just as Helen's audience turned
on her, you go right for the jugular when you think someone
is trying to run your life or tell you what to do—even when
you asked for their advice in the first place. You launch a
counterattack. "What I do is none of your business," you say,
or "Don't you tell me how to handle my relationship. Your
marriage isn't exactly made in heaven, you know." Or "Who
died and appointed you God?" Or "You could use to lose a
few pounds yourself."

In an attempt to defend yourself you may make some

incredibly hurtful and accusatory statements. You reason that if the helpers are obviously flawed, so is the help they offer. Their inadequacy is your perfectly good reason *not* to change. You let them know you see right through them, so they will take their know-it-all attitude and lousy advice someplace else.

Few people will subject themselves to your wrath more than once. They will back away and become decidedly reluctant to offer their support or respond to you when you seek them out at a later date. If this happens, your need to defend yourself against change will cost you a valuable resource person.

But you need not verbally attack the well-intentioned people in your life to alienate them. You can also drive them away by burning them out. Unhappy with yourself or your circumstances, you share your feelings with people you trust and believe to be emotionally supportive. They hear your tales of woe and watch you resist change by rejecting all alternatives (for perfectly good reasons, of course). They listen to you make one excuse after another. You decide your situation is hopeless. They decide you do not really want to change. Their patience wears thin. They sympathize with your plight, but it becomes increasingly difficult to sympathize with *you*. You sing the same old tune, sometimes for years on end, but you never *do* anything except explain your perfectly good reasons not to change.

Everyone has their limit. When your emotional support people reach theirs, they turn you off, avoid you, change the subject when your problems become part of a conversation. Sometimes they lose their temper and yell at you. Like the boy who cried wolf, when you decide to really change, no one believes you. The people who could help you have been burned out by your stuckness and are nowhere to be found.

**4.** *Time, energy, and emotional resources that could be used to get unstuck are wasted on defending a current practice or finding perfectly good reasons not to change.*

Helen's audience spent fifteen minutes of a three-hour seminar defending the practice of watching eleven P.M. newscasts, a practice they later agreed was of relatively little importance to them. They mobilized the energy to be angry and argumentative, more energy than they had exhibited during earlier portions of the seminar. The time and energy was largely wasted, however, since no conclusion was reached and no new stress-management strategy learned. They could have used their time and energy to learn more about overall wellness or to brainstorm more peaceful, positive, or relaxing things to do before going to sleep at night.

Similarly, Carol, the Minnesota social worker dissatisfied with her job, constantly feels drained and lethargic. She uses her energy to complain about her job in one breath and convince herself to keep it in the next. She is too tired and empty to consider alternatives, set goals, or get unstuck.

If Julie spent half as much time testing her alternatives as she spends making excuses *not* to try them, she might have met several men by now and perhaps settled into a relationship with one of them.

I know countless therapists who wish their clients could be as focused and creative about exploring options and attempting new behaviours as they are when they defend themselves and the way things are. Every minute you devote to defending what is and creating elaborate rationales for staying the way you are, you *could be* coming up with creative solutions to your problems, pursuing new alternatives, and moving closer to the life you really want.

In case you have not yet seen yourself in the picture I have painted or still are not sure if barrier number four is impeding your progress, here are some of the most commonly used reasons *not* to change. How many have you used?

I tried that, but it didn't work.
Some people can do it, but I can't.
My situation is unique.

It's not as bad as it looks.

You're blowing this way out of proportion. It's really no big deal.

I can quit anytime I want.

I know what I'm doing.

I have it under control.

There are extenuating circumstances.

Right now I don't have the time (energy, money, freedom, etc.) to change.

I don't drink (smoke, spend, overeat, gamble, hit my kids, etc.) half as much as some people I know.

People in glass houses shouldn't throw stones.

Did I ask for your opinion?

There is absolutely nothing I can do about it.

It must be my karma.

It's not my fault.

It's just the way things are. Some things will never change.

These and other reasons not to change are used daily by you and everyone you know. They counter every imaginable reason *to* change and eliminate all avenues—except staying the same, settling for half a loaf, or putting up with the way things are. If you truly believe that is enough, then you *do* have a perfectly good reason *not* to change. But you opened this book and read this far because you wanted more. To get it, you must dismantle barrier number four and learn to let go of your defensiveness.

---

### DISMANTLING BARRIER #4:
### LETTING GO OF DEFENSIVENESS
### SO YOU CAN TRY SOMETHING NEW

As Cleveland State University professor Hanoch McCarty's motto goes: *"If you always do what you've always done, you will only get what you always got."*

In this statement lies the reason to dismantle barrier number four. You have a choice to make. You can settle for what you already have (and fight to the death for your right to keep it) or reach for something better. You dismantle this barrier by becoming more aware of its presence in your life and learning to counter reasons *not* to change with equally persuasive reasons *to* change.

### Recognizing When Barrier #4 Has a Hold on You

Barrier number four is such a powerful obstacle to change because it comes into play *automatically* almost every time you consider the mere possibility of change. You defend the way things are without thinking about whether or not you like, value, or really want what you have. You find perfectly good reasons not to change without knowing that you are doing it. The walls go up, the drawbridge closes, the claws come out, the counterattack is plotted—involuntarily, almost unconsciously, as if an early warning device had been triggered and your normal thought processes overridden by an automatic defense system. To offer a perfectly good reason *not* to change can be as automatic and as natural as breathing.

"You don't have to take that kind of abuse," a mother tells her daughter.

Automatically her daughter replies, "I know, BUT he always apologizes. He feels really bad about it and tries to make it up to me."

"You could go to your supervisor," a husband says, suggesting a solution to his wife's work problem.

"I guess, BUT she probably wouldn't do anything about it," the wife counters immediately.

"Have you thought about telling Billy how you feel?" a counsellor advises a mother having trouble disciplining her twelve-year-old son.

"Yeah, BUT he never listens to me," the mother instantly offers as a reason not to try.

You do not need someone else to trigger your defence system. You defend yourself against your own ideas about change.

"Sure, I know I should lose weight, BUT diets never work for me."

"Yeah, I know I want to exercise, BUT I don't have time."

"I suppose we could see a marriage counsellor, BUT the Martins went to a counsellor and now they're getting divorced."

"I know I really need a vacation, BUT there would just be more work to catch up on when I got back. Still, it would be nice, BUT money is kind of tight right now and the kids are at that awkward stage and . . ."

These examples illustrate a practice those of us in the helping professions call "yeah, but-ing." Each alternative or possible behaviour change is considered for as long as it takes to say, "yeah, sure, I know," "I suppose," "I guess," or "you're right." Then an excuse is made or a perfectly good reason not to change is given. In between the grunt of agreement and the counterargument is the word BUT. A "yeah, but" is a sure sign that you are defending a practice or resisting a change.

When you "Yeah, but" every alternative, you give additional power to the obstacle to change instead of empowering yourself to succeed or get unstuck. In one way or another, you are saying that the reasons to stay the same mean more than your desire to reach your goals and aspirations. You are more committed to keeping things the way they are than to trying to make them better. You may not mean that. You may not know *why* you defend yourself and block that change. But you do it. And you do it automatically.

To begin letting go of your defences, you must recognize when you are becoming defensive. Your "yeah, but"s serve as warning signals. The next time you hear those words coming out of your mouth—STOP!

Ask yourself—Am I looking for perfectly good reasons *not* to change? Am I defending the way things are so I can convince myself it is okay to be stuck? Do I *really* want to continue this practice and maintain the status quo? Or do I want something better than I already have?

Your body and emotions also can let you know you are getting defensive. Pay attention to your physical and emotional reactions the next time you think about or discuss change. You may feel angry, offended, confused, irritated, tense, or anxious. You might feel an urge to change the subject, criticize or verbally attack the person with whom you are talking, storm out of the room, or escape through drinking, eating, shopping, gambling, or getting into your couch potato mode. Your palms sweat or your heart beats faster. You clench your teeth so tightly that your jaw begins to ache. Perhaps you feel tears welling in your eyes or you start to hyperventilate. These feelings and physical symptoms could be signs of defensiveness. Once again, STOP!

Ask yourself—Why am I reacting this way? What am I afraid of or angry about? I feel threatened, but is there really any danger present? Why does it seem so important to protect myself and defend what I do? Do I actually need to calm down and face this issue head on?

Both your "yeah, but" statements and your automatic physical and emotional reactions tell you that your defensive walls are going up and the drawbridge is closing. If you STOP and ask yourself the questions I suggested, you can diminish the power of this barrier. Then you can counter your perfectly good reasons *not* to change with plausible reasons *to* change.

## Ten "Yeah, But"s Make a Go for It!

Finding reasons *to* change is not nearly as automatic as finding reasons not to change. You will have to work at it and work hard. You must begin to counter your excuses with motivating statements. In a sense you must learn to "yeah, but" your "yeah, but" statements. Then you once again see your alternatives.

Below are ten commonly used "yeah, but" statements. They may or may not apply to your life or your present state of conflict and confusion. However, you can use them to practise the art of letting go. Counter each perfectly good reason not to change with a positively motivating statement, one also beginning with "yeah, but." I have done the first one for you.

**1.** I know, but if I want something done right, I have to do it myself.

I know, but as overwhelmed as I am, it won't get done at all unless I delegate it to someone else.

**2.** Yeah, but I don't have time to exercise . . .

**3.** Yeah, but the last counsellor I went to was a real jerk . . .

**4.** Yeah, but I can't afford to take a vacation . . .

**5.** Yeah, but I like watching the eleven o'clock news . . .

**6.** I guess, but they probably want someone with a college degree . . .

**7.** Yeah, but he never listens to what I say . . .

**8.** Yeah, but I'll gain weight if I quit smoking . . .

**9.** I know, but nothing ever changes in this company . . .

**10.** You're right, but it really is not so bad . . .

## Now Try It on an Actual Change You Want to Make

Choose an aspect of overall wellness or an area of conflict and confusion (from Chapter Two) or an alternative you generated as part of the strategies presented in Chapter Four.

At the top of a sheet of paper, write your choice in a sentence beginning with the words I REALLY WANT TO . . . Under that headline sentence, list every imaginable excuse and perfectly good reason not to change (or pursue the alternative). Leave several lines between each reason/excuse. When you finish, go back and cross out the excuses that are relatively meaningless (i.e., they would be highly unlikely to actually prevent you from taking action). The excuses that remain are your strongest reasons *not* to change. Contradict each with with a plausible, positive reason *to* change. Write your reason in the space you left.

If you immediately think of a "yeah but" for your newly listed reason *to* change, write it down. Then go back and "yeah, but" your "yeah, but" statements. Continue arguing with yourself until the reasons *to* change outnumber and outweigh the reasons *not* to—or until you realize what a tangled web you weave when you devote your time and energy to finding perfectly good reasons *not* to change.

Think of all you can do with the time, energy, and creative ideas you will have once you dismantle barrier number four. You can discover new alternatives, pursue different options, achieve new goals, and move ever closer to the life you truly desire and deserve.

## A Success Story

As described in Chapter Two, Marilyn, a registered nurse and mother of three, was forced to change after her husband left her. She describes herself as having no choice except to change, take a nursing refresher course, get a job, and go on with her life. The demand to change was clear-cut and obvious, yet Marilyn did not change immediately. She had a number of perfectly good reasons not to.

"As soon as the shock wore off," says Marilyn, "I got

very depressed. My friends and family were understanding and sympathetic at first. But after a while they began telling me I had to 'snap out of it.' I was appalled at their insensitivity. How can you expect me to go on as if nothing happened?" she moaned. "I'm in pain. My husband left me. My life is ruined."

Then she got angry. "I'll be damned if I'm going to change my lifestyle," she growled. "I'll call my lawyer. I'll get more child support. I'll make him pay. Why should I be the one to go through hell—I didn't desert *my* family."

But Marilyn's husband refused to pay more child support, and he was not exactly the model of punctuality when it came to sending the amount he had agreed to pay. Her friends confronted her with reality, but she was not ready to accept it. "I told them I didn't have the energy to look for a job," she recalls. "That was no lie. I was so depressed I barely had enough energy to get out of bed."

Marilyn doubted her ability to get a decent job. She had been away from nursing for nearly a decade. No hospital would hire her unless she took a refresher course. She would have to work at some menial job until she passed the course. It seemed too difficult. It would also mean she would be out of the house for hours at a time, time she would normally spend with her children. She couldn't do it, she claimed, because her kids needed her.

"Your kids need to know where their next meal is coming from!" shouted her mother, who had had about as much as she could take of her daughter's excuses.

"We'll get by," Marilyn sighed.

But Marilyn and her children were not getting by. Bills went unpaid. The electric company threatened to cut off their service. Winter was coming and the children needed coats and boots. They were frightened by their mother's behaviour. She rarely bothered to get dressed or comb her hair anymore. One day Marilyn's oldest daughter came to her.

"Mum," she said. "Maybe it would be better if we went

to live with Dad. You could go live with Grandma until you felt better, and you wouldn't have to worry about the bills."

Marilyn felt terrible, but still could not stop defending the way things were. "Things will be okay, love," Marilyn reassured her. But her daughter didn't believe her any more than she believed herself.

"No, they won't. Things will not be okay and I wish you would stop saying that because it just isn't true!" Marilyn's daughter stormed out of the bedroom.

"My daughter was right," Marilyn admits now. "I was lying to myself about being able to make ends meet. When I realized that, I also saw the lies in my other excuses. I don't know what I was thinking, except that if I could fool myself into believing everything was under control, I wouldn't have to *do* anything. When I finally got my head out of the clouds, there were more reasons to get my act together than there were reasons to stay in the hole I'd dug for myself. So finally, after four months of wallowing in self-pity, I decided to climb out and rejoin the human race."

It was a struggle every step of the way, but Marilyn got an aide's job in a nursing home, completed her refresher course, and moved on to an intensive care nursing position at a hospital near her home. She works a seven A.M. to three P.M. shift, which allows her ample time with her children after school and evenings free to date occasionally.

"We're not on easy street by any means," says Marilyn. "If I had my way, my husband would never have left me, and the five of us would be living happily ever after like The "Cosby Show" family. If I had my second wish, I'd fall madly in love with a very wealthy man. He would take the four of us with him to his mansion where his servants would wait on us hand and foot and I'd never have to work again. But hey, until that happens, I'll do the best I can and *never* let myself get that stuck again."

As with most people, when Marilyn recalls the time she spent being stuck, she has a hard time believing she sank so low or why she felt so afraid to let go of the way things were. I mention this feeling because cold, raw fear is a powerful obstacle to change. That change makes up barrier number five, which will be described and dismantled in the next chapter.

# 7

████ █ ████ █ ████ ████ █████████████████████████

# *Change and Fear*

Fear comes in many flavours:

| | |
|---|---|
| Fear of failure | Fear of success |
| Fear of pain | Fear of rejection |
| Fear of embarrassment | Fear of being hurt |
| Fear of hurting others | Fear of disappointment |
| Fear of being different | Fear of loneliness |
| Fear of seeming stupid | Fear of becoming dependent |
| Fear of being misunderstood | Fear of losing what you already have |
| Fear of not measuring up | Fear of the unknown or unfamiliar |

Nothing blocks change quite the way fear does. Cold, raw fear freezes you in your tracks. It paralyses. It keeps you from moving forward. When its power exceeds your power to push through it, fear is devastating.

Fear is a powerful and quick teacher. Its lessons are learned on the gut level—and rarely forgotten. There are no slow learners when fear is the teacher. Think of the young child who learns not to touch a hot stove. The very first time he touches the stove, he gets the message—and he does not have to think long and hard about it. He gets burned and immediately decides that he does not want to feel pain like that again. So, he stops touching hot stoves.

Throughout your lifetime you learn similar lessons in the same way. You learn to fear—and avoid—much more than physical pain, however.

## MARTHA

Martha has been hurt in the past and does not want to be hurt again. She fell in love for the first time when she was sixteen, but the relationship did not last. Neither did the love relationships she had at eighteen, twenty, or twenty-one. All her relationships have followed the same pattern: She gave unselfishly to the man she loved, trusted him, and made herself vulnerable. At this point she began thinking in terms of marriage. Then in each case her lover left her for another lover, for a job three thousand miles away, or because of his need for space and freedom that baffled Martha. Her love relationships always turned out the same way, but the hurt never became easier to handle.

Martha brings her past experience to each new love relationship. As a result, the ending to the relationship is written before the affair begins. No matter how well the relationship starts off, Martha fears she will be hurt again and abandoned once more. So, at the first and slightest sign that her usual fate might be on its way, she walks away from the relationship. Without discussion or explanation she tells her lover the affair is over.

Not about to wait for her lover to hurt her, Martha wants

to "get it over with" immediately. By leaving before she is left, Martha believes that she at least retains control and her dignity even though she is hurting the men she loves. Martha followed this self-destructive pattern in six short-term relationships in two years' time before she finally stopped dating altogether. But that is not a solution either. Now she is lonely and feels isolated. But Martha also feels that she is safe, protected from the possibility of being hurt again.

## WHAT ABOUT YOU?

You too have been hurt before. You have been disappointed, rejected, embarrassed, or belittled. You have lost things you cherished and failed to get what you wanted. When you remember these experiences, they stimulate all sorts of painful, negative emotions. The thought of feeling those emotions again frightens you, and you begin to avoid any situation or circumstance that presents the *possibility* of disappointment, rejection, embarrassment, belittlement, loss, failure, or anything else you fear. As a result, your fears and avoidance behaviours limit the number and kind of risks you are willing to take. Like Martha, you learn to play it safe and protect yourself. Consequently, you get less out of life and you get stuck.

Fear can be a reasonable response to a real situation. If a mugger holds a knife to your throat, if your car skids out of control at an ice-covered junction, if the flood waters rise to the second storey of your house, or if the baby's temperature reaches 102 degrees, you experience a real threat and feel fear. Indeed, in such life-threatening situations any normal human being would be frightened and traumatized. Although it feels very much the same, this kind of fear is *not* the kind that blocks change and keeps your from pursuing viable alternatives and unpleasant circumstances.

Let me illustrate the difference by telling you a very

condensed version of an old folk tale called "The Three
Sillies":

Once upon a time on a fine summer's afternoon, John
paid a visit to his fiancée, Mary, and her parents, Mr. and
Mrs. Smith, and was invited to stay for supper.

As the foursome took their seats, Mr. Smith realized
there was no wine on the table. Mary offered to correct the
oversight and went to the wine cellar. Considerable time
passed, but Mary did not return. Mrs. Smith went to see what
was keeping her. When the two women did not return, Mr.
Smith went to the wine cellar to get them. John waited and
waited until he could wait no longer. He too went to the wine
cellar and, much to his surprise, found Mary and her parents
weeping and wailing as if their hearts would break.

"Whatever is the matter?" he asked.

All three sobbed and pointed to the ceiling. John looked
up. Stuck in one of the beams, where it no doubt had been
lodged for years, was an axe. John stared at the axe. Then he
stared at his fiancée and future in-laws. He could not fathom
why they were so upset.

Seeing John's confusion, Mary tearfully explained, "What
if you and I were to marry and have a son? He would grow
tall and handsome like his father and be adored by his grandparents, would he not? And they would want us to visit as
often as we could and invite us to stay for supper. Our beautiful, wonderful, kind, and loving son would one day come
down to this very wine cellar to fetch some wine—*and what if
that axe fell and killed him?*"

The prospect of such a horrible disaster's coming to pass
set off more mournful crying by Mary and her parents. Nothing John could do would console them, and they refused to
leave the cellar where the imaginary son might one day meet
his imaginary demise.

In exasperation John declared his belief that they were
the three silliest people in the world and refused to marry

Mary until he had searched the world over to find three people more ridiculous than they were.

John found them eventually, but that is not why I told this story or why I like it so much. I tell it because it makes people laugh. How truly absurd Mary and her parents acted. Yet it is exactly what each of us do when we fear *possible* negative outcomes. We predict disaster, visualize catastrophes, and our fears about what *might* happen mushroom to outrageous proportions and block change.

## CATASTROPHIZING

Carol keeps her dismal social work job because she fears the alternatives. She is afraid she will fail at any other job. She wishes she could devote herself to a full-time private therapy practice, but every time she thinks about doing that, she is plagued by fears of financial ruin. First she is sure that she will not be able to pay her bills, then she just knows she will lose her home. Her husband will then sue for custody of their children and win. Finally Carol will have to go on welfare and end up spending her old age as a homeless bag lady.

From your point of view, Carol's fears may seems as absurd as the axe's falling on the imaginary child, but to Carol they are very real. She believes she cannot risk leaving her job and persuades herself to hang on to what she has no matter how much she hates it.

As Jack's stress and anxiety increases, he becomes acutely aware of his need for professional help. He knows that he must consult a therapist, yet he is afraid of what a therapist will tell him. At best, Jack expects to hear that his life is messed up beyond repair and he will have to give up the accounting job that he has worked so hard to get. At worst, he believes that the therapist will take one look at him, call for the men in the white coats, and commit him to the nearest mental institution. Because his fears are so strong, Jack does not call the therapist to make an appointment, and stress and anxiety continue to plague him.

You imagine your boss's reply to your request for a pay rise. "Forget it," he says. "What makes you think you deserve a rise? You are not a valued employee. In fact, I've been meaning to tell you just how disappointed I am by your work."

Because of low self-esteem combined with fear, your thoughts turn to every mistake you have made during your tenure with the company, and you figure you are lucky to have a job at all.

You worry about the party you plan to attend. You worry about what to wear. Then you worry that whatever you choose will be the exact opposite of what everyone else is wearing and you will feel embarrassed and out of place. You worry about conversing with people you do not know very well and saying something stupid or offensive or not knowing what to say at all, which will make you look like an idiot. Then you worry that no one will start a conversation with you in the first place, making you feel like a loser, just like you used to at those high school dances. You feel doomed to stand alone and miserable while everyone else is having fun, "as usual." As a result, you wonder why you subject yourself to such humiliation and decide not to go to the party.

In each instance you do not fear a clear and immediate danger. Instead, you fear *possibilities*—possible pain, possible rejection, possible failure, possible embarrassment. In your imagination you conjure up the worst-case scenario and fear it will become a reality. All the while, however, you overlook the *probability* that what you so desperately fear will never come to pass.

Carol is not going to become a bag lady. Jack is not going

to be committed against his will to a mental hospital or be forced to quit his job. You might actually get the rise you request or have a good time at the party. But ruled by your fears, you sacrifice probable gains to protect yourself from possible loss—a decision that is going to get you stuck.

---

## TEN WAYS FEAR BLOCKS CHANGE

*1. Fear persuades you to set easier goals and do less than you are capable of doing.*

I started this book by telling you how close I came to not writing it. Fear played a role in getting me stuck. I feared every publisher in America would reject the manuscript, that no one would read the book if it was published, and that someone else had already written a better book about change. I feared criticism from book reviewers and my colleagues in academia. I was afraid that the time I spent writing the book would have a negative impact on my family and my other work and that I would run out of things to say halfway through the project. I almost convinced myself to limit my writing to journal articles.

*2. Fear triggers internal defence systems and fools you into thinking that you have perfectly good reasons not to change.*

In the previous chapter you met Jennifer, the doctor's wife who fears losing what she already has. If she files for divorce, insists on marital counselling, or otherwise challenges her status quo, she may end up alone and stripped of the perks, privileges, and status of a doctor's wife.

When she thinks about change, Jennifer sees a painful, unappealing picture. To counter her fear, she paints a rosy picture of her present situation, trying desperately to convince herself that marriage to an unfaithful husband is "not so bad."

*3. Fear—especially fear of failure or disappointment—reduces the number of available alternatives or keeps you from pursuing them.*

Julie fears she will be alone and lonely for the rest of her life. What she fears even more, however, is the possibility that she will try to improve her situation, be disappointed by the results of her change effort, and *still* be alone and lonely. Therefore, to reduce the chances of being disappointed, she searches for a perfect solution, rejecting any alternative she perceives to be flawed or apt to fail. The trouble is, Julie perceives *all* alternatives that way.

*4. Fear—particularly fear of making mistakes—causes indecisiveness and confusion. It stops you from knowing what you* really *want.*

After discussing his concerns with trusted friends, Steven, the plumbing contractor whose problems include cocaine and women, lists several ways to feel more in control of his own life. He lists actions he could take immediately, such as organizing and computerizing his business ventures, delegating responsibility, and managing his time. He also lists options that offer long-range benefits, such as seeing a therapist, starting an exercise programme, and cutting down his cocaine usage. Unfortunately, having options only increases Steven's despair.

Steven cannot decide what to do first. He does not trust his own instincts or abilities and is terrified that he will make a dumb mistake or impulsively choose the wrong alternative, as he has done so often in the past. So, he waffles and procrastinates.

*5. Fear warps your perception of your life and what you can do to make it better.*

A realistic assessment of her situation would show Carol that she has proven talent as a therapist, many professional contacts and potential client referral sources, valuable expertise, and a great geographic location for her private practice, which is highly likely to thrive and flourish. If she approached her financial situation rationally, she would see that she does indeed have alternatives. If she wants to leave her savings and pension fund untouched for emergencies and future retirement, she can get a small business loan to cover her initial expenses. If she could think clearly, Carol would also know that her job stress and burned-out condition could damage her health, her personal relationships, and her family. If she viewed her situation objectively, she would choose to change. But seeing only what she fears—failure, financial ruin, and humiliation—she chooses not to change.

*6. Fear keeps you from asking for help when you need it or benefiting from the emotional support offered to you.*

As you may recall from Chapter Three, prior to the onset of anxiety attacks that prompted her to change, Cindy's self-esteem was extremely low. She assumed she was unlovable. From childhood experiences she came to believe her acceptance by other people rested on being cute, funny, and amusing all the time. She thought people would ignore and abandon her if she let them know how she really felt. Long before her anxiety attacks began, Cindy knew she was depressed, confused, and having difficulty coping. But fearing that even the people who loved her most would reject her, criticize her, or stop caring about her, she kept her pain and her problems to herself—until an emotional crisis forced her to seek help.

It's true that to ask for help is to risk losing face or hearing something you do not want to hear (as Jack did). To delegate responsibility, seek practical assistance or emotional support, is to possibly appear weak, incompetent, dependent, or needy. You risk rejection as well. So you decide to "go it alone." But that often turns out to be the most difficult way to go.

*7. Fear keeps you from asserting yourself and persuades you to settle for what you feel you must settle for instead of going after what you want.*

Although she had years of sales experience when she began her new job, Lisa is new to the office supply business. She is the only sales representative without a college degree and the only female. In addition, Lisa's colleagues seem so smart and confident and form a tight-knit group.

Fearing she will look dumb, naive, or incompetent, Lisa is reluctant to ask questions, offer opinions, or make suggestions. She works hard and keeps her mouth shut. Soon she knows the ropes and has a sales record comparable to her male colleagues, but her fears persist. She does not communicate her needs or problems, however, or question the policy decisions made without her input. She does not complain when she does not get the rise she is promised or is not considered for promotions. Consequently, with each passing day Lisa feels more unhappy, but she is scared to do anything about the situation.

*8. To calm your fears, you develop (and get stuck with) unhealthy habits and behaviour patterns.*

Melanie is painfully shy and has been since early childhood. At first her shyness was not a problem. She rather enjoyed being by herself and occupying her time with imaginative fantasies. However, once she entered high school, she realized she might be missing something, but by then she had become too shy to make friends or socialize. Then a new family moved in next door, and their fifteen-year-old daughter befriended Melanie. The girl was Melanie's opposite in every way—outgoing, confident, and never at a loss for words. Melanie's friend dragged her along to parties where Melanie always felt uncomfortable and out of place.

Sometimes beer or wine was served at these parties, and Melanie's friend suggested she drink to relax and have a good time. Melanie resisted at first, but soon gave in and discovered the power alcohol had to loosen her tongue and boost her courage. After a few drinks Melanie was not timid anymore. She was not afraid of rejection or embarrassment or long awkward silences when she ran out of things to say. In fact, she became amazingly bold and witty. To this day in any social situation, whenever she feels insecure or fearful, Melanie drinks—a lot—since it takes more alcohol to loosen her up than it did when she was fifteen.

Similarly, Steven uses cocaine to feel the rush of power and confidence. To avoid the panic she feels in public places and behind the wheel of her car, Patty rarely leaves her house. In spite of her desire to lose weight, Karen goes on eating binges while she waits to hear about a writing assignment she really wants but fears she will not get.

*9. Fear often makes you give up just one step short of your goal.*

Newly identified and added to the menu of fears that block change is the fear of success. It is a common fear for the achievement-oriented woman, whose power, status, and wealth sometimes threaten the man in her life. This woman has worked hard to achieve her goals and aspirations, but just as she reaches the pinnacle of success as she always envisioned it, she asks herself, "What if I get what I really want only to lose the man I really want?" It is then that her fear of success overwhelms her, and she may stop achieving, sabotage her own career goals, or leave the "rat race" to pursue less demanding and threatening interests.

Fear of success is also at work when you ask yourself, "What if I get what I want but I am no happier than I was before?" This is a question well-known to anyone who attempts a change effort in one specific area. For instance, fear of success plagues Karen each time she nears or reaches her goal weight.

"People start treating me differently," she explains. "They pay more attention to me. They are nicer. Men come on to me and I have to deal with all the complexities of male/female relationships. There seem to be a million things I have to deal with that I didn't have to deal with when I had the wall of fat to protect me. I got what I wanted and I should feel good about it, but I don't. Life isn't better, it's more complicated. At the same time I get angry that people can't see I'm the same person on the inside as I was when I was fat. As a result, I get myself all worked up and start overeating again."

*10. Fear keeps you from taking risks.*

Anything you do to change or improve yourself involves risk—the chance of injury, damage, or loss. With every step forward you risk failure, disappointment, rejection, pain, or any other feared negative outcome. When change is involved, the most common fear of all is fear of the unknown or unfamiliar.

Nine times out of ten, change leaves you better off than you were before. Nine to one are terrific odds at the racetrack, in the gambling casino, or on the stock market. However, when you attempt change, the risk you take involves *your* life and *your* future and the stakes may seem too high. In addition, you have personal choices to make (which you naturally fear will be the wrong choices), and you alone are responsible for making your effort to change work (which you naturally fear you will fail to do over the long haul). Suddenly, the nine-to-one probability of success no longer reassures you. The one in ten chance for failure, disappointment, loss, or pain frightens you. It frightens you enough to keep you from taking the risk.

Fear of unknown and unpredictable outcomes of a change effort can freeze you in your tracks. Afraid to enter unfamiliar territory, you get stuck where you are. Fear in any flavour can keep you from getting unstuck.

## Fear Can Control Your Life If You Let It

In my youth, I heard President Franklin Delano Roosevelt declare, "We have nothing to fear but fear itself." At

the time it made a modicum of sense to me. Over the years
it has grown ever more meaningful. Fear can, and often does,
take on a life of its own. As its power increases, it can take
over *your* life as well.

The physical and emotional reactions to fear are extremely uncomfortable. Fear itself is frightening, escalating
the pain over your situation that you already feel. Whether
you fear a very real and life-threatening mugger who con-
fronts you at knifepoint or the mere possibility of an unpleasant occurrence, your body mobilizes its energy to fend
off an attack. Your muscles tighten, your breathing becomes
rapid and shallow, your heart beats faster, and adrenaline
rushes through your veins. Fear can also take you by surprise
when no tangible threat is present.

When a physical threat passes, your body returns to
"normal." However, when what you fear is intangible and
relates to a problem, a pending decision that will not go
away, or something of which you are not even consciously
aware, fear turns into anxiety. It hangs around persistently
or appears unexpectedly, perhaps blossoming into full-fledged
panic or anxiety attacks, causing dizzyness, hyperventilation, tingling or numb hands and feet, pounding headaches,
and other painful, frightening symptoms.

With or without panic attacks, fear and anxiety cloud
your thinking and produce a sense of dread and impending
doom that reduce your ability to make decisions or take
action. You feel paralysed and powerless because of your
fears.

The most common reaction to fear and anxiety is to
avoid anything that frightens you or makes you anxious. This
avoidance is most clearly and dramatically seen in people
who suffer from phobias—irrational, overpowering fears of
flying, closed places, crowds, heights, and many other things.
The most severely afflicted phobics create specific safety
zones for themselves. These may be a two-mile or two-block
radius around the home, the inside of a house, or sometimes
only one floor or several rooms inside the house. Agora-

phobics move outside their safety zones very rarely—if at all. Their life in its entirety is turned over to their fears.

Most of you do not suffer from debilitating, life-restricting phobias. However, your reaction to fear differs only in degree. Like the phobic, you avoid what you fear. If decisions bring on anxiety, you avoid making them. If social situations frighten you, you do not socialize. If asserting yourself causes stress and tension, you keep your mouth shut and go along with what others say, even if you disagree. If lovers hurt you in the past and you fear you will be hurt like that again, you avoid intimacy. Your fears dictate how you live your life, limit your enjoyment or satisfaction, and hamper your ability to change for the better.

Quite logically you may conclude that the best way to rid yourself of fear and anxiety is to avoid the situations and abandon the behaviours that cause fear and anxiety. But the truth of the matter is that to overcome fear and get on with your life, you must FACE FEAR HEAD ON AND PUSH THROUGH IT, reclaiming the power and energy it stole from you.

## DISMANTLING BARRIER #5: PUSHING THROUGH FEAR

Pioneers in the treatment of phobias, behavioural scientists often compare fear to a monster living in a cave. Periodically the monster comes out into the open to attack you and bring on the painful, panicky symptoms I described earlier. To avoid these feelings, you do anything and everything you can to make sure the monster stays in his cave— where you cannot see him and are unlikely to be hurt by him. Of course, the monster is perfectly happy to stay in his cave, because he knows he still controls your life and your behaviour. In fact, he is quite pleased with himself. Without lifting so much as a finger he has you where he wants you —stuck and afraid to do anything to get unstuck.

To rid yourself of fear and regain lost control, you must

lure the monster out of his cave and whack him on the head until he can no longer harm you. You must take a good long look at your fears and see how they limit you. Then you will be able to take steps to counteract those fears, control your anxiety, and move forward once again.

### Learning to Relax

As previously noted, the painful physical symptoms, thoughts, and emotions activated by fear and anxiety are themselves frightening. Often they hit you without warning, wake you in the middle of the night, or automatically escalate when you think about change. Because they seem to occur spontaneously, you may think such stress and anxiety reactions are beyond your control. This is not true.

You can learn to control your physical symptoms and actually create a state of being that is the exact opposite of distress and anxiety. You can learn how to relax your body and your mind. Relaxation techniques give immediate, measurable relief, and they contradict your beliefs about fear. If your reaction to fear can be controlled, so can anything else you do or do not do when you feel fearful. If fear is a monster, it is one of your own making. You can alter its existence or eradicate it altogether.

There are any number of resources available to teach you relaxation techniques. There are books, courses, and even anxiety-reduction clinics that use biofeedback machines to measure relaxation. I lean toward the use of audio tapes myself and recommend you get one and follow its instructions. You can also relax without electronic devices or audiovisual aids.

## A PHYSICAL RELAXATION EXERCISE

Sit in a comfortable chair (recliners work well) or lie down. Close your eyes.

Focus your attention on your breathing. Think of nothing

else. Other thoughts may intrude. Acknowledge them. Let them pass through your mind, but do not focus on them. Return your attention to your breathing. Continue this until your breathing is calm and rhythmic (as opposed to rapid, tight, or strained).

Then, beginning with your toes and moving upward one muscle group at a time, *tense* the muscles—*hold* for a slow count of three—then let go and *relax* the muscles. You will feel the distinct difference between tension and relaxation. Repeat the *tense-hold-relax* sequence on the muscles in your calves, thighs, buttocks, abdomen, chest, back, shoulders, arms, hands, neck, and face. If you still notice tension anywhere, tense-hold-relax those muscles, so that your entire body is completely relaxed.

## A MENTAL RELAXATION EXERCISE

Once you remove physical tension from your body, take your mind on a short vacation. Think of a place (real or imaginary) that is particularly calm and soothing for you and place yourself in it. You might be lying on a deserted beach, floating in a canoe on a calm lake, strolling through a garden, sitting on the porch swing at your grandmother's house, or any other place that symbolizes peace and serenity for you. Imagine it with all your senses. Relax and enjoy being there. Then, slowly return your attention to the here and now.

Taking only fifteen minutes, this technique offers physical and emotional relaxation. It brings anxiety down to level one or two on a scale of ten. It can be used to ward off a pending anxiety attack, prepare you to sleep through the night, or rejuvenate you to face the rest of the day or evening.

### Confronting the Monster

Once you learn what relaxation feels like and how to control your level of relaxation, you can use what you learned to reduce fear's hold on your life. First make yourself relaxed and focus on your calm scene until your stress/anxiety level rates a one on a scale of one to ten. Then begin thinking about a stressful situation in your life, one that conjures up fear in the flavour of your choice. This may be asking for a pay rise, going to a party, broaching the topic of marriage counselling with your spouse, attending your first therapy session, going on a diet, or any other area of conflict and confusion.

As you think about the stressful situation, your anxiety level will rise. When it reaches a three or four level on your one to ten scale, *stop* thinking about the problem and focus once again on your breathing. Relax any muscles that feel tense and visualize your calm scene, bringing yourself back down to level one.

Over the course of several days or weeks, repeat this process. Each time, think about the situation for a longer period of time and allow your anxiety level to get higher before returning to level one. After you have worked yourself up to level ten a few times, you will make an interesting discovery. It becomes *more difficult* to reach level ten. The same catastrophic thoughts and dreaded outcomes do not frighten you *as much* as they once did. Soon they hardly frighten you at all.

More importantly, you realize *you are in control.* During these sessions, *you* create high anxiety levels and you reduce your anxiety. If you can do it during a relaxation session, you can do it as part of daily living. When you face a decision, a problem, or a possible effort to change, *you* control the amount of fear and anxiety you feel. If you notice yourself becoming fearful, you can reduce the amount of fear you feel. You can reduce it enough to push right through it and do what you really want to do.

With practice you can become sensitive to the slightest increase in fear or anxiety, and you can do something about it. The next time you fear *possible* failure, rejection, disappointment, or any other dreaded outcome—SLOW DOWN!

Take a few deep breaths. Relax your tense muscles. Take a quick peek at your calm scene and push past that fear.

## Imaging for Success

Thoughts are powerful. You know that because you have watched your thoughts block change. You have seen how thinking of the worst-case scenario stirs up fear and self-doubt. You have used thoughts to reframe reality and convince yourself that things are not so bad. Your thoughts have lowered your self-esteem. All too often how you think about change blocks change and gets you stuck.

*Positive* thoughts are powerful too. You can visualize success as well as failure. If your mind can picture the way you really want your life to be, you vastly improve your chances of actually achieving your goals.

Once again bring yourself to a relaxed state. Visualize a success. Picture yourself shaking your boss's hand after he says, "Of course you can have a rise. You've earned it." Imagine yourself enjoying a party. See yourself ten or twenty pounds thinner. What are you wearing? How do you move? What do you do that you did not do before? Envision yourself celebrating the six-month anniversary of the day you quit smoking, receiving your college diploma, having a love relationship, crossing the finish line of a five mile road race, or achieving any other goal. Visualize each step along the way. Create a detailed image of yourself as you will be when you get what you want. Savour it and return to it at the end of each relaxation session.

Imaging predicts success and motivates you to reach for the real thing. Imaging trains you to think and act positively, to say "I can" and "I will" instead of "I can't" or "I'll never." Imaging helps you push through fear so that you stop looking at the worst possibilities and focus instead on how good life can be.

## Affirmations

Imaging works best when accompanied by *affirmations*—positive statements reinforcing your beliefs about what you *can* do and how good you *can* be.

Once you have visualized achieving a goal or taking a positive step toward your goal, repeat several affirmations about that goal. Begin your affirmations with:

I can . . .

I will . . .

I deserve to . . .

I owe it to myself to . . .

Success will be sweet when I . . .

Write down your affirmations. Read them before you go to sleep at night, when you awaken in the morning, and anytime your fear monsters come calling.

## Taking Action to Push Through Fear

I can fly an aeroplane. I learned several years ago. I did not know exactly why I wanted to fly, but the thought of being airborne behind the controls of a small plane thrilled me. If I learned to fly, I knew I would have mastered a truly marvellous skill, one that I had never done before. The challenge excited me and also frightened me.

Flying a small plane is a big risk. It involves the possibility of mechanical failures, sudden storms, gusts of wind during takeoff, and making mistakes at some crucial moment. Yes, there is a great deal of risk involved.

I did not *have* to learn to fly, but I still really wanted to risk it. I would achieve a new goal, conquer a new frontier. I knew I would feel more capable and more powerful. I was correct on all counts.

But I must admit I had my doubts when my flight instructor turned out to be just twenty years old. He assuaged some of my fears the first time I flew with him, however, flying with grace, precision, and confidence, as if flying were something he was born to do. Yes, he could fly, but could he teach? I had to be sure of that. For flying to be a reasonable risk rather than a foolish one, I had to know this young man could teach me superbly.

I had been a teacher all of my professional life, so I knew a thing or two about teaching. I knew for example that good teachers do not just teach, they teach to accomplish an objective. Half-joking and maybe a little nervous, I playfully asked what his objectives were. He took me seriously, however. "I have just one objective," he answered. "It's to teach you how to keep yourself alive."

That was exactly what I wanted to hear. It told me he understood risk. He knew about the wisdom and skill that must illuminate all risk taking, and he was well aware of the balancing act of pushing yourself to get what you want while still protecting yourself from harm. You must account for the chance of injury, damage, or loss inherent to any risk, yet you cannot become so fearful of the possibilities that you do not risk at all.

## MORE ABOUT RISK TAKING

To be healthier and happier as well as to get what you really want, you must push through fear by taking well-chosen, carefully considered, and wisely executed risks. Let me review four types of risks, three of which were presented as self-esteem building blocks in Chapter Three. All four promote growth and change, and all produce an exhilaration that gives life a certain spice.

*INTELLECTUAL RISKS* expand awareness, acquaint you with new ideas, reactivate your brain cells, make you more open to the world around you and more accepting of the positive possibilities life offers. To risk intellectually, read more demanding books, see more challenging films, drive miles if need be to hear a provocative speaker, subscribe to magazines and newspapers that stretch you intellectually and sometimes even threaten your opinions.

*PHYSICAL RISKS* push your body to its limit, increase your endurance, test your agility, your courage, and your survival instincts. Physical risks are tangible proof of your current capabilities and your potential to do more today than you did yesterday.

Included in the physical risk category are those activities that present some physical danger, activities where injuries can occur unless skill, knowledge, and wisdom are employed. When done correctly and responsibly, these "edge sports" let you experience the thrill, sense of accomplishment, and sheer exhilaration that comes from successful risk taking. Edge sports include everything from rugby to rock climbing, from hang gliding to waterskiing. My edge sport may not be yours. There are countless areas of physical risk from which to choose, including learning to drive a car, dirt biking, running a mini-marathon, or diving from the high board at the community swimming pool.

*SPIRITUAL RISKS* ask you to explore your faith and dare you to meet your God in ever more meaningful ways—ways that go beyond the boundaries of traditional religion. By exercising faith and discovering the realm unexplainable by your five senses or the marvels of modern technology, you expand your world tremendously and conquer fear. When you live your life by faith instead of fear, you make no excuses. You do whatever it takes to be the best you can be.

*EMOTIONAL RISKS* are the most frightening. So many fears are reactions to the possibility of emotional pain. Emotional risks are taken when you dare to meet new people, deepen existing friendships, ask for emotional support or seek counselling, repair broken family ties, face conflicts head-on, or ask brave questions about the future of a relationship. The greatest emotional risk of them all is to move toward genuine intimacy, to allow another person to see all of you, including your fears and vulnerability.

## LISA'S RISK

Risking genuine intimacy was something Lisa and Bob were afraid to do. They met at a social function sponsored by a company to which Lisa sold office supplies. There was real chemistry between them, and by the end of the party they had plans to see each other again in the near future.

Dinner and a concert led to more dates. Soon they were spending every weekend together, then weekends and two or three nights each week. After a year Lisa wondered why she rented her own apartment, but Bob had never mentioned living together, and marriage seemed to be an off-limits topic.

"When I met Bob, he was dating several other women," says Lisa. "They were tall, gorgeous, and sophisticated. Bob's friends never failed to mention how I was not his usual type, and it got to me. He was this rich, powerful lawyer who had travelled all over the world and knew lots of important and famous people. I loved to listen to his stories, but at the same time they made me feel insecure. What was this hotshot doing with a boring sales rep like me?"

Further fuelling Lisa's fears was the fact that Bob did not have a terrific track record when it came to relationships. "By the third month we were dating, I had heard about all his old girlfriends," Lisa continues. "And there were plenty of them. They came with the same basic story. In the end they all turned into clingy, demanding shrews. Bob tried to let them down nicely but eventually had to hurt them to free himself."

Determined *not* to be like her predecessors, Lisa made no demands. She was supportive and understanding and flexible. She never shared her problems with Bob, seeking emotional support from her girlfriends instead. Whatever time they spent together was at Bob's suggestion, not Lisa's.

"It was easy to let him call the shots, because he was really good to me. We had a great time together and I loved him dearly. Besides, even if he did not say it, I was pretty sure he was in love with me, too. But after about nine months it started to get to me. I couldn't go on pretending what I needed did not matter or keep things from him because I did not want to look demanding or dependent. And I needed to know if the relationship was going anywhere, if it had a future and what the future was."

It took Lisa three more months to "get up the nerve" to say anything. She was afraid he would reject her, abandon her, or hurt her. Finally she told him what she had been doing and why she had done it. Then she took a deep breath and asked him where he saw their relationship going.

"I braced myself for the response I expected," Lisa recalls. "I thought he would say 'Why does it have to be going anywhere?' and launch into a lecture about freedom and no commitments and going with the flow. Instead, he said he would have asked me to marry him six months ago, but he didn't think I was interested."

Fearing rejection and the possibility of being hurt, Lisa had behaved with calculated nonchalance. Responding only to what Bob wanted, she had asked for nothing and gave no indication that she wanted anything of significance from the relationship. Fearing the same possibilities, Bob thought Lisa did not need him, that she could take or leave their relationship and would indeed walk away one day. He assumed she would say no to a marriage proposal or an offer to live together, so he did not ask either. For at least six months they both allowed their fears to convince them to settle for what they had and reach for no more.

Then, fortunately, Lisa took a huge emotional risk. Everything she believed about Bob told her he would run as fast and as far as he could if she used words such as "future" or "commitment." Asking her brave question *could have* turned her fears into reality. On the other hand, she could have settled for less than she wanted and *still* been hurt if their relationship had ended one day.

"The biggest risk I ever took had the best results," says Lisa, who has been married to Bob for two years now. "I don't know if risk taking always works out that way, but I can't imagine what my life would be like today if I had not taken that risk when I did."

Lisa took a risk and came out ahead. Much of the time, risks work out that way. You may not get all you want, but you generally get more than you had before. And you give that fear-monster a hefty whack on the head, reducing fear's control over you.

---

### TO PUSH THROUGH FEAR—TAKE MORE RISKS

WE ALL TAKE RISKS. If you think *you* do not, reread the list of successes you compiled while reading Chapter Three. You *have* taken risks before. You will take them again. To get unstuck, you must. Risks teach valuable lessons, not the least of which is how to risk successfully in the future.

#### Five Risks Already Taken

On a sheet of paper, list five risks you have taken in the past. Remember, a risk is anything that includes the chance of physical or emotional injury, damage, or loss. Your risk could have been taken at work, in your family, or as part of a love relationship. The risk might have been intellectual, physical, spiritual, or emotional. Leave seven or eight blank lines between each risk.

Now think about how you felt *before* you took that risk. What did you fear? Directly below each risk, list your fears.

In spite of those fears, you went ahead and took the risk. What did you do to push through fear? What did you think, say, and do to get yourself to take the risk? Write your answers in the remaining space below each fear.

## Five Risks You Want to Take

Of course, there are many other risks you will take during your lifetime. The next risks you take may result from your desire to move closer to overall wellness, get something in your lifeline net, clear up an area of conflict and confusion, or pursue an alternative to a specific problem. Using your ideas about change found in the strategies you did in Chapter Two or the alternatives you listed in Chapter Four, select five risks you need to or want to take now or in the near future. List them on another sheet of paper. As you did before, leave space between each risk.

What fears come to mind or well up in your gut when you think about taking the risks you have listed? What possible physical or emotional danger, injury, or loss do you fear? List those fears. How will you push through your fears and actually take those risks? Using what you have learned from past risk taking as well as ideas you found in this chapter, make notes to yourself about how to push through fear.

## Creative Worrying

You may want to go one step further and do some *creative worrying* about the risks you want to take. When you worry creatively, you let your imagination run wild, catastrophize prolifically, and think of all those worst-case scenarios.

List *everything* that could go wrong.

For every potential disaster, ask yourself what you can do to make sure the catastrophe you fear does *not* happen.

List one or more contingency plans for each imagined disaster. Then—like the flight instructor whose objective was to teach me how to keep myself alive—you will be able to risk wisely, with your eyes open wide and your anxiety under control.

Whenever you risk, pushing through fear is easier if you have the cooperation and support you need. Without other people's help, support, validation, and cooperation, you will get stuck again. Chapter Eight describes this next barrier and shows you how to dismantle it.

# 8

||||||||||||||||||||||||||||||||||||||||||||||||||

# *Change and Cooperation*

In previous chapters I have described Carol, who is stuck in a job she detests, and Marilyn, who returned to the work force after her husband unexpectedly left her. Both are divorced working mothers and have three children living at home. Carol's sons are nineteen, sixteen, and thirteen years old. Marilyn has sixteen- and fourteen-year-old daughters and a twelve-year-old son. With a full-time job and a part-time private therapy practice, Carol spends as many hours outside the home as Marilyn, who works full-time and takes nursing refresher courses. Yet, although their basic situations are quite similar, Marilyn and Carol run their households very differently.

Once Marilyn was no longer immobilized by depression, she tried to be superwoman. She works, goes to school, takes care of all homemaking chores, and is an active, involved parent. "The demands are endless," she sighs. "I have to be mum, dad, housekeeper, cook, dishwasher, chauffeur, cheerleader, seamstress, and breadwinner."

Marilyn's days begin at five-thirty A.M. She straightens

the house, does a load of laundry, and irons school clothes and nursing uniforms. Then she wakes the kids, makes breakfast, checks homework, packs lunches, and sends the children off to school. After that, she showers, dresses, drives to work, works her shift, runs errands, starts dinner, drives the kids to afterschool activities, helps with homework, serves dinner, and cleans up after the meal. She also goes to class three nights a week, invariably returning to find her house a mess or her children in the midst of some crisis. After they go to bed, she studies, pays bills, does more laundry, and falls into bed by midnight.

Weekends offer little relief. She must catch up on all the housekeeping and errands she could not get to during the week as well as spend as much "quality" time as possible with her children. "I don't know how other single working mothers handle it," she groans. "Being all things to all people is making me crazy. I'm running myself ragged.

"But it all *has* to get done somehow. Asking the kids to help is more trouble than it's worth. They moan and groan and never do things the way I like them done. Most of the time I have to go back and redo what they've done. Then they moan and groan some more, asking why I didn't just do the job myself in the first place.

"I used to be too depressed to do anything. Now I do it all and I'm a raving maniac. Instead of whining and crying, I yell and criticize. I lie in bed after the alarm rings each morning and don't know how I'm going to make it through another day. I pray that things won't be like this forever, but I don't see any end in sight."

On the other hand, Carol has worked and single-handedly raised her children for close to a decade. At first she handled her many roles and responsibilities in the same way Marilyn does and also felt overwhelmed and resentful. Now, Carol and her sons work together to complete household chores and coordinate their hectic schedules.

"It's a matter of survival," Carol explains. "If you want clean clothes, a house that isn't a pigsty, food to eat, and a clean fork to eat it with, you have to pitch in. It isn't fair to expect me to do it all just because I'm the mother.

"It's also about family harmony," she continues. "We each have things we have to do and things we want to do. The boys have sports and dates. They want to hang out at the shopping precinct. The oldest has a part-time job. I have work and friends and errands to run, clients to see. Three of us can drive, but there are only two cars. If any of us are going to get at least some of what we want, we have to join forces and work together."

In Carol's house, each family member has several permanently assigned responsibilities. Particularly distasteful chores, such as vacuuming, dishwashing, and cleaning bathrooms, are assigned on a rotating basis. A multicoloured housework schedule hangs on the kitchen wall so that everyone can see who is supposed to do what. Next to the work schedule is a large calendar. As soon as any family member learns of a scheduled appointment or activity, he or she writes it on the calendar.

Once a week a family meeting is held at which the calendar is reviewed and transportation arrangements made. Failure to complete assigned tasks is also discussed, and conflicts between two or more family members are resolved.

"We talk about fun things, too," Carol explains. "Like how to spend money left over from the household budget and where to go on vacations. The point of everything we do is to avoid turning minor disagreements into major arguments and prevent any one person from feeling abused or unappreciated."

Disagreements do occur, of course. Plans or schedules are not always followed to the letter. One family member can ask another to do his chore—usually in exchange for cash, a ride, or some other favour. The bartering system occasionally gets out of hand, however, and inequities must be corrected at the next family meeting.

"There are always little crises," Carol admits. "Someone decides they just *have* to go somewhere right away, or that an item of clothing they neglected to put in the clothes hamper needs to be washed and ironed immediately because it is the *only* thing they can wear that day. We're not perfect. But our system works for us. Everything that needs doing gets done, and no one feels overburdened or taken for granted."

The difference between Carol's family harmony and Marilyn's family chaos can be summed up in one word— COOPERATION.

---

### BARRIER #6: A LACK OF COOPERATION

To cooperate is to act or work *together* with another person or other people. People who cooperate join forces to reach a common goal or solve a mutual problem. They unite to emotionally support one another, share wisdom, and benefit from each other's experiences. Cooperation creates partnerships. Each partner brings something into the cooperative effort and gets something out of it. They pull together and as a result achieve more than they could if they worked alone.

Carol gets cooperation. With each person contributing to an effort that benefits them all, Carol's household runs smoothly and to everyone's satisfaction most of the time. Marilyn, however, lacks cooperation. Household chores get done only because Marilyn overextends herself to do them all. She feels overwhelmed, resentful, and trapped—feelings that detract from her relationship with her children and her ability to enjoy life.

Barrier number six—a lack of cooperation—slows and complicates change efforts. It does this by preventing you from getting the help you need, creating new problems or unexpected obstacles. It may also strain relationships with people who matter to you, sometimes prompting them to work *against* you rather than *with* you.

## Why You Need Cooperation

Change does not occur in a vacuum. From the moment you decide to change, while you progress toward your goal, and after you reach it, people are drawn into your change effort. Some participate at your request. Some become allies, encouraging and supporting you. Some are automatically affected by what you do, such as friends, family, co-workers, and others who feel the impact of your effort to change and must adjust accordingly.

With cooperation you get more of what you need and move steadily toward your destination. Without cooperation you get less help, support, or encouragement, make much slower progress, or get stuck altogether.

> COOPERATION gets you the emotional support or practical assistance you need to succeed. A LACK OF COOPERATION limits the help you receive and the success you are able to achieve.

In many cases, in order to succeed, you *must* act or work together with other people. Simply put, you may need help. You need the services of a professionally trained therapist or the emotional support and advice of other recovering alcoholics, addicts, overeaters, or compulsive gamblers. Or you may need a "change partner" who goes on a diet with you, attends the same aerobics class, runs with you each morning, or edits the great romantic novel you have always wanted to write. Cooperation may also take the form of practical assistance—help with household chores, transportation, child care, typing, finances, or the planning of your father's sixtieth birthday party.

When you know how to cooperate, you get the help that allows you to change successfully. If, for reasons I will present later, you try to change without cooperation, you are liable to fail or get stuck.

COOPERATION supplies encouragement or backing
from allies. A LACK OF COOPERATION leaves you with
discouragement and more problems.

Jack, the accountant, has started a step-by-step stress
management plan and is pleased with the progress he has
made. He assumes other people will be pleased too, but finds
that just the opposite is true. Jack's friend and drinking buddy,
Kevin, tries to get Jack to "loosen up and party." He says the
new, improved Jack is boring and less fun than he used to
be. Jack sometimes believes Kevin's assessment, and it takes
all his strength to *not* get plastered with Kevin on a Saturday
night or keep his therapy appointments instead of "playing"
with his friends.

Jack's business colleagues also notice the change in Jack.
They too are put off by his new mellow approach because
they still run around like chickens with their heads cut off
and feel their blood pressure rise each time a work-related
problem presents itself. Although Jack expects his cohorts
to admire and respect his self-improvement and perhaps ask
how they too can reduce stress, he instead hears put-downs
and comments about how he is "losing his competitive edge
and killer instinct."

"Other people's reactions are a whole new source of
stress for me," Jack says. "I'm sticking to my programme, but
it would be a whole lot easier if people didn't give me such
a hard time about it."

The amount of cooperation you ask for and receive influences the level of success you achieve and your desire to
continue moving forward. Cooperative people say, "Go for
it. You can do it. We're behind you all the way." Hearing
these enouraging words, you want more than ever to forge
ahead and reach your destination. When you lack cooperation, however, you hear, "Give it up. It isn't worth it. Why
can't you leave well enough alone? Your ridiculous notions
are ruining our lives." Understandably, your desire wanes

and your determination wavers. You are quite likely to give in, give up, and get stuck.

COOPERATION helps you contend with new or unexpected obstacles and problems. A LACK OF COOPERATION often prompts you to turn back at the first sign of resistance.

Change can create unanticipated problems or present unexpected obstacles. Any goal you pursue, bad habit you alter, or self-improvement effort you undertake touches the lives of the people around you. Accepting the job you *really* want means you will have to relocate, travel extensively, or work longer hours. Now your family faces the prospect of uprooting their lives to relocate with you, or your lover must adjust to seeing you less often.

Similarly, a return to the work force alters relationships with your spouse and your children. Newfound assertiveness confounds your friends and co-workers. Giving up drugs or drinking alters your social relationships. Getting involved in a love relationship threatens friends who see you spending more time with your lover and less time with them.

In these examples you can see change's domino effect. Altering and improving *your* life starts a chain reaction. Your success or a step toward it will subtly or dramatically change your relationships with the people around you. They must adjust, and you, in turn, must adapt to their adjustment.

When you approach change cooperatively, other people have a better idea of what to expect from the change effort and are more willing to work together to resolve the resulting problems or obstacles. On the other hand, a lack of cooperation turns obstacles into barriers and problems into crises. Working through the conflicts can become so painful and complicated that you abandon your effort.

COOPERATION is the difference between being supported or being sabotaged.

Sometimes people who are stuck themselves feel threatened by your self-improvement efforts. Your time-management plan may work brilliantly for you. Unfortunately, your co-workers feel your efficiency makes them look bad, and they decide to give you the silent treatment.

Your diet may be a terrific success. Compliments on your appearance abound. As a result, your spouse cannot help but notice your renewed desirability to other men. This consciously or unconsciously frightens him, and the next thing you know, he brings home devil's food cakes and ice cream. He finds ingenious reasons to celebrate by taking you to fancy restaurants that serve rich, tempting foods. He decides to learn to cook and appoints you his chief taste-tester. A day does not pass without his asking when the diet will end or mentioning how much he misses having "love handles" to grab.

Or perhaps, for the first time in years, your life seems to be going the way you want it to. You work part-time, take courses at the local community college, and date or socialize with friends on Saturday nights. Unexpectedly, however, your son begins to suffer headaches of unknown origin, your daughter misbehaves at school, both children's grades drop, and they complain every time you leave the house. They enlist grandma as an ally and she heaps on the guilt. Feeling bad, you limit nights out to once a month. Then you drop your night courses. Finally you quit your job. Without knowing how you got there, you find yourself back at square one.

When you lack cooperation, your best-laid plans get you nowhere. Instead, your best efforts run you smack into a brick wall of resistance from the people who matter to you. They want to reinstitute the old you—the person they were used to and comfortable with, the person they could relate to without having to change themselves in any way. In this way they are subtly or obviously sabotaging your change efforts.

### But It's Their Fault, Not Mine. The People in My Life Are Not About to Cooperate!

Barrier number six comes with a ready-made reason *not* to change. When you take a quick inventory of your friends, family, lovers, and co-workers, you easily see that most of them are completely uncooperative. You believe that because they have their own problems or they are set in their ways or they never really understood you, you cannot force them to cooperate.

Each year, Christmas Day is a disaster. Your mother criticizes your cooking. She argues with your mother-in-law, who thinks you should have used *her* recipes. Children, screaming like wild banshees, race through your home knocking over furniture and breaking things. The meal is wolfed down between TV Christmas specials and films. Even so, there is enough time to start a vicious political discussion or bitterly rehash a wrong done by one family member to another. Someone leaves the table in tears, someone spills red wine on your antique oriental carpet, and as soon as you finish washing dishes and wrapping leftovers, someone walks into the kitchen and asks to take home some turkey, stuffing, and plum pudding. Each year, the best you can say about Christmas is that it is over. You dearly wish you could do things differently, but sadly sigh, "It will never happen. *They*'ll never go for it."

Although you want more from your marriage and you and your husband have reached an impasse, you reject counselling as an alternative. "He would never agree to it," you claim.

You do not present your plan to improve job satisfaction because your boss "is not open to employee suggestions" and your co-workers "would never get behind the idea."

You want to go into business for yourself and know you can succeed. All you need is five thousand pounds in start-up funds, but you do not ask your father for it because "he doesn't lend money to his children, never has and never will."

You want to start a support group for working mothers, but you can't seem to get it off the ground. You decide the women you want to join your group "are all too busy for something like this. They'd never get it together."

I could go on endlessly about the dreams and goals that fall by the wayside because you assume you cannot get the cooperation you need from the people you know and/or love. You honestly believe they will *never* agree to cooperate. Of course, *you* do not actually ask for their cooperation. Instead, you blame a lack of cooperation on the people whose cooperation you need, assume you will not get what you want, and give up without trying to change. Consequently, *you* give barrier number six the power to get you and keep you stuck.

Now, before you discount what I'm saying because I don't know your friends, family, or co-workers, let me reassure you that their lack of cooperation is not entirely *your* fault either. But the real reason barrier number six impedes your progress is because you DO NOT KNOW HOW to get the cooperation you need. Few of us have mastered the art of cooperation.

## WHY YOU DO NOT KNOW HOW TO COOPERATE: MYTHS ABOUT SUCCESS AND SELF-RELIANCE

### MYTH NUMBER ONE—I don't need anybody.

"I used to think there were two kinds of people in the world," Cindy explains. "Givers and takers. I was a giver.

Givers are strong, independent, and reliable. We're like cactus plants—we survive without much care or attention. Givers never take," she says, relating the details of the belief system that contributed to her downfall and brought on her anxiety attacks. "We never ask for anything. We think we don't need much, and to tell you the truth, we'd rather suffer in silence than let other people think for a second that we are weak or needy. No matter what the problem is, we think we should be able to handle it ourselves."

You may not divide people into two mutually exclusive categories the way Cindy does, but I suspect you agree with the basic point she makes—that to ask for help is to admit weakness, failure, or inadequacy.

It is almost universally accepted that a "good" and strong person succeeds and gets unstuck on his own. This philosophy works better in principle than in practice, however. While working as a public relations director, Cindy was in pain. She doubted her ability and was confused about her identity and where she belonged. No one knew about her feelings, however, because she kept them well-hidden, giving the impression that she needed no one's help, support, or cooperation. In fact, she resented even minor suggestions. To Cindy, input was the same as criticism.

"Whenever anyone was sensitive enough to ask if something was wrong, I denied it," Cindy recalls. "I cut them off, changed the subject, or told them to mind their own business. I really thought I had to get my act together all alone." Of course, Cindy did not get better by herself. In fact, she got worse.

When you cling to the myth that only the weak and inadequate ask for help, you make the mistake of deciding to go it alone. You do not actually go anywhere, however. You are stuck without emotional support—other people's knowledge, optimism, and life experience. You reject people who could help you and sincerely want to cooperate, all because you believe you do not need anybody.

**MYTH NUMBER TWO—If you want something done right, do it yourself.**

This popular misconception is wreaking havoc on Marilyn's household. Like Cindy, Marilyn wants to manage without assistance. In addition to thinking she does not need anybody, she believes no one's help can meet her standards. The few times she has delegated responsibility, she has been dissatisfied with the result. More aggravated and overwhelmed than ever, she redid the job and decided not to bother asking for help again.

How many of you have fallen into the same trap? You could delegate tasks to the workers you supervise. You could ask your husband to do laundry, grocery shop, or prepare meals. Your kids could vacuum, dust, or make their own lunches. Each relative coming to your house for Christmas dinner could bring part of the meal. You do not have to handle all the details for your father's sixtieth birthday party. You could ask your siblings to help or hire professionals.

You do not do any of these things or seek cooperation in countless other ways because you believe you will not get *exactly* what you want unless you get it yourself. By believing myth number two, you are unwilling to compromise or give up the smallest bit of control. Determined to do it all, do it right, and do it yourself, you become more overwhelmed and experience more stress, and of course, such a state is not conducive for starting or sticking to a self-improvement plan.

**MYTH NUMBER THREE—I shouldn't have to ask.**

Marilyn believes that if her children really cared about her, they would know she is overworked and would volunteer to help with the housework. She believes that she should not have to ask for their help.

Likewise, on more than one occasion, Cindy thinks her friends and family should sense her life is not all she makes it out to be. Even if she denies her feelings, she believes they should keep trying to get to the root of her problem. She believes that she should not have to ask.

You think you should not have to tell your lover you want more intimacy and communication. He thinks he should not have to tell you he needs space after a hard day at work. You think your boss should know you want positive feedback on a job well done. You believe your mother should be sensitive to your weight-loss efforts and know not to tempt you with fattening food. Your relatives should realize Christmas dinner at your house every year is a tremendous burden. You think that someone should volunteer to have the family come to their house for a change. But you also believe that you shouldn't have to ask for any of those things.

So many of us honestly believe the people we love, respect, and work beside week in and week out *should* know what we need and *should* cooperate without being asked. Whether they should or should not is irrelevant—usually, they do not. And expecting to get cooperation without asking for it almost guarantees disappointment.

As a rule, human beings are lousy mind readers. Other people simply won't understand how you feel or what they can do to help you feel better—*unless you tell them.* They cannot give you what you need—*unless you request it.* Even if they try to be cooperative and supportive, they will continue to miss the mark—*unless you clearly communicate your desires.*

Of course, asking for cooperation does not guarantee that you will get the exact amount and kind of cooperation you *want.* However, *not* asking assures you of getting less cooperation than you *need* and, in most instances, no cooperation at all.

**MYTH NUMBER FOUR—Success is achieved through COMPETITION.**

To COOPERATE is to act or work together.

To COMPETE is to be in a rivalry, participate in a contest, or vie for a prize.

When you COOPERATE you join forces and combine strengths to achieve a common or mutually beneficial end. Everybody gains something. When you COMPETE, on the other hand, you win only when your opponent loses. You both want the same thing, but only one of you can have it. When you compete, getting what you want depends upon your ability to beat, overpower, outwit, or eliminate the other guy. The last thing you want to do is cooperate with him.

From preschool playground games to insider trading on the stock market, from outperforming the next kid on the geography quiz to outselling the next guy in order to win a trip to Hawaii, from making the best birthday card for your mother to getting your toddler into the "best" nursery school, the belief that success comes through competition is deeply ingrained in our culture and characters.

Throughout your life you hone your competitive abilities and reinforce the belief that being your best means proving that you are better than someone else. Unfortunately, this killer instinct and your competitive edge are not very helpful when you need cooperation. The deep-seated desire to win, win, win, stifles your ability to cooperate. Indeed, it keeps you from seeing cooperation as a viable alternative for reaching your goal.

But you must remember that you do not get emotional support or practical assistance by competing against the person whose help you need. Someone you try to outwit, outdo, beat, or eliminate is not about to work with you to achieve a mutually beneficial goal or willingly adapt to life with the new you. Competition is not conducive to personal growth and self-improvement—cooperation is.

To get the cooperation you need, you must compete less and cooperate more. You must counteract your own misconceptions about self-reliance, competition, and going it alone. Then you can learn new skills and approaches that promote cooperation and help you work *with* other people to attain the kind of life you desire and deserve.

## DISMANTLING BARRIER #6:
## GETTING MORE COOPERATION

Just as you learned to compete, you can learn to cooperate. The following suggestions and strategies help you get *more* cooperation than you get now or have received in the past. But *please*, do not think for an instant that you will get *all* the cooperation you want each and every time you seek it.

We live in an imperfect world populated by individuals who do not always speak or act precisely as we wish they would. That will not change. People who know little or less than you do about cooperation will be uncooperative at times. Well-intentioned friends and relatives will do the best they can and still fail to fully meet your expectations. And people accustomed to hearing you say that you don't need anybody, or people whose help you previously rejected, may hold back when you attempt to gain their cooperation now. But that is reality, and if you learn to work within its limits, you will get the cooperation you need to improve your life.

So, please remember, you must dismantle barrier number six in order to get *more* cooperation, but that cooperation does not necessarily have to be *perfect* and *complete* in order to work for you.

### Eight Ways to Get More Cooperation

Let's assume that one reason you lack cooperation today is because, in the past, you did not cooperate often or easily. You may be the product of a family that valued achievement and competition. Perhaps your educational experiences included rewards for getting the highest marks in the class or winning athletic competitions. Or you may be a perfectionist or a control artist who does not trust other people to do things the way you want them done, or you may be a loner who prefers to keep some distance between yourself and other people. Whatever the reason, your past behaviour did not foster cooperation.

Consequently, the people around you may be surprised by your present attempt to cooperate. Questioning your "real" motives or thinking that you are going through some kind of "phase," they may disregard your overtures and continue their old uncooperative ways. As a result, both you and the people who matter to you have to get used to the idea of cooperation before you embark upon cooperative change efforts. The first three ways to foster cooperation, listed below, lay the groundwork and set the stage for working together harmoniously.

### 1. Be open to suggestions and support when they are offered.

You must immediately begin to overcome success myth #1, I don't need anybody, and success myth #2, If I want something done right, I have to do it myself. Try not to be so hell-bent on getting unstuck *your* way that you reject or alienate people who sincerely want to cooperate. Do not bite the hand that brings you alternatives, advice, encouragement, or assistance—even if the unsolicited support is not exactly what you want at that moment.

In addition, listen for ideas that have not occurred to you and ignore the devilish voices that tell you accepting help is the same as admitting weakness. These are the people in your life who want to cooperate. Let them help you.

Maybe they are making their approach at the wrong time. Maybe the suggestion they are giving isn't really the right one for you. Perhaps you are getting advice when you want sympathy, or friends want to talk when you want something more tangible. Poor timing or an offer that misses the mark is no reason to callously dismiss someone who wants to be your ally and your friend.

You must lay the groundwork for cooperation by remaining open to emotional support, practical assistance, and advice when it is given voluntarily. If you cannot take the advice or follow their lead at the present time, let them know you appreciate them for caring. They may surprise you by adapting to your real needs now, and they certainly will be more likely to cooperate in the future.

### 2. Give cooperation.

This approach is so logical that it ought to occur to each and every one of us. In biblical terms, you reap what you sow. You get cooperation from the people with whom you cooperate.

Start looking for opportunities to help other people. Find the time to listen to their concerns. Carol did. From experience, her children knew that their mother was available to them—to hear their problems, answer their questions, and help them to make decisions. She gave her support without expecting to be paid back someday. She gave them concern and cooperation for its own sake. As a result, when, out of necessity, she asked for concern and cooperation from her children, they were willing to give it.

There are countless small ways you can cooperate. You can help with the housework even though it is not traditionally your primary responsibility. You can allow a co-worker to run ideas past you, watch your neighbour's children, offer a ride when a friend's car is being repaired, bring dessert or wine or the turkey to Christmas dinner, accompany someone to an Alcoholics Anonymous meeting, or listen to the speech your husband has to give the next day.

Don't keep a tally sheet or fill a green stamp book full of favours. I know I am not the only one who cooperates reluctantly with people who remind me of everything they did for me in the past. Cooperate for cooperation's sake, to model and experience the joys and benefits of working together. Once partnership and harmonious relationships become familiar and comfortable for all involved, cooperation becomes easier to obtain. You will pave the way for future cooperation by being cooperative today.

### 3. Decrease negative criticism and increase validation.

You undermine cooperation with negative criticism and all the nagging, harping, and nit-picking you do in the name of building character and improving performance.

Negative criticism erodes self-esteem. Someone who feels unloved, unworthy, or inadequate whenever he is around you is not going to stick around to cooperate with you. In addition, someone regularly subjected to your negative criticism may come to believe that your efforts to better yourself are, in fact, thinly disguised attempts to make him look worse. This may lead to sabotage instead of cooperation, and your put-downs and "constructive" feedback will only set an example of noncooperation. If you habitually criticize and complain about the help you *are* given, you will convince others nothing they can do will satisfy you. Why should they even try to cooperate?

Cooperation increases when your criticism decreases. If negative criticism worked, you would not spend so much of your time nagging, complaining, and repeating yourself. The next time you feel the urge to criticize—STOP. Instead, ask yourself: Will what I am about to say *really* help the other person? Will it *really* get me more of what I want? Is the damage it might do to my relationship in the long run worth the short-term benefit of being right or feeling superior to the person I am about to criticize?

If the answer to even one of these questions is no, bite your tongue and keep the peace. Try a little validation instead.

Validation is the opposite of negative criticism. When you validate someone, you tell him what you admire, appreciate, respect, love, celebrate, applaud, and enjoy about him as a unique and worthwhile human being. Look for opportunities to show that you value the people in your life and stay away from those validations that can be construed as backhanded compliments or poorly hidden criticisms, such as "It makes me so happy when you put your socks in the hamper" or "What a thrill to see you here on time." Start small if you must, but give the people you value at least three validations a day, preferably more.

You will be amazed to see how far a true validation goes to create bonds between people and foster cooperation. Think how much *you* would like to hear someone say, "I love seeing your smiling face in the morning" or "I appreciate how thoughtful you are. You always remember to ask how I'm feeling" or "I know how much work you put into that proposal. I really do admire your creativity and stick-to-itiveness."

A validated person is less likely to resist your efforts to change. Unlike the overly criticized person, someone who is validated has healthy self-esteem and is less threatened by your change effort. If you knew someone truly valued you, wouldn't you want to support and cooperate with him?

Accepting suggestions and support when offered, giving your cooperation willingly, reducing negative criticism and increasing validation, all set the stage for cooperation for your change efforts. Cooperation itself becomes an integral part of your life and the lives of those around you. Consequently, asking for help, support, encouragement, or adjustment to the new you fits you and your lifestyle, and because it does, it is much easier to come by.

### 4. Account for change's domino effect.

Consider in advance how your change effort will affect the people around you. If you can anticipate resistance or sabotage, you may be able to prevent it.

On a sheet of paper, make a list of people who play a significant role in your life. They can be family, friends, lovers, colleagues, or anyone else. For the most part they should be people you come in contact with at least once a month.

Which of these people will have to change in some way as a result of your change effort? Put a capital *C* beside their names.

Which of these people seem to be stuck themselves and

may feel threatened by your attempt to get unstuck? Put a capital *T* beside their names.

Who might try to sabotage you? Put a capital *S* beside their names.

Who are the adaptable people on your list? Even though your change effort may present them with an unexpected need to change, who will nonetheless try to cooperate? Put a double asterisk (**) beside their names.

This inventory of people in your life helps you in several ways. "C" people need to know from the outset what you plan to do and what impact it may have on them. Then you can work together to iron out the details. "T" people can also be informed of your intentions. But keep in mind that, for the most part, these are people whom you cannot expect to give you encouragement or praise and you must learn to accept that. People marked with a double asterisk (**), however, are your front line for cooperation. They have demonstrated their willingness to cooperate with and support you and should be the first people you consider when you want to ask for cooperation.

On the other hand, "S" people pose a tangible threat to your self-improvement effort, and their reaction or behaviour has the potential to halt your progress or send you back to square one. As you did when you were "creative worrying" at the end of Chapter Seven, think about potential problems or possible sabotage and come up with contingency plans.

For example, after Lisa quit her second sales job, she was hired by another firm as a sales manager. She knew she was brought in to reorganize a department. The people she would supervise knew changes were coming, and one person—who wanted the job Lisa got—was particularly unhappy and vocal about it. But Lisa anticipated resistance and resentment and expected to be sabotaged. After consulting people who had been in similar situations, she decided that her best bet was to make change a group effort. So, she brought her group together, outlined the goals she was given by her superiors, asked for input, and formed committees, making sure to have the disgruntled employee head one of those committees.

By getting everyone actively involved in the effort, Lisa gave them a feeling of ownership. As she realized, people are less likely to undermine something they "own." What Lisa did to prevent sabotage is only one kind of contingency plan and it may not be the one you choose. However, you must try in some way to anticipate how change will affect the people in your life and plan to overcome problematic reactions.

### 5. Know what you want from whom.

In order to dismantle other barriers you have on several occasions reviewed the strategies found in Chapter Two (Why Change?). By now you have identified one or several benefits from your lifeline net you want to get or areas of conflict and confusion you would like to resolve. Now, from these possible change efforts, choose one you *really* want to pursue.

To improve the odds that you will get enough cooperation to succeed, before you begin a change effort, think about the cooperation you *wish* you could have. Luckily, what you wish is generally more than you absolutely need and almost always more than you will get, but it is nonetheless a good place to start identifying *kinds* of cooperation your change effort will require.

KINDS OF COOPERATION include:

Emotional Support (in the many forms described beginning on page 68 of Chapter Three)

Change Partners (people who will undertake the same self-improvement effort along with you)

Practical Assistance (help with tasks that are overwhelming or frustrating you)

Instruction (formal or informal)

Advice or Alternatives

Self-help/Support Groups

Professional Services
Adaptation to the New You
Encouragement/Gentle Pushes
Honouring Specific Time-Limited Requests (such as
keeping quiet while you study for an exam or loaning
you fifty dollars until payday)

Thinking about the change effort you intend to pursue, list every imaginable kind of cooperation you *wish* you could have. Be as specific as you can. For instance, if you are a wife and mother of three children who wants to return to college for paralegal training in hopes of returning to the work force, you may want, among other things—

—your husband to encourage you and let you use a portion of your savings to pay tuition;
—your children to give up part of their playroom for you to set up a desk;
—your neighbour's to keep an eye on your children on afternoons you must attend classes;
—your family to cook dinner and clean up afterward several evenings a week;
—to be left alone to study whenever you ask.

For whatever change you hope to make, try to anticipate the kinds of cooperation you will want and make an extensive cooperation *wish list.*

As you may recall from Chapter Three (Self-esteem), you will rarely get all the support or cooperation you need from a single person. Some people in your life can give emotional support but are unreliable when it comes to helping with child care or transportation. Others will drive, cook, watch your kids, or loan you money, as long as they do not have to hear you say you are hurting. Still others are great cheerleaders or great brainstormers.

After reviewing the emotional-support-people strategy found in Chapter Three, identify a minimum of three people you know or could find to cooperate in each of the ways written on your wish list. Each person can be listed beside more than one kind of cooperation.

Give each of your three potential cooperators an A, B, or C rating. An A person is the most likely to cooperate and the person whose assistance you will request first. Bs and Cs are backup people or those who could do part of what you ask, if not all.

You may have difficulty completing this task. You may rack your brain but be able to think of no one who can cooperate in just the way you want. This is a clue that your standards and/or expectations are too high. Remember, you cannot expect all your desires of cooperation to be fulfilled. Now is as good a time as any to start seeing things more realistically.

### 6. Be realistic.

Karen really wants to develop healthy eating and exercise habits so she can lose thirty pounds and maintain her weight loss. Previously, in all her other attempts to achieve her goal, she never considered cooperation. At most she got help from a medically supervised weight-loss programme, relying on one weight-loss counsellor to meet all her needs. This time, however, she is making a cooperation wish list and immediately notices she cannot get all she wants in several areas. Particularly unrealistic is her wish that someone commit to walk with her for one hour every day, and her wish that no one tempt her with sweets or fattening foods. To get what she needs, however, she has to alter her idea of what she wants. She has to be more realistic.

DIVIDE AND CONQUER: To make expectations more realistic, consider getting *all* of what you want by combining the contributions of several people. It is easier to get a little cooperation from a number of different people than to get a great deal of cooperation from one person.

With this in mind, Karen, who wants to walk every day

*and* wants a walking partner, lines up several friends to walk with her on different days. Having the more flexible schedule, Karen walks at the time each friend wants to and goes to the location of *their* choice. Through compromise, therefore, Karen gets all of what she wants—although not in the exact way she originally expected to get it.

Are there ways *you* can divide and conquer? Could you rotate responsibility for distasteful chores the way Carol does? Could you get emotional support by discussing some concerns with friends, some with your spouse, and some with the members of a support group? If you reach an impasse when seeking cooperation, consider asking more people to do less rather than expecting a few people to do more than makes them comfortable.

COME DOWN FROM THE CLOUDS: Karen wishes no one would ever tempt her with sweets or fattening foods, which is obviously an unrealistic expectation. In order for that to work, she would have to inform everyone in her life (family, friends, and co-workers) of her goal and her wish for cooperation and that everyone would keep her diet in mind when serving food. Not even dividing to conquer could get Karen all of what she wants. She has to come down from the clouds and look at her need for cooperation realistically.

In order to look at cooperation realistically, you first need to be more specific about your needs. Break the cooperation you want into smaller pieces. When you say you want more help with housework, specify the help you need—someone to cook dinner twice a week, someone to do the laundry, someone to wash dinner dishes, someone to vacuum three times a week, someone to clean the bathrooms, someone to take out the rubbish each morning, and so on. If you want Christmas dinner to be more harmonious, specify what you want from your family—each person to bring a covered dish, to go to a different home each year, direct supervision of the children, a cleanup crew, and requests for leftovers made before leaving the table. List your exact wishes as clearly as you can.

On another sheet of paper, write numbers down the left side of the page, beginning with number one and continuing until you get to the number of items on your list of exact wishes. Then rank each item. Write the cooperative act you *need* the most to succeed beside number one, the next most *needed* item next to the number two, and so forth.

Next, review your list. At what point would you actually have what you need to change successfully? If items one, two, and three would be enough, draw a line across the page under item number three. If the top five are essential, draw a line under item number five. Anything *above* your line represents cooperation you *really* need and should be the cooperation you request from the people you previously identified as likely to give it.

### 7. Ask for what you need.

Sadly, most of you have a horrible time asking for what you need. The thought of revealing that you need anything, let alone asking for help, is terrifying. I recommend you use what you learned about conquering fear (Chapter Seven) to reduce your anxiety level about asking for cooperation.

*How* to ask for what you need is an assertiveness skill. If asking for cooperation is very new to you, in addition to using the approach described below, I suggest you consult one of the many books about assertiveness that are available in most libraries or bookstores.

When you ask for cooperation, also help people understand *why* you need their cooperation. Tell them what you want to accomplish and how much achieving your goal means to you, as well as explaining what you actually need from them. You can clarify this for yourself by finishing the following sentence stems:

I want to . . .
It is important to me because . . .
I need you to . . .

Be specific and honest. And use what you have written as the basic for what you will say when you make your actual request. It also may help you to *rehearse,* especially if you fear you will get a negative response. Have someone you trust play the part of the person whose cooperation you seek. Make your request and have the actor respond in several different ways so you can work out contingency plans.

Remember, other people will not know what you need unless you tell them. Even if what you want is something you *think* you should be getting already—if you are not getting it, you have to ask. Remember, too, that asking *does not* guarantee your request will be granted. If you get a negative response on your first attempt, you need not allow the situation to be a total loss.

### 8. Be willing to negotiate.

Always, always, always approach cooperation with an open mind. Accept that other people will not meet your every need simply because you want them to. Do not *demand* cooperation or you will not get it. Instead, present your needs and discuss various alternatives until you arrive at a mutually agreeable solution. The process will not be painless, and it may be time consuming, but in the end you will have something you did not have before and might never have had if your concept of cooperation remained non-negotiable. So, be willing to negotiate, to compromise, to trade favours, make concenssions, and receive any *some* of what you need. That's still better than getting nothing.

One way to approach negotiation is to sit down with another person or other people and exchange descriptions of what each person sees as the optimal outcome to a particular situation. Each person asking or being asked for cooperation should complete the following sentence stems:

In my opinion the best possible outcome would occur if
I would . . .

You would ...
We would ...

Each response defines the distance between individual positions and reveals points of compromise or potential to trade favours. For instance, a husband and wife, having reached an impasse in their marriage, complete the sentence stems in the following manner.

In the wife's opinion, the best possible outcome would occur if she asks her husband to get counselling, if he hears what she has to say and agrees, and if they go to a counsellor together. In the husband's opinion, the best possible outcome would occur if he does not have to involve strangers (i.e., a counsellor) in his private affairs, if his wife would spend weekends at home with him instead of working or socializing, and if they could work through their problems by talking honestly with each other.

After some negotiation the wife agrees to reserve one weekend a month exclusively for her husband. They also both agree to spend one hour twice a week discussing their problems and feelings the way they would if they were seeing a counsellor. And the husband agrees to go into therapy with his wife six months from now if the situation has not improved. By negotiating, both get part of what they want and build a foundation for future cooperation.

### Can Someone Who Gets Little or No Cooperation Really Improve the Situation?

Marilyn did. Using the same ideas you read about in this chapter, Marilyn got the cooperation she needed to get unstuck. She sought out other single working mothers and solicited their advice and suggestions. She also made a list of household chores she wanted her children to perform and held her first family meeting. Each child accepted two permanent chores and the rest were rotated weekly, with Marilyn included on the schedule. When her children complained that she was never satisfied with their work, Marilyn agreed to show them how she wanted things done. If they still did not perform to her standards, however, she would not criticize. Instead, she would bring it up for discussion at the next family meeting and promised to seriously consider being less of a perfectionist.

At first, Marilyn did not know quite what to do about constantly having to drive her children to afterschool activities or attend all of their school or extracurricular functions. Then her oldest daughter suggested asking Marilyn's father to help. It turned out that grandpa, recently retired and restless, was thrilled to oblige.

"We haven't worked all the bugs out of the system yet," Marilyn reports. "There are still things I need help with and things the kids want that I cannot give them. But life in our house is one hundred percent better than it used to be— and six months ago you could never have convinced me it was possible."

As Marilyn learned, you can't always get exactly what you want. But if you try, you may be able to get what you need. The truth of that premise was demonstrated throughout this chapter. It applies to cooperation *and* every other facet of any effort to change. Unfortunately, when we cannot get what we want, many of us give up without trying to get what we need. We see change as an all or nothing proposition. Why? Because we are plagued by the curse of perfectionism—barrier number seven and the subject of the next chapter.

# 9

███████████████████████████████████

# *Change and Perfection*

Dave, a thirty-two-year-old architect, and his wife, Alison, a thirty-year-old graphic artist, are a two-career couple planning a family and looking for their dream house. Both work in the city and want to live within a reasonable commuting distance in a community that is attractive, has a small-town feel to it, and offers superior schools for the children they hope to have. Property is quite expensive in communities meeting this description, however, and saving money to buy their first house took longer than they had originally expected.

The years of scrimping, saving, and tripping over each other in their one-bedroom apartment gave Dave and Alison plenty of time to visualize every detail of the house they would one day own. Now they have finally begun house hunting in earnest and have a long list of requirements for their perfect home. They are determined to find a house that matches their description exactly.

After explaining to the estate agent where they want to live and how much they want to spend, Dave and Alison present their list of non-negotiable criteria. Unfortunately, the estate agent looks at the list and shakes her head. She does not think she can find a house they can afford that has *all* of these features, and she asks if there is anything on the list they would be willing to do without. But Dave and Alison insist that the list describes the home they *really* want. They ask the estate agent to find *that* home–no matter how long it takes.

The estate agent does the best she can, and over the next few months she shows Dave and Alison dozens of wonderful homes but none is *exactly* what they envisioned. Finally they grow impatient and try a different estate agent, who reacts in much the same way as the first. He too cannot seem to locate the house of their dreams. Dave and Alison are upset and disappointed. Still, they will not settle for less than their original vision.

By the time they move on to their third estate agent, Alison is pregnant and the prospect of bringing a baby home to their already cramped quarters is very unappealing. The third estate agent knows this, and unlike her predecessors, she convinces Dave and Alison at least to consider a compromise. She hands them a pad of lined paper and asks them, just for the sake of argument, to list their bottom-line requirements for a home: those features that make a home safe, comfortable, and functional.

Dave and Alison struggle with the task but eventually draw up a list describing a simple four-bedroom home with those features that are actually essential for a young couple starting a family. The estate agent looks over the list and smiles. She can think of half a dozen houses that meet their basic needs *and* include over half of the extras found on their first list. In addition, many of the special features these homes now lack can be added at a later date.

It is only after making that list that Dave and Alison discuss the matter and decide that, in fact, they can live with the compromise. Ironically, they end up buying a home quite similar to one the first agent showed them and are able to move into it long before the baby is born. They do add a few extras, but forgo others. The funny thing is that they can't imagine why they ever thought they could not live without them.

Based on what you have read in earlier chapters of this book, I bet you think I am going to tell you Dave and Alison are still stuck because they settled for less than they *really* wanted. But if you guessed that, you would be wrong.

Dave and Alison were stuck when they would not compromise on *any* aspect of their perfect house, holding firm to their stubborn decision that they would buy the exact home they wanted or no home at all. If the third estate agent had not pushed them to be more realistic, they still would be living in a one-bedroom apartment and desperately looking for their dream house, no better off than they were before they started house hunting.

---

### BARRIER #7: THE CURSE OF PERFECTIONISM

Dave and Alison were plagued by the curse of perfectionism. The curse of perfectionism sets up all-or-nothing propositions. Either you achieve your ultimate goal or you do nothing. Of course, this would not be a problem if your goal was attainable and realistic. However, when cursed by perfectionism, you set goals that are inordinately high and standards that are impossible to meet, expecting more of yourself than is humanly possible or insisting that everything else in your life must be in perfect order before you change. While under this curse, you will not even consider smaller steps toward a larger goal, and you reject opportunities to be better off than you are. You want it all or you want nothing—and nothing is what you get.

You may be confused by this idea. After all, I was the one who told you to go after the best life has to offer. I still think you should. When I speak of the best life has to offer, however, I am referring to your personal best, something that is—in a specific way—exceptional and very, very good, yet not necessarily perfect in all respects all of the time. True perfection is rarely, if ever, attainable. The chances of achieving it are so slim that the pursuit of perfection is a waste of your time and energy, particularly if you postpone the pursuit of goodness or excellence while you wait around for the perfect answer, the perfect change effort, or the perfect moment to begin that change effort.

## THE PERFECT ANSWER

Once Harry made up his mind to exercise regularly, he was determined to find the perfect exercise programme. Thinking the most hassle-free exercise programme will be the one he sticks with, Harry did some creative worrying and listed criteria for a programme that presents no obstacles at all.

He wants to exercise indoors, so that he does not have to battle the weather, and he wants to exercise with other people so he can make new friends and meet women. In addition, the facility must be near his home because he does not want to waste time driving, and the programme must not be too expensive or require that he buy costly equipment or sportswear. It must also be noncompetitive, take no more than forty-five minutes to complete, and be something he can do when he is on the road peddling his photographs. Instructors—if he needs them at all—cannot be pushy or hypercritical.

As you can see, Harry gave his exercise programme a good deal of thought and covered all contingencies. His list is long and detailed and describes what he *really* wants. Unfortunately, his requirements are so stringent and inflexible that no exercise programme can live up to them. He has searched high and low for the perfect programme, but there is always something missing, some criterion unmet. His quest has continued for several months—during which time he has not exercised at all.

Julie has not always been alone and lonely. At one time she was in a terrific relationship with a kind, attentive man who was deeply in love with her. Brian was a few years younger, attractive, intelligent, sensitive, and quite ambitious. At the age of twenty-four he was the general manager of a very successful restaurant. He earned a handsome salary, much of which he was saving to open his own restaurant and nightclub before he turned thirty.

At first Julie was in seventh heaven. Brian was wonderful. He made her laugh, listened to her concerns, and accepted her for who she was. He spent all of his precious free time with her and even rearranged his work schedule and made as many adjustments as humanly possible to be with her as often as he could. Not one to try to impress Julie with lavish gifts, extravagant dates, or expensive getaway weekends, he still went out of his way to make their time together adventurous and romantic. He got along with her friends and was not intimidated by her mother or her wealth. He was even good in bed. Indeed, Brian was as close to Julie's ideal as any man she had ever known.

But he was not perfect. Julie cared for Brian and enjoyed his company, but she could not help thinking that there might be someone better out there somewhere, someone with a little bit more of Brian's good qualities who also had a less demanding job or more money and the desire to spend it to pamper her. The more Julie thought about how nice the perfect man would be, the more she began to dwell on Brian's imperfections.

The fact that Brian worked Friday and Saturday nights began to seem like a bigger and bigger problem. She wondered what good it did her to have a boyfriend if she still had to amuse herself on the weekends. He was consumed by his ambition, she thought, forgetting how she had complained about her previous boyfriends' lack of ambition. And she was unhappy that he rarely had the energy to go dancing or stay until the end of a party.

Eventually Brian's flaws, although few in number and minor in comparison to his positive attributes, were all Julie could see. She nagged and criticized him incessantly. And when Brian called to say business was slow and he could leave work early, Julie had worked herself into such a state that she refused to see him.

"Why should I go running whenever he calls?" she asked.

"Because you want to be with him," her mother suggested.

"That's not the point!" Julie groaned.

The real point is that Julie managed to sabotage her relationship by refusing to compromise on any matter or discuss ways to resolve their problems. In Julie's mind the problem was that Brian was not perfect, and if she could not have all and exactly what she wanted, then she wanted nothing at all. Consequently, she ended the most satisfying love relationship she ever had and returned to complaining about being alone and lonely.

For a moment, think of what you miss when you live by all-or-nothing propositions. While you wait for the perfect job, you stay in a job you hate even though you are offered jobs that are better in countless ways than your present job. But you reject them because they do not meet every one of your exact requirements. Or you look for the perfect college—one near your home and offering *all* the courses you want to take. But not finding that perfect school, you take *no* courses and get no closer to earning your degree. Or you seek the perfect therapist. That therapist must be the right age and gender, come from the same socio-economic background as your own, have a perfect track record for treating problems like yours, and not charge a lot of money. You search, but you can't seem to find him. In the meantime, you receive no therapy and your emotional problems are no closer to being resolved.

You are looking for the perfect answer to your prayers. Being better off than you already are is simply not good enough for you. When you hold out for the unattainable, however, you get no further on life's journeys than you would have if you had set no goals whatsoever. You are still stuck and you stay that way because you stubbornly refuse to take a single step forward unless you can "have it all."

I truly believe you deserve to "have it all"—as long as "all" falls within the boundaries of reality, does not become part of an all-or-nothing proposition, and does not prevent you from getting something here and now. Letting life pass you by while you wait for the one right and perfect solution to all your problems is the essence of the curse of perfectionism.

## THE PERFECT CHANGE EFFORT

When Karen diets, she accepts nothing less than perfect adherence to her food plan. Unfortunately, she makes this extremely difficult for herself by choosing an extremely restrictive diet of one thousand calories or less per day. She sees the slightest deviation as a complete dieting failure, and her disappointment with herself leads to brutal self-criticism that in turn leads to frustration and despair. She sighs and asks herself why she bothers to diet at all since it seems that she can never do it right. The trouble is that for Karen "right" means perfectly.

Thus, if Karen eats so much as one cream cracker she had not planned to eat, she declares the entire day of dieting a failure. She does not consider that the few extra calories will have no meaningful effect on her weight loss if she otherwise adheres to her diet or compensates by eating fewer calories at another meal. No, eating that cracker means her effort is imperfect and imperfection is unacceptable. Her day is ruined and she might as well eat whatever she wants and start over tomorrow. Unfortunately, her one-day binge turns into a two-, three-, or four-day binge, and as a result, she finds it even more difficult to get back on track. When she does, her perfect effort lasts a few days. But invariably she slips up and starts the cycle once more.

In another overzealous attempt to manage stress, Jack follows the advice he finds in a magazine article. He accepts the idea that improving his physical health will automatically improve his mental health, and—all on the same day —he stops smoking cigarettes, gives up drinking, starts a macrobiotic diet, and begins a rigorous exercise programme. Like Karen, Jack embarks upon this drastically altered lifestyle fully expecting to adhere perfectly to his new regimen. He wants to rid himself completely of every unhealthy habit, make all these changes at once, and do so perfectly on his first attempt.

But unfortunately, Jack trips over his own expectations, by trying to do too much too quickly and leaving no room for human error. His life becomes a hell while he simultaneously contends with nicotine cravings, refusing alcohol at social functions, and scheduling time to exercise during his impossibly busy workday. During frequent business lunches in restaurants, he agonizes over what to eat. In addition, he has to learn to shop for and cook macrobiotic meals. Ironically, instead of reducing stress, his change effort and unrealistic demand for perfection place additional pressure on him. Jack does not get what he wants. But instead of stepping back and taking one change at a time, he decides the entire effort is too stressful and abandons it completely. Cursed by perfectionism, he wants all or nothing—and gets nothing.

Cindy's anxiety attacks are barely under control and her recovery is just beginning when she takes a new job. Not quite ready for the stress of a new job, she finds her first day of work leaves her disheartened and panicky. She arrives at her therapist's office and immediately bursts into tears.

"I can't do the job," she claims. "I don't know why I took it in the first place. It looked so easy. I thought I could handle it, but I can't. I've never felt so confused and incompetent. You wouldn't believe all the mistakes I made today—at least a dozen major ones before I stopped counting."

"Only a dozen?" Her therapist chuckles. "Listen to yourself. Did you really expect to learn everything you need to know and do a brand-new job perfectly on your very first day?"

But Cindy believes that if you cannot do something right, you should not do it at all. And like Jack and Karen, Cindy thinks doing something "right" means doing it perfectly, the first and every time. While Karen could not accept a single deviation from a diet programme that was probably too restrictive to begin with, and Jack tried to do too much at one time, Cindy expects to immediately (and flawlessly) master all facets of a new job and instantly adapt to a new situation. After a rough and imperfect first day she is ready to quit. All or nothing, the curse of perfectionism, strikes again.

Perhaps you too apply all-or-nothing standards to change efforts, demanding perfection right away and all the time. In doing so, you invite disappointment, disillusionment, and disaster. When you cannot adhere *perfectly* to a self-improvement programme, break a habit *completely* the first time you try, or adjust *flawlessly* to a new situation or lifestyle, you throw the baby out with the bathwater. Instead of slightly altering your course or modifying your expectations, you abandon the change effort entirely. Consequently you end up back at square one—no better off than you were before. This is the second way the curse of perfectionism gets you stuck.

## THE PERFECT TIME AND THE PERFECT CONDITIONS FOR CHANGE

"As soon as I lose ten more pounds, I'll quit smoking."

"These holiday parties are just too tempting. I'll go on a diet after the new year begins."

"Things will settle down at work soon. Then I'll sign up for those business courses, take that vacation, move to a new flat, etc."

"Let's give this time to work itself out. If the relationship isn't better six months from now, *then* we can see a counsellor."

"I can't leave him now. The kids are too young. When they get a little older, then I'll leave."

"If only I didn't spend so much time on the road. I'll get a promotion to management soon. Then I'll have more time to spend with my kids."

"This project is all I can think about right now. I'll worry about a social life and getting into a love relationship later."

"If I had ... the money
the time
the freedom
a better job
fewer problems at home ... I would change."

"When I ... am more financially stable
get over this cold
know my kids are okay
find a better apartment
turn twenty-five, thirty, forty, etc.
... then I will change."

These are the sounds of procrastination. These are the reasons you do NOT take action *today*. Something always happens *today* that proves change should wait until another day, until you think the time is right and the conditions are perfect. You believe that a perfect time is one that guarantees success. At the perfect moment there will be no temptations, no interruptions, no unanticipated events, nothing to disrupt or undermine your change effort. Unfortunately, there will never be such a perfect moment, but you nonetheless wait for it to arrive. And it is just that waiting for perfect conditions that gets you stuck.

While you postpone and procrastinate, your life does not

get better. Often, it gets worse. The ten pounds you wanted to lose become twenty pounds or thirty. You withstand *more* criticism and abuse from your spouse. With each passing day it becomes more difficult to see how you—an obviously unworthy and unlovable person—can improve your life. Your co-workers become accustomed to your nonassertiveness and take advantage of you at every opportunity, and you put up with it until you can no longer stand it. Then, without trying to improve the situation, you walk out on the job.

Procrastination erodes your motivation to change. If you have hung on for this long, you figure, what is another day or month or year? So, you spin your wheels, digging a hole so deep that the prospect of climbing out of it seems all the more difficult—maybe even impossible. You become paralyzed, impotent, unable to do anything more or better than the dissatisfying status quo—all because you refuse to take a single step forward until the perfect moment arrives and the rest of your life is in perfect order.

The curse of perfectionism turns you into a modern-day Scarlett O'Hara. "I'll worry about this tomorrow," you say. But the perfect tomorrow never comes and you never take action. You do not get out of the starting blocks. You cannot get unstuck.

## THE PERFECT BARRIER

The curse of perfectionism undermines change so brilliantly because this barrier never works alone. It teams up with other barriers to more efficiently get you and keep you stuck.

*This barrier invites the return of barrier number one, believing you do not deserve better.* If you look for the PERFECT, spouse, job, exercise programme, house, social life, or answer, you will not find it. If you expect your change effort to be completely flawless every moment of every day, you will fail to achieve the perfection you want. You fail to get what you think you want, and you decide that a failure is a failure. You believe you failed because you personally were not good enough and therefore do not deserve success. Self-esteem takes a nosedive and stops you cold. The sad thing is that, because of your obsessive attitude toward perfectionism, you were doomed before you even began your effort.

*Barrier number seven is almost always tangled up with barrier number two—not seeing your alternatives.* In the same way you look for perfect moments and perfect conditions for change, you seek perfect alternatives. Excellent alternatives are not good enough and not worth pursuing. You want one right and perfect solution to your problem or one right and perfect path to your destination. You cannot find it because you spend so much time rejecting all the "imperfect" alternatives you do find. The end result is that you do not change.

*Barrier number seven reactivates barrier number four— finding perfectly good reasons not to change.* The curse of perfectionism demands a perfect rationale for why you should change. It asks for proof that self-improvement is actually needed and accepts only an airtight case in favour of change.

You may really want to change jobs, go back to school, fall in love, or lose ten pounds. You may really want to stop hurting yourself or other people. You may be as close to the end of your rope as you want to get. But unless the arguments are perfect and cannot be countered in any way, you decide that they are not good enough. If you can find one reason, no matter how lame, NOT to change, the curse of perfectionism tells you not to bother trying.

*Barrier seven would be insignificant without barrier number five—cold, raw fear.* Fear and anxiety run rampant when you set up all-or-nothing propositions. The curse of perfectionism with its unrealistic expectations sets you up for a fall. You reach for something you may not be able to attain in a lifetime and expect to get it immediately and flawlessly on the first attempt. In your heart you know you can't succeed perfectly, and so fear steps in to prevent the failure, disappointment, rejection, or loss you have practically guaranteed by such unrealistic expectations.

You fear the disappointment you will feel if you cannot find the perfect job, spouse, social life, or any other perfect answer you seek. You fear you will fail to change perfectly. You fear you will choose the wrong moment to start a self-improvement effort. Perfectionism leads to procrastination, and fear turns procrastination to paralysis. It is a deadly one-two punch.

---

## ARE YOU PLAGUED BY THE CURSE OF PERFECTIONISM?

Perfectionism is puzzling. At first glance you may be unable to distinguish perfectionism from high standards. You may think your expectation to go for the best life has to offer is realistic, when in fact you are seeking the unattainable. You may claim you are carefully, conscientiously planning the change effort most likely to succeed for you, when what you are really doing is procrastinating and perpetually waiting for perfection.

How do you tell the difference? How do you know if you are cursed by perfectionism? LOOK AT WHERE YOU ARE.

Are you still in the same dissatisfying job, hanging on to what you have until you find another job that meets every single one of your exacting requirements? Have you rejected options that offered more than you now have because they were not perfect? Are you still looking for the perfect spouse, exercise programme, diet, social life, home, or alternative? Have you maintained the status quo in the meantime? Has anything about your life got better?

Are you back at square one? Did you attempt change but fail to flawlessly adhere to your self-improvement programme? Did a single setback convince you that the entire effort was not worth the time and energy? Did you try to do too much too quickly and give up when you did not succeed immediately?

Are you still waiting to take the first step? Do you know exactly what you want to do but have yet to do anything? Can you list all the little things that have happened to keep you from starting your change effort?

If what you want, how you expect to get it, and when you will take the first step have kept you from moving forward at all, then you are cursed by perfectionism. You set your sights TOO high, asked TOO much of yourself, and wanted TOO many conditions to be met before you would change.

LOOK AT WHERE YOU ARE. If your original expectations had been realistic and attainable, by now you would be at least a step or two closer to your destination. On the other hand, you will know perfectionism and procrastination are blocking change *when you know what you want but are NOT a single step closer to getting it.*

## DISMANTLING BARRIER #7: AIMING FOR EXCELLENCE

To open this chapter I described Dave and Alison's search for the perfect house. They looked everywhere for the exact replica of their dream house. Unfortunately, no such house existed. Now, there *was* a remote possibility that if they waited long enough, a house meeting all of their requirements would be put on the market at a price they could afford. But there was a much greater chance that no matter how long they waited they would never find the perfect house of their dreams. They had a choice. They could hold out for perfection or they could compromise. Fortunately, they chose the latter option and bought a home that met their basic needs and included most—but not all—of the features they wanted. It was a wise and realistic choice. Now Dave and Alison love their new home and hardly miss the extras they once believed they could not live without.

Dave and Alison escaped the all-or-nothing trap set by the curse of perfectionism. By lowering their expectations slightly and becoming more flexible about what they would accept, they opened themselves up to all the possibilities that lie between all or nothing. Yes, they settled for less than perfection. But they got a great deal more than nothing.

## PERFECTION VERSUS EXCELLENCE

According to the dictionary definition, to be perfect is to be *"complete and flawless in all respects."* If you ever become perfect by this definition, pull off a change effort that is perfect by this definition, or find an answer, a time, or a condition for change that is perfect by this definition, I want you to write me a letter and tell me about it. I will be the first one to celebrate your good fortune. In the meantime, I hope you do not mind it if I do not hold my breath.

Excellence is defined as something *"outstandingly good or of exceptional merit."* Each and every one of you have the potential to achieve excellence as it personally applies to you. The first difference between perfection and excellence is that excellence is a realistic expectation and a worthy goal. Perfection is neither.

Perfection is a condition that neither you nor anyone else in the entire world can find fault with or criticize in any way. It is a state described by absolutes. A perfect person *never* errs in his own eyes or anyone else's. A perfect job *never* gets boring, stressful, overwhelming, or frustrating. The person who holds the perfect job loves going to work *every single day* of his life, *never* disagrees with a co-worker or a policy, and gets paid the *exact* amount of money he wants, as well as automatically receiving pay raises whenever he asks for them. The perfect couple *never* argues or disagrees about *anything*. Each partner anticipates and meets the other's *every* need. Neither one *ever* squeezes the wrong end of the toothpaste tube, steals the blankets in the middle of the night, or sleeps with the window open if his partner wants it closed. They *never* feel grouchy, insecure, frustrated, or confused. No remark is ever misinterpreted. No hurt is ever felt. And of course, the couple's parents, children, and home are perfect, too.

The perfect person, job, and couple are figments of my imagination—and always will be.

Excellence, however, does exist in the real world. An excellent human being conducts his life to the best of his ability—but he sometimes makes mistakes. An excellent job has a few bad days mixed in with the good. It has a few flaws. However, for the person whose job it is, even with its flaws the job is outstanding and exceptional. Any couple who get along half as well as the imaginary perfect couple I described have an excellent relationship. That very same relationship might not work for you or me, but for the people in it, it is wonderful and satisfying—even though it is not complete and flawless in all respects.

Perfection is an end state, while excellence leaves room for growth. You can achieve excellence and decide you want to be even better. You can create an excellent career, then go on to develop an excellent love relationship. You can continue to grow and experience success.

In addition, aiming for excellence allows forgiveness. When you seek excellence, you accept the fact that there are no absolutes. There will be bad days and you will make mistakes. There will be setbacks and temptations you should, but do not, resist. The perfectionist focuses on the flaw and rejects the whole. The seeker of excellence looks at the big picture, recalls the good already done, forgives the error, and gets back on track.

Perfectionism is rigid and uncompromising, while excellence is flexible. Sometimes everything you want simply is not available, so you adjust, compromising and negotiating. But if you cannot have it all, you give up what you must to get most of what you want. The result may not be perfect. Instead, it is outstanding, exceptional, and much, much more than you already have—a great deal if there ever was one.

Perfectionism negates the value of progress, while aiming for excellence rewards progress. To achieve your personal best you simply try to get a little better each day. You may be a long way from your destination, but each time you master a step and achieve excellence at that level, you have cause for celebration. You have progressed and progress is excellent. What might have happened to some of the people I described earlier if they had aimed for excellence instead of demanding perfection?

If he had aimed for excellence, Harry would have been exercising regularly. Instead of waiting until he found a programme that met all of his stringent requirements, he would have chosen the option that met all of his basic needs and some of his preferences. And most importantly, he would have discovered that even though the programme was not perfect, it suited him well and he could stick to it.

Karen would have been well on her way to losing weight. She would have chosen a more flexible eating plan, one that fits her lifestyle. She would have kept her eye on the big picture, noting progress as she made it and reminding herself of it when she deviated from her diet. And instead of going on a binge each time she dieted imperfectly, she would have looked at what she did right and been motivated to stick with her eating programme.

Jack would have chosen one self-defeating habit to conquer at a time and persevered until he achieved his goal. Then, with one success under his belt, he would have attempted to rid himself of the next unhealthy habit on his list, and so on until he achieved excellence in each of the four areas he had failed to change when he demanded perfection.

Cindy would have avoided the agony she felt when she could not master a new job immediately. She would have seen what she did right on her first day and have set realistic goals to improve her performance one day at a time until she achieved excellence.

If you had not been procrastinating, you would have taken your first step by now. An excellent time to change is the present—before matters get worse or stuck becomes a lifestyle.

In each case described above as well as in Dave and Alison's, something had to be sacrificed in order for change to be set in motion. Dave and Alison's house did not have everything they originally wanted. The exercise programme Harry eventually chose did not satisfy his every desire. And Karen ended up losing weight at a slower pace than if she had adhered perfectly to a very restrictive diet. It also took Jack longer to "get clean." And Cindy had to admit she was not perfect.

## COMPROMISING VERSUS CAVING IN

Throughout this book I have told you to pursue what you *really* want and go after the best life has to offer. By lowering your standards and aiming for excellence instead of perfection, aren't you doing exactly what I've been saying you should not do?

No. No. No. If you review the chapter on knowing what you really want, you will recall that you should only choose what you want after considering the consequences. One consequence you must consider is your ability to achieve your goal, given the resources available to you. If you honestly evaluate perfection as a goal, you will see it is unrealistic. Are you doing what you *really* want when you pursue something you cannot get? I think you are doing yourself a disservice and setting yourself up for failure when you expect to achieve perfection. That is NOT a consequence you *really* want.

As far as the best life has to offer is concerned, life offers many things, but perfection is not one of them. What's more, while you sit around waiting for your perfect dream to come true, countless pleasures and opportunities are escaping you. If compromising your vision means getting *some* of life's goodness—while refusing to accept less than perfect answers, change efforts, or conditions for change means you get *nothing*—which will you choose? I hope you will choose to compromise.

When I suggest compromise, I do not mean caving in or giving up or settling for something you do not want. I do mean toning down your expectations and seeking excellence instead of perfection. You must set goals that are realistic and attainable. Yes, you can reach for more than you now have, but you should not reach so far beyond your grasp that you fall flat on your face. Instead, consider your own uniqueness and take one step at a time toward your ultimate destination.

Compromise is a nebulous concept and a bit frightening. It requires you to sacrifice something in order to get something else. How do you know when you are giving up too much or getting too little in return? The third estate agent Dave and Alison consulted showed them how to achieve the balance between holding on and letting go. Perhaps a similar exercise will show you how to compromise and free you from the all-or-nothing trap of the curse of perfectionism.

## Compromise Strategy

On a sheet of paper draw a four-column chart. Leaving the first column blank, label the second column "Perfection," the third column "Bottom Line," and the fourth column "Excellence"—as I have done on the next page.

|  | Perfection | Bottom Line | Excellence |
|---|---|---|---|
|  |  |  |  |

On the first line of the blank first column, write the word HOME. In the "Perfect" column, list five to ten words or phrases that describe the perfect home. When you finish the list, draw a line across the page, write the word CAR in the first column, and list five to ten attributes of the perfect car. Repeat the process for the perfect RELATIONSHIP and the perfect JOB.

Now go back to the top of the page and consider the *least* you would accept in a HOME, a CAR, a RELATIONSHIP, and a JOB. This is your "Bottom Line." It can be exactly what you have now or a little more. It should *not* be less than you already have. List five to ten bottom-line standards in each area.

Review your descriptions of perfection and your minimum bottom-line requirements. Somewhere between the two lies "excellence." Give the matter some thought and then realistically describe a HOME, a CAR, a RELATIONSHIP, and a JOB that is *more* than the least you would accept and *less* than perfect.

By setting goals that exceed your bottom line but are less than perfect, you can overcome the curse of perfectionism. Your expectations will be more realistic, and you can give up those awful all-or-nothing propositions, opting for reasonable gains attained one step at a time.

Approaching change one step at a time makes compromise easier to swallow. Once you reach the level of excellence you have defined by compromising, you can take new steps forward to obtain things you gave up when you first compromised.

### Aiming for Excellence in a Change Effort You Want to Make

Let's apply the same compromise process to a change you personally want to attempt. First, review the overall wellness strategy in Chapter Two and choose an area that you would like to improve. Use one you have used in other chapters, if you'd like, or choose a new area. What is your ultimate goal and the perfect outcome of improving this area of overall wellness? Write your answer in as much detail as possible.

On the other hand, what is the *least* you would accept in this area? Remember, your bottom line should *not* be less than you already have. Describe your bare minimum in this overall wellness area.

Now compare your idea of perfection with your bottom line. Consider what you *really* want and what is realistic to expect to achieve in this area *in the next year*. Write a goal for achieving excellence in this area.

This same process can be used to tone down your expectations of any effort you're making to change. First, list what you would do if you were to adhere to your self-improvement effort perfectly. Then set a bottom line, and finally, identify a middle ground, leaving room for flexibility and human fallibility.

## A Realistic Goal is Not Enough

The curse of perfectionism affects more than the outcome you have come to expect from a change effort, however. It also influences the conditions that you decide must be met before you take your first step.

List the PERFECT CONDITIONS for change. Include any task you want to complete before initiating a change effort, any personal or professional matters you want to have in order, any upcoming events you want to get through, and any requirements for the change effort itself (such as Harry's conditions for his exercise programme). You are describing the best possible circumstances for self-improvement, those which you believe will ensure a successful change effort.

When your list is complete, give each item on it an A, B, or C priority. "A" priority items are those that are absolutely essential, items that you will *not* sacrifice for the sake of compromise. It is in your best interest to also make sure that all "A" priority items are realistic and attainable in the foreseeable future. Waiting for someone else to change before changing yourself or finding a diet that allows you to eat unlimited quantities of everything you love are both unrealistic and unattainable conditions. They should not be given "A" priorities—no matter how much you would like such conditions to be met. "B" priority items are those you really want but could live without if you had to. "C" priority items are the least significant and easiest to give up in order to make real gains. As you did with your alternatives in Chapter Four, code all the items on your list so that you have an *equal number* of A, B, and C items. This forces you to seriously consider compromise and shake the curse of perfectionism.

When you look for a self-improvement programme or the right moment to change, you must willingly sacrifice your "C" priority requirements and be prepared to give up a few "B" priority items (or all, if need be). Remember that an excellent time to change is as soon as possible, and that the fewer conditions for change you set, the less likely you will be to postpone, delay, or procrastinate.

Once you learn to reject all-or-nothing propositions, your need for procrastination will naturally decrease. You will become less likely to slide back to square one. Sometimes, however, you will be tempted to do both. Those are the times when you must depend on the will and energy to change. They are also the moments in which you may encounter the eighth and final barrier—a shortage of will and energy. The next chapter tackles this ultimate barrier to change.

# 10

## The Will to Change

Karen feels terrific. Alone in her parents' seaside apartment while they are out of town, Karen has completed the chores she promised she would do in time to watch a magnificent sunset. Now, in the comforting quiet of the apartment, she settles into a reclining chair and reaches for the magazine section of the Sunday newspaper. She will work on the crossword puzzle, watch some TV . . .

Suddenly, however, thoughts of strawberry ice cream intrude upon her serenity. She visualizes the brand-new carton tucked behind the bread rolls and frozen peas in her mother's freezer, and it is calling her name.

"Stop that," she tells herself. "Don't ruin what you've got going."

What Karen has going is a sensible nutrition programme. Having considered the alternatives, she decided to strive for overall wellness instead of quick weight loss. She has stopped eating sweets and fried or fatty foods. As a result, she is losing weight and sees a dramatic improvement in her overall disposition. She has every reason to continue her change effort and no reason to go back to her former habits. Yet she feels an overwhelming urge to eat the strawberry ice cream.

Karen tries to focus her attention on the crossword puzzle, but she is distracted by the battle raging in her mind. The voice of temptation bombards and tries to seduce her. "A little bit of ice cream won't hurt just this once," the temptress argues. "You've been so good. You deserve a treat. You worked hard today. Reward yourself. You really want that ice cream. You know you're going to eat some before the night is over. Why torture yourself? You can get right back on track tomorrow, can't you?"

The more Karen tries to resist, the stronger her craving becomes. She cannot stop thinking about the ice cream. She can practically taste its sweet deliciousness melting on her tongue ...

Harry's alarm clock wakes him at six on a winter morning. His bed is warm and cozy. From it he sees that a thin layer of ice has formed on the windowpane. According to the radio announcer, it is a chilly thirty-three degrees outside. Harry groans.

Last August, Harry began a programme of regular exercise. After several false starts, he settled into a routine of working out at the gym three times a week and running two miles every morning. But this particular morning is a cold and dreary one. The sun has not yet risen, and Harry's bed feels like a warm, comforting cocoon. He is not thrilled by the idea of throwing off the covers, donning layers of clothing, lacing up his running shoes, and logging his daily miles. He wants to roll over, yank the blankets over his head, and go back to sleep.

Harry's inner dialogue goes like this:

"One day off won't kill me."

"But I made a commitment."

"But I'm not perfect. It's not like I'm in training to run a marathon or anything. I only run for my health."

"And it's working. Look at how much better I feel."

"But it's cold out there. I'll probably catch pneumonia. I was sniffling last night and my throat feels scratchy. It really does."

To prove his point, Harry coughs. Then he sighs, lifts the covers, and slides one leg toward the floor. Then he changes his mind, lifts his leg back onto the bed, replaces the covers, and sighs again.

It took some doing, but Jack found a therapist who specializes in stress-related problems. He is scheduled to see the therapist for the first time at seven o'clock tonight. All day Jack has second thoughts about keeping his appointment. His resolve fades. He figures that a man of his age and position should be able to handle his problems without outside help. He argues with himself until his motivation returns, realizing that being a successful accountant does not necessarily qualify him to figure out new directions for his own life. He knows that his previous single-handed efforts failed miserably. Yes, he concludes, therapy is the right first step and he is ready to take it.

At six o'clock Jack's will to change wavers again. He paces in his living room, wringing his hands and chain-smoking cigarettes. He tries to strengthen his resolve. He gives himself pep talks. Therapy may not be easy or painless, he argues, but it will help him in the long run. He is reluctant to take the step now, but one day he will be glad he did.

The telephone rings. Jack's friend Kevin tells him he has an extra ticket to a sold-out soccer game and a six-pack of beer chilling in the refrigerator.

"Come on over," Kevin says. "We'll kick back, drink some beer, and go to the game. It will take your mind off business. You haven't cut loose for a while. It will do you good."

Kevin has a point, Jack thinks. He reminds himself that he hardly ever gets a chance to unwind. A soccer game and Kevin's good-humoured company sound great right now. The therapy appointment *could* be rescheduled.

"I can see a therapist anytime," Jack thinks. "But tickets to a sold-out football game come along once in a blue moon. I could go to the game tonight and start therapy next week—unless I have to work late on that audit next week. Okay, so I'll make an appointment for the week after that . . ."

Karen, Harry, and Jack are beginning to get unstuck. They understand the first seven barriers to change and work to dismantle the ones that influence them. Karen gives up old eating habits. Harry starts a new exercise programme. Jack considers his options and devises a step-by-step plan to manage stress. Now each faces a moment of truth–and one last barrier.

Torn between a powerful craving for strawberry ice cream and her commitment to better nutrition and control over her eating habits, can Karen find the will and energy to resist temptation? Or will she slip back into old behaviour patterns?

As part of his commitment to exercise regularly, Harry runs two miles daily. He wants to continue what he started, but does he have the will and energy to leave a warm bed on a cold day? One day without running may not hurt him, but Harry will face the same choice every morning all winter long. Does he have the inner strength and discipline to stick to his plan over the long haul?

Seeing the immediate benefits of a night out with his friend and having his doubts about therapy anyway, Jack is tempted to procrastinate. Can he find the resolve and inner resources to take a step in the right direction today? Or will he postpone change until a later date?

Change is not easy. Life's journey presents an endless array of choices and dilemmas to divert you from the route you have chosen. That's why you must reach deep inside yourself for the force to propel you toward your goals. If you find that inner strength, you can leap the hurdle and surge ahead. If you come up empty-handed, you will give in to temptation or postpone the action you planned to take. You have reached barrier number eight—a shortage of resolve and energy.

## A MATTER OF WILL

Every change effort leads to a moment of truth. Many moments of truth, actually, moments when you act upon your choices or do not act, when you move forward or turn back, when you take a step or postpone it. You may know what you really want and believe you deserve it. You may conquer your fears and disarm your defences. You may clear all other obstacles from your path. But when all is said and done, at a moment of truth change becomes a matter of will.

You muster resolve to take your first step and stay on course. You exercise resolve so you can adopt a new behaviour or way of living and stick with it over the long haul. You activate resolve to resist temptations to return to old habits. When it is far easier not to, resolve is what gets you to actually DO what must be done.

### But What Is Resolve, Anyway?

Resolve, or will (the two are interchangeable), is an invisible hand pushing you forward. It is a jumper cable feeding power to a dead battery. You need will to start your engine and keep it running.

Will is the commitment that turns a pipe dream into a plan. It supplies the energy to turn visions into reality. Resolve is a fire burning inside you. With it, you ignite new fires and begin new change efforts. You produce enough energy to stay with any course of action you choose. Without it, you give in, give up, procrastinate, and get stuck.

*Resolve is the deciding factor each time you face a mo-*

*ment of truth,* stopping you from slipping backward. A moment of truth arrives each time you feel an urge to return to old ways of thinking or acting. Temptations present themselves. Someone offers you cocaine. You walk past the same store every day, wanting to spend five hundred pounds you don't have on the leather coat on display in the window. For your birthday your mother bakes your very favourite banana cream cake just after you tell her you are on a diet. You hear the winner of next week's lottery drawing will rake in six million pounds and feel the urge to blow one hundred pounds on tickets. Having made a commitment to be drug-free, stay within a budget, not eat sweets, or abstain from gambling, it takes will to say no to such temptations.

Old habits and behaviours offer comfort and escape when you are tired, lonely, angry, or sad. In the midst of a work crisis you crave a cigarette. Your lover leaves you and you want a drink. Your child throws a tantrum and you want to hit him. You wreck your car and want to feel the shelter of someone's arms, anyone's arms. You previously stopped smoking, drinking, hitting your children, settling for one-night stands with strangers. However, in stressful situations you need extra will and inner strength to keep from going back to old behaviours or losing the ground you gained.

*Will helps you stay on any new path you choose for yourself.* Having adopted a new behaviour pattern or way of life that requires discipline and stick-to-itiveness, you will face many moments of truth when NOT sticking to your commitment seems easy and appealing. There are those hectic, harried days when you have been one step behind from the moment your alarm clock rang. So, you think about not going to a support group meeting or a therapy session. With a party you could attend or a great movie you could watch, you feel like skipping a weekly class. But you don't. Instead you go to your therapy session or class because you've resolved not to fall back into your old, destructive behaviour patterns. Whenever you come to a crossroad where you can keep moving forward or turn back, your will to change is what keeps you on track.

*Will pushes you to take the first step in a new direction.* The greatest moments of truth are those that confront you when the time comes to actually do what you have planned. Today is the day you planned to go on a diet, quit smoking, or stop drinking. Will counters those "perfectly good" reasons not to change and makes you take action. You drive to the support group meeting location. Resolve opens the car door, walks you to the building, and carries you to your seat. It stops you from turning your car around or convincing yourself to attend next week's meeting instead of this one. You have updated your résumé, read the job ads, and composed a letter of resignation. When the time comes to leave your job, resolve helps you do it. Without sufficient resolve you are likely to decide to give the job another month or six more months to become fulfilling (even though you already gave it twelve of the best years of your life). The first step of any change effort is a real killer, and you need resolve to take it.

### Do You Have the Will to Change?

I suspect by now all this talk about the will to change is making you uncomfortable. When I say will or resolve, you think about your old nemesis—willpower. Just the thought pushes your panic buttons and tears open old wounds. References to willpower dredge up some decidedly unpleasant memories of all the times you needed willpower but did not have it.

Karen's reaction is typical. "Oh, that's just terrific!" she groans. "I work my tail off trying to get unstuck, go through all those strategies, reorganize my life, my thinking, my priorities, and *now* you tell me that what I need is willpower.

If I *had* willpower, I wouldn't be in this mess in the first place!

"I hear willpower and I think failure," Karen continues. "Show me someone who says dieting only takes a little willpower and I'll show you someone who never dieted a day in her life. I wish I had a pound for every time my mother got that pained expression on her face and asked, 'Where's your willpower?'

"I don't know where it is. It sure isn't around when the Christmas cookies are. It takes a leave of absence at midnight when I want to raid the refrigerator. It goes on vacation every time I do—which is why I gained seven pounds on a six-day cruise last year. You'll never see willpower hit the highway faster than mine does when there's chocolate cake in the cupboard or strawberry ice cream in the freezer."

Obviously Karen knows what it feels like to look inside herself for the will to change and not find it. In the past she has reached for the strength she needs and watched it slip through her fingers.

Resolve *is* slippery. Perhaps it has eluded you in the past. Resolve has an infuriating tendency to evaporate into thin air at the precise moment you most need it. Perhaps you think you have no willpower at all. I think you do, however. You have merely forgotten how to awaken it and use it.

---

## WILLPOWERLESSNESS

Will is like a muscle. It gets stronger when you exercise it regularly. It lifts more, pushes harder, and carries you further than a muscle weakened and limp from long periods of inactivity. If you only use your legs to carry you from the car to the garage door or from the TV to the refrigerator, you cannot expect to run a four-minute mile (or make it even once around the track for that matter). Similarly, if you have not exercised your will in a while, you cannot expect it to be available at full strength and in plentiful supply when you face a moment of truth.

Most of the time it seems to be easier and faster *not* to exercise your will, so you choose not to. Or sometimes you muster the will to start a change effort but run out of steam somewhere down the line. In either case you fall into a trap set by barrier number eight and get into the habit of not exercising your will often enough or at all.

*Exercising your will pays long-term dividends, but you want immediate rewards.* Ours is an instant gratification society. We want it all and we want it now. So, we look for the easiest, shortest, fastest route to our goals. We feel a pain, we take a pill advertised to produce instant relief. We drink instant coffee, eat fast food, play "instant lottery" games, buy diet products that promise fast, effortless weight loss.

If resolve was needed for an effort that guaranteed instant results and immediate rewards, you would rarely experience a shortage of it. But most efforts requiring willpower are efforts that promise future rewards or gains that are not immediately apparent. The payoff will come eventually, the relief will be longer lasting, and the benefits will be greater in the long run. Still, more often than not, you opt for immediate, albeit temporary, relief.

Think about Jack's dilemma. He can keep his therapy appointment and begin a change effort that six weeks, six months or a year from now will have dramatically improved his life and his ability to manage stress. Or he can drink beer with his buddy and go to a soccer game, a form of immediate relief because Jack won't think about his problems at the game. Instead, he will laugh, relax, and have a good time. But what about when the game is over?

In general, Jack leans toward instant gratification. As you may recall, when Jack first felt stress overpowering him, he looked for quick fixes, easy answers, and fast cures. When an action did not bring instant benefits, he abandoned it.

With conscious effort Jack has reoriented his thinking about change. He accepts that real relief and a better life will require time and effort and has devised a step-by-step plan to achieve stress management. But old habits die hard and slow deaths. Each step of his plan brings him to a moment of truth. Will he take action today to receive benefits in the future? Or will he, out of habit, postpone a step, take an easier route, and go for an immediate pleasure?

If you seek immediate relief and instant gratification or want your rewards right away, you probably choose not to exercise your will. Unfortunately, quick and easy is not necessarily healthy or better. The long haul is a rough road to travel, and a better life somewhere down the line is not as motivating as instant gratification of an immediate need, especially when easy answers and fast relief are close at hand. In addition, you may have forgotten what willpower feels like and how to find it. From lack of exercise your resolve weakens and eludes you the next time you really want to change.

*Maybe you* can *mount will to start a change effort—but can you maintain the energy to see it through?* Will is like a furnace. It needs constant refuelling. You get stuck when you stoke up the fire to take a first step and then forget to tend the flame. Uncared for, it flickers and dies. To move forward again you have to start a new fire from scratch.

"I started managing my time with a vengeance," says Janet, who was determined to have more time to do what she really wanted. "I made lists, delegated responsibility, turned over one of my groups to another therapist and stopped teaching courses at the Y for a pitiful five pounds an hour. I discontinued Saturday hours. I even hired a secretary to help with the paperwork. Things were going great."

Janet pursued new interests. A portion of her time was devoted to learning new therapy methods, and she could hardly wait to put her new ideas into practice. If she received a call from someone who had a problem in her new specialty area, she automatically scheduled an appointment—even if it meant working one of her free evenings or on Saturday. Then she began to lead a new group on the night her old one used to meet and began teaching a college class about her new area of expertise.

"I was flattered by the university's offer," she says. "I was excited about my new clients and my new approach. But the next time I stopped to catch my breath, I realized I was as overcommitted and overworked as I had been before. Again I had no time to relax, go to movies, dance, see my friends, or do anything else on my list of fun things to do. I had to start my time-management plan all over again."

Janet found the will and energy to start a time-management programme, but she could not sustain that energy. Instead, she lost track of her commitment and slid back to square one. It happens to us all.

You start diets fearlessly and begin to lose weight immediately. Basking in the success of a rapid ten-pound loss, you figure you can get away with some extra dressing on your salad. You continue to lose weight, so you decide dessert once a week would be okay, and a day off your diet completely now and then wouldn't hurt. You might even treat yourself to one binge day each week. As a result, your weight loss slows to a halt. You cannot understand it. It must be the diet. You abandon it, find a new diet, and start over again.

In the beginning you and your partner worked hard on your relationship. You communicated and did little things to surprise and please one another. You each bent a little bit to accommodate the other. You even rearranged your schedules so you could spend more time together. Once you felt comfortable, loved, and secure, however, one by one those special efforts fell by the wayside. You believed love conquered all, and that rationale allowed you not to devote as much will and energy to the relationship or work as hard to demonstrate your caring and commitment. Then one morning you discovered your relationship no longer felt close, comfortable, or satisfying.

Life promises goodness but does not deliver it automatically. Any pleasure, achievement, or change worth pursuing requires work and sustained effort. Your initial burst of will and energy may get you moving in the right direction, and you may even reach your destination, but you will not stay there or continue to grow unless you continue to exercise resolve and tap your internal energy supply.

The times you chose instant gratification instead of committing yourself to long-range, lasting benefits, and the times you got yourself moving on the right track only to run out of steam, may have convinced you that will is elusive and largely unavailable to you. Like Karen, you may believe you simply do not have enough willpower to face your moments of truth and take action to get unstuck. If this is the case, your willpower failures have become self-esteem wrecking balls.

### The Ultimate Barrier

Barrier number eight is the ultimate obstacle to change because it impedes your progress at the most crucial point in your journey. You face a moment of truth and you do or you do not take action. You will or you will not continue on the course you have chosen. You are or you are not able to get unstuck.

If you exercise your will and mobilize energy, all the work you did to clear other obstacles from your path will pay off, and you will truly be on your way to the life you desire and deserve. If barrier number eight appears and you experience a shortage of will and energy, however, it will make no difference that your road is clear of obstacles. You will not move forward.

Logically speaking, if you cannot move, you are stuck. Those old stuck feelings, thoughts, and behaviours reappear. This barrier is the ultimate block to change because it reconstructs the other barriers, most notably barrier number one—believing you do not deserve or have what it takes to be better.

Each time Karen tries to lose weight but her willpower evaporates into thin air, she likes herself a little less. She feels like a failure.

Each time Carol thinks about changing jobs but doubts she has the inner resources and does not mobilize the energy to take action, her self-esteem suffers. She feels inadequate.

Each time Steven swears he will stop using cocaine but cannot muster the will to resist it, he damages his self-image. He feels weak and unworthy.

Each time Janet tries to manage her time but sees her resolve and control slip away, she feels the full force of a self-esteem wrecking ball. She feels powerless.

Each time *you* say you will—but you don't—you think less of yourself. You come to believe you do not have what it takes to get what you want and that you personally do not deserve better. Allowing your inner resources to remain untapped, and letting resolve elude you when you need it most, can send you directly back to the starting line where you find barrier number one waiting for you.


## Don't Turn Back Now

Regardless of the reason you come up short in the will and energy department, the outcome is the same. A moment of truth arrives. You know where you want to go, but you DO NOT GO. You know what you must do, but you DO NOT DO IT.

But you have worked long and hard to decide what you want and plot the course to your goals and aspirations. Why see the effort wasted? Having come so far, you do not *really* want to turn back, do you? I hope not. Instead, let's work together to dismantle barrier number eight right now and finally send you on your way to your desired destination.

## BARRIER DISMANTLER #8:
## TRICKS AND TREATS TO STRENGTHEN WILL

Will makes or breaks a change effort. The work already done and the barriers already dismantled put you back on the main road and set the course you will travel. Resolve is what gets you out of the starting blocks and pushes you onward to the life you really want for yourself. But how do you find the will to change, and having found it, how do you use it?

Remember, will is mysterious and elusive. It is as slippery as an eel and as wily as a con artist. It hides from you and dodges your attempts to grasp it, and so you must draw it from its hiding places and tease it into working for you. You can do this by employing several "tricks of the trade" to mobilize your resolve and then "treat" it well so it does not slip away from you.

### First, You Practice

Let's compare will to a muscle. Let's also say that you are a runner intent on competing in the next city marathon. You do not rush out, register, and simply show up on the day of the race. There is no way you could reach the finish line if you did that. Instead, you must practise running, building your strength, stamina, and endurance a little more each day. You start on flat ground and run a single mile. Then you add miles slowly and start running up hills. What's more, you do not just jump out of bed and hit the pavement for your daily practise runs. You do warm-up exercises, loosening and stretching your muscles so they can tackle your effort without injury.

The same holds true for mobilizing your resolve. You do not go straight to the moment of truth, reach down inside yourself, and hope for the best—especially if you cannot remember the last time you exercised your will. Instead you nurture and fortify your inner resources through practice, practice, practice.

If you doubt you have the will to change, practice proves otherwise. If will has eluded you in the past and left you feeling like a failure, practice lets you rediscover success, build confidence, and identify your personal trouble spots so you can overcome them.

Practising exercising your will is a hands-on lesson. You can't just *think* about using willpower—you have to actually *use* it. You have to take every opportunity to experience will-power in action. Sometimes you have to create opportunities. That way you recognize the factors that sap your will—and learn to compensate. You become familiar with the dialogue between your little devil on one shoulder and your little angel on the other. The little devil, using tricks he has learned from other barriers, tries to convince you that you do not need to change and do not really want to, while the little angel reinforces your honest desire to change and encour-ages you to exercise your will. Sometimes you may feel like a ping-pong ball in a table tennis match. Do it. Don't do it. Do it. Don't. Do.

With less at stake, practice lets you feel the pull of op-posing forces and make a choice. If your will eludes you, you practise some more—until you get it right. And what tremendous joy and excitement you feel when you do get it right. Taste it, savour it, remember every detail. The small successes will persuade you to try more difficult tests of will.

## WARM-UP EXERCISES

I sometimes ask my students at the University of Mas-sachusetts to test their willpower by participating in a group experience I arrange. One such test of their resolve has stu-dents walk to a nearby doughnut shop. Baking is done on the premises, and the aroma reaches them while they are still a block away from the shop. I encourage them to let the smell of fresh-baked doughnuts tease and entice them.

Then they enter the doughnut shop and stare into the glass cases at all those glazed doughnuts, jelly doughnuts, doughnuts covered with powdered sugar, cinnamon doughnuts, chocolate-coated doughnuts with sprinkles on top, and every other imaginable kind of doughnut. If they could buy five different doughnuts, which five would they choose, I ask them. They talk about their very favourite kind of doughnut and take one last fond look at the doughnuts before they file out of the shop—without buying anything.

Now, doughnut shops may or may not test *your* will. But had you been on the field trip with my students, I'll bet you would have heard a few choice words from your will-weakening devil and few desperate pleas from your will-strengthening angel. Ultimately you would have walked out of that doughnut shop savouring a sweet willpower victory.

Here are six additional will warm-up exercises followed by a series of thought-provoking questions to help you maximize the benefits of your willpower practice sessions.

**1.** Attend a Friday "happy hour" at a bar or cocktail lounge of your choice with co-workers or friends—BUT DO NOT DRINK an alcoholic beverage. Stay at the bar for at least one hour.

**2.** Go to the grocery store and purchase a box of cookies, a carton of ice cream, a bag of potato chips, or some other munchie-type item that you really like. Bring it home, put it in the freezer or cupboard, but DO NOT OPEN OR EAT any of it for at least forty-eight hours.

**3.** The next time someone comes to you with a piece of juicy gossip, tell him NOT TO TELL YOU THE RUMOUR until at least twenty-fours hours have passed.

**4.** Go to a department store and try on clothes until you find an outfit that fits well, looks terrific on you, and that you would really like to buy. DO NOT BUY IT that day.

**5.** Spend an evening at home and DO NOT TURN ON

THE TELEVISION SET. If you get through one evening without watching television, try two days or an entire weekend.

**6.** Practise developing a new behaviour pattern. Each night before you go to bed, empty the coins from your pockets, wallet, or purse and put them into a jar. Do this every night until the jar is full.

After you finish some willpower warm-up exercises (and you may have to make several attempts before you succeed), answer the following questions:

—How did you feel right before you tested your will; while you were testing it; after you passed the test?

—What part of the will test was most difficult for you?

—When, if at all, did it seem as if will would elude you?

—What did you do or say to strengthen your will?

—What discouraging words/thoughts tried to sap your will?

—If you were faced with this temptation again, what could you do to make it easier to resist?

—On a scale of one to ten (with one being least tempting and ten being most tempting) how would you rate the will test the exercise provided?

—In the same kind of situation, what circumstances would test your will a bit more?

—Next, test yourself under those conditions.

### Taking One Step at a Time

Three years ago Eleanor lost fifty pounds and has maintained the weight loss ever since. Karen, seeing Eleanor has done something she too wants to do, chose Eleanor as a mentor. Karen asked about willpower and this is what Eleanor told her:

"Finding enough willpower to lose fifty pounds was practically impossible. The goal seemed so big and so far away that I couldn't believe I would ever do it. But finding the willpower to lose ten pounds seemed easy enough; to lose one pound was simpler still. Willing myself to stick to the diet for twenty-four hours seemed like a cinch, and I figured anyone could wait an hour before digging into the leftover lasagne. So that's how I looked at it—one step at a time. When I thought I was going to lose my willpower, I moved back and looked at the smallest possible step—a teeny tiny baby step. I took it. Then I took another and another until I'd got through the day."

Eleanor's advice is similar to the suggestion made by twelve-step recovery programmes such as Alcoholics Anonymous, Overeaters Anonymous, or Al-Anon. Participants are encouraged to progress one day at a time.

The idea of looking at a major change effort as a series of smaller, more manageable steps is a sound one. The philosophy of succeeding "just for today" teaches a valuable lesson. Why are change efforts easier and more likely to succeed when taken one step at a time? Well, remember your need for immediate results and instant satisfaction? It is not about to disappear. Dividends payable in the distant future will never be enough to entice your resolve out of hiding or persuade it to stick around. But when you accomplish a little bit at a time and stick to your change effort for one day at a time, you feel pride and experience success often enough to gain momentum for the next leg of your journey. As twelve-step recovery programme participants discover, eventually it is easier and more satisfying to stay on course than to go astray.

Additionally, looking only at the big picture can be frightening and stir up self-doubt. To be completely drug-free for the rest of your life seems impossible. That you one day will find the right partner, marry, and raise a family seems doubtful. To manage stress under all circumstances seems more than you can handle. To get out from under all the debts you have accrued over years of uncontrolled spending seems beyond your capabilities. Just at the thought of all the changing you have to do, your confidence wavers and your will weakens.

However, you know you can abstain from using cocaine or drinking alcohol for one day. You can start a simple conversation with someone or attend a singles group function. You can learn and use a new relaxation technique. You can cut up your credit cards or use coupons when you grocery shop and immediately put the amount of money you saved into a special savings account. These steps take willpower too, but they take less of it. These steps do have long-term benefits, yet you also see the short-term results. You did *something,* and no matter how small that something might be, it is better than nothing and proof you can do more.

## BREAKING DOWN THE BIG PICTURE

Think about a change you want to make. It can be an item on your Overall Wellness inventory, something in your lifeline net, or an alternative you identified when you confronted barrier number two.

State your ultimate goal and put it in writing. For example, Janet's goal is "to manage my time so I have three evenings a week and the entire weekend available to do things I want to do." Karen's goal is to "figure out and stick to a lifelong nutrition programme that brings me to my goal weight, keeps me there, and helps me be healthier and happier."

Think about all the steps you must take to reach your ultimate goal. What is the first step you must take; the second; the third; and so on? Write each step on an index card.

Janet decided her first step would be to move all her Saturday clients to appointment times during the week. Karen's first step was to eliminate foods containing white sugar from her diet. It was a step requiring stick-to-itiveness, one she would have to take every day, so she phrased what she put on her index card like this: "For today I will not eat anything with white sugar in it."

Put away all index cards but the one with your first step on it and keep that first-step card with you as a willpower reminder. If your first step is a one-time step such as "ask friends to recommend a therapist" or "cut up credit cards," when you complete the step, write "DONE" across the card and hang it somewhere to remind you of your success. Then, when you are ready for the next step, go to your index cards and repeat the process with the card for the next step.

### Offer Rewards for Willpower Achievements

Like anyone else, I experience willpower shortages. I most often notice them when I am in the middle of a project—such as when I was writing this book—or when I have to complete a task I find particularly unappealing—such as paying bills or answering the mail I have allowed to accumulate on my desk. From such experiences I have learned that resolve sometimes needs to be poked, prodded, or outright bribed.

Exercising will, regaining control over your life, or completing a project is its own reward. So is losing weight, earning a college degree, finishing a writing assignment, or running a 5 mile road race. There can be doubt about the inner satisfaction and sense of accomplishment you feel when you finally reach your destination. It is a wonderful natural high. Unfortunately, the promise of future gains and the pleasant feelings produced by achieving a long-term goal are not enough to counter willpower shortages you are experiencing here and now. Sometimes even the price and confidence boost found in completing a small step toward your goal is not enough either. In those instances your will must be pushed into action by offering yourself tangible rewards for progress made.

For instance, on a bright, beautiful day such as today I have difficulty disciplining myself to work on this book. I just do not feel like writing. At this particular moment I am bored or frustrated by the project. The right words do not come to mind immediately, and I am not in the mood to push myself to find them. It is such a lovely day. I would rather be riding my bicycle, hiking through the woods, or rowing my canoe on the lake.

But, I have to write. I committed myself to the project. There are deadlines to meet. The time I scheduled for writing is the only time I have available for the next few days. I cannot postpone or procrastinate any longer. Besides, I really want to write this book, and I knew when I started it that I would have days like this.

Reminding myself of my commitment, the deadlines, and my schedule, however, is not enough to restore my willpower. So, I make a deal with myself. If I have a chapter to finish, I promise myself I can go to the movies after I finish it. If I want to organize my notes and outline the next chapter, I offer myself a bicycle ride as a reward. Sometimes I put in two solid hours of work so I can relax in an easy chair and listen to my favourite record for the next twenty minutes. I keep a whole list of tangible rewards and willpower enticements, and the payoffs I promise and give myself push me forward when inner discipline is nowhere to be found.

Tangible rewards bolster shaky willpower and get you beyond the rough spots in any change effort. Perhaps you *should* be able to force yourself forward without external rewards or bribery. Yet, realistically speaking, there will always be times when you just cannot find the inner strength and willpower you need. Those are the times to call for reinforcements in the form of tangible rewards.

Willpower rewards can be *things* you give yourself—a paperback novel, a new hat or pair of shoes, a cassette tape, a new piece for your collection of glass miniatures, or some gimmick or gadget you want. The item often is something you already want and plan to get. So, to strengthen willpower, wait to buy these little luxury items until you need a willpower reward.

*What are some gifts you would like to give yourself that could also reward a willpower success?*

Willpower rewards can be *activities* you enjoy—hot bubble baths, long walks in the woods, viewing a videotape of an old movie, listening to music, visiting a friend, reading part of a mystery novel, or taking a nap. When you feel your will weakening, set an achievable goal and offer yourself this activity as a reward.

*What activities pamper and please you that can be used as willpower rewards?*

Rewards can also be words of praise, encouragement, and support delivered by friends, family, colleagues, or bosses. Go public with a step toward improvement that you have taken. Tell one of your emotionally supportive people (see Chapter Three) about it. Or call one of your support people and ask them for encouragement or to help you celebrate your success.

*What people can you call upon to deliver a well-timed pat on the back or encouraging words?*

## Temptation Alternatives

Temptation alternatives are similar to willpower rewards. Both work when inner resources dwindle. While rewards get you to do something you cannot find the resolve to do, temptation alternatives stop you from doing something you have an irresistible urge to do. Rewards are delivered after you complete a task, while temptation alternatives are employed as soon as you realize you are at a moment of truth.

Perhaps you feel stressed, fatigued, angry, or sad, and those old negative self-esteem messages are echoing through your mind. Hoping to silence them, you think about smoking cigarettes or marijuana, taking a drink, picking up a stranger, or buying something you do not need and cannot afford.

Or maybe you are bored. Eating ice cream, wandering through shopping arcades, or going to see your abusive former boyfriend seems better than boredom. Or on a special occasion you might want to treat yourself to a drink, a slice of German chocolate cake, or a day off from running, therapy, or night school. Perhaps an unexpected opportunity to indulge presents itself.

Temptation taunts you and the more you try to resist, the harder it tugs at you. At times like these you need alternatives to switch your focus from the temptation to something else. Distraction often works where sheer will cannot. So, take your mind off the battle of will and occupy yourself with another activity. By the time you complete your temptation alternative, you may find the urge to cheat, indulge, or break training has passed.

Instead of giving in to temptation, you can make a telephone call, go for a walk, write in your journal, go to the library, visit a friend, clean a closet, sort through old photographs, do a crossword puzzle, watch a movie, or play a cassette tape and dance until you drop. The activity you choose must meet one basic requirement, however. It must occupy your mind and/or body sufficiently to distract you from thinking about the temptation you want to resist. It also does not hurt to choose temptation alternatives that take thirty minutes or more to complete, or ones that strengthen one of the seven self-esteem building blocks described in Chapter Three. In addition, be prepared at times to employ a second or third temptation alternative if the first does not completely squelch the urge to "cheat."

*What can you do to resist temptation and call a temporary cease-fire in your willpower war?*

When it comes to temptation alternatives, it is best to think ahead. Identify the potential trouble spots in any change effort and plan your own detours and diversions. For help in planning your temptation alternatives, turn back to Chapter Three and consult your list of support people. You can ask one of them to help you brainstorm temptation alternatives.

Then make a list and memorize it. Then when you feel willpower weakening, do something on your list. If the urge persists, try another temptation alternative and another. Eventually, either the urge will leave you or you will get tired of distracting yourself. Your resolve will return when you say, "Enough already. This compulsion is ruining my day and I won't put up with it for one more minute!"

### Forgive Yourself

The final will booster I suggest is forgiveness. Forgiveness prevents a single willpower failure from ruining an entire change effort.

No one is perfect. Indeed, expecting perfection is a barrier itself. Because you are human, you will make mistakes. Because you have not exercised will regularly in the past, you can expect it to elude you at least once and possibly many times.

When it does, you can view your willpower shortages and imperfect efforts as evidence of your own unworthiness and inadequacy. When you falter or fall, you can say to yourself, "You weak, incompetent son of a gun, look what you did. Things were getting better—but could you hang on? No. You blew it. You always blew it. You'll never change."

Expertly beating yourself for an indiscretion and reminding yourself that you obviously do not deserve a better life, you polish off the whole carton of strawberry ice cream go on a three-day binge, abandon your diet completely, and regain the weight you lost. Not only do you not run today, but you do not run tomorrow or the next day or the day after that, until you give up running altogether—all because you could not forgive one little mistake.

Or, when you're at the exact same crossroad, you can

FORGIVE YOURSELF. Grant yourself the right to be human and therefore imperfect. Acknowledge where you went wrong, but also remind yourself of all the right moves you made before. And let go of those negative messages and self-propelled wrecking balls. Tell yourself you succeeded before and can succeed again. Instead of taking a long, self-destructive detour back to square one, forgive yourself and get right back on track.

Without forgiveness you see every misstep as evidence of inadequacy. When that happens, your self-esteem drops and barrier number one halts your progress. You get stuck —again.

But you do not want to be stuck anymore. So, do the very best you can. Practice will. Take one step at a time and reward willpower successes. Employ temptation alternatives and *still* be prepared to mess up once in a while. Also be prepared to forgive yourself, restart your engine, and get moving once more on the road to change.

### What Now?

You have read about eight barriers to change and how to dismantle them. Now you have all the pieces of the puzzle. If you also have the resolve and desire to change, the next and final chapter will help you put the pieces together and actually plan the change effort *you* really want to undertake.

# 11

![decorative bar]

# *Getting Unstuck*

You now know a great deal about change and the eight barriers to change. You have plenty of information about getting stuck as well as tools and ideas you need to get unstuck. Will you do it? Will you change? Will you go after the life you desire and deserve?

I cannot answer that question for you. The choice is yours. Others before you have faced the same choice. Some chose to get unstuck. Some did not.

Before adding the final touches to a blueprint for change, let's catch up with some of the people whose lives and struggles appeared as examples throughout this book.

Carol no longer works for the child welfare bureaucracy. Instead, she serves as a consultant to smaller, privately run organizations, conducts training seminars for social workers, and is writing a textbook on child sexual abuse. She shares an office with two other therapists and conducts a modest but profitable private counselling practice.

Once doubtful about her ability to be anything but a petty

bureaucrat and fearful of financial ruin, Carol is thrilled with her accomplishments. "For the first few months I was in a constant state of panic," she admits. "New clients were not coming in fast enough, and I really thought all my fears were going to come true. But I was determined not to let them get the best of me. I pounded the pavement, knocked on doors, and called everyone I had ever worked with to try to get consulting contracts. When I finally got my first contract and knew I had at least one source of steady income, I relaxed, and one thing after another fell into place."

Karen has yet to lose all the weight she originally set out to lose. She is proud of the progress she *has* made, however. "I'm down twenty pounds so far," she reveals. "I'll lose the last ten eventually. I don't make myself crazy about it the way I used to. The pounds are not as important as the programme, and I'm sticking to that."

Karen created her change by obtaining valuable information about nutrition and using it to create an eating plan that suited her. She has eliminated sugar from her diet and rarely eats red meat or foods that are fried or have a high fat content. She takes one hour walks at least five times a week and works out with an exercise videotape on the days the weather keeps her from walking outdoors.

"I think I'm proudest about not eating as an emotional outlet anymore. It's not my main form of recreation either," she says. "I eat at mealtimes and I eat what's good for me. Oh, I blow it every once in a while. But I stop before I go on a true binge. I ask myself if I really want to go back to the way I used to be. I don't, so I make sure to get right back on track. It's amazing how much happier I am, and I now have the energy to follow through with other plans that have nothing to do with dieting."

Cindy worked as a freelance publicist for a while before returning to full-time employment with an established public relations firm. "Hustling for clients and bidding against other people to get a contract wasn't my cup of tea," she explains. "I don't count it as a failure though, just something I learned I didn't actually want to do."

Cindy no longer sees her therapist, but she would return for counselling if she reached another impasse in her life. She is involved in a "terrific" love relationship, has deepened old friendships and made new ones. Job offers poured in as soon as word got out that she was looking for employment.

When asked why people are drawn to her professionally and personally, Cindy—who once wondered if there was anything about her anyone could ever love or appreciate—replies, "Hey, what's *not* to like?"

Harry now gives himself "A in exercise and a B-plus in relationships." He continues to work out three times a week and runs daily, although he admits he does not stick to his programme religiously when he is on the road. And yes, on some winter mornings, he rolls over and goes back to sleep.

He grins sheepishly and says, "What can I say? Nobody's perfect."

But boy, has he progressed. He even thinks about entering some mini-marathons and imagines winning one someday. "The headlines will read: 'Former Couch Potato Makes Good,' " he says, laughing.

Harry has not found a lasting love relationship—yet. "But I will," he states confidently. "In the meantime I am meeting a lot of great people—male and female—and I have a whole lot of fun."

"I'm working on self-esteem mostly," Steven reports. "There's more stuff for me to work out than I thought."

Steven is in therapy. Where his business and life are concerned, he is taking "small steps in the right direction." He is more organized than he once was and more apt to initiate things rather than simply drift into them. "I guess I'm better," he admits. "Yeah, I *am* better. There's a long way I have to go yet, but at least now I think I have a chance to come out ahead."

After taking time off to have a baby, Lisa now works part-time as a sales rep. "Just to keep my hand in, and I want to hang on to my business contacts," she explains. "So that when I return to work full-time, I can be even more successful. I have it all mapped out. It's going to happen, you'll see."

Confidence to reach for ever higher goals has been an unexpected benefit of getting unstuck for Lisa, who once was too timid and intimidated to express an independent idea in the workplace.

Marilyn lives with two of her three children (the oldest is away at college most of the year) and supervises a hospital intensive care unit. She is amazed at how much she enjoys working. She also dates a high school teacher who is ten years younger than she is.

"I met him at one of my son's soccer games," Marilyn explains. "Our relationship caused quite an uproar with my kids and parents at first. But we worked it out. I deserve a little happiness, right? And I am pretty happy. Not every minute of every day—but when I think about how I used to be . . ."

Thinking about how he or she used to be is something everyone who got unstuck has in common. When Jack thinks about how he used to be, he is "surprised I *lived* long enough to get it together."

Jack has reached step six on his twelve-step stress management plan. He sees a therapist, no longer drinks or uses drugs, and tries to exercise three times a week. He uses relaxation techniques each morning and whenever he feels his stress level start to soar. Instead of treating every decision or dilemma as if it were a crisis, he carefully evaluates the situations he encounters at work and at home. His most recent change effort was to cut his coffee intake to one cup a day.

Jack recalls, "I had to figure out new ways to have fun, which was tough at first. Still is sometimes. I lost a few friends. But all things considered, it was a small price to pay."

Not everyone who attempted change succeeded, and some folks chose not to take a single step forward. Lorraine, at age forty, earned her master's degree and became a family therapist. However, she got stuck when her husband suffered a heart attack and his computer software business failed. The last time I spoke to her, she could not see any alternatives to her painful situation and was very depressed and waiting for a job with a school system to become available.

Having chosen not to do anything about his marriage, Len is in the same place he was in Chapter One, And Julie still pursuing stuck as a lifestyle, has got worse, Her desperate search for the perfect man has led to numerous casual sexual encounters, jeopardizing her physical health as well as her emotional well-being.

Everyone you read about in this book had a choice to make. Those who got unstuck chose to take the first step forward. Then they chose to keep moving in their new direction.

"The first step was the killer," Carol recalls. "I started to take it so many times but always lost my nerve. Finally I got sick of myself and my excuses. It just got to the point where I was going to do it now—or never do it. So I *made* myself do it."

Harry adds, "It's not like I jumped in with my eyes closed. I thought it through and worked out the details ahead of time. Or as you put it, I plotted my course, figured out which barriers were in my way, and dismantled them—either up front or when I got to them. Then I kick-started the old engine and took off down the road."

Harry and others "took off down the road" even though

no one guaranteed they would reach their ultimate destination. They moved forward even though they knew they would hit a few bumps and encounter a few obstacles along the way.

"Movement is movement," says Janet, who judges herself to be halfway to her goal of having enough time to enjoy life. "As long as I'm moving, I'm not stuck. I'd rather change my course along the way than have to start over again from a dead stop."

The points made by Harry, Carol, and Janet are worth repeating. *The first step IS a "killer."* However, if you want to get unstuck, you have to take it. But taking the first step and continuing to move forward is easier when you plan for self-improvement, identify potential barriers, and begin to dismantle them. Finally, *imperfect movement is better than perfect paralysis.* You cannot completely dismantle every barrier before you take your first step, and if you wait for perfect conditions to change, you may never actually start to change. And keep in mind, once you start moving, it's easier to alter your course a little than to stop and start again. With these points in mind you can pull together information about change and barriers to plan the change effort most likely to succeed.

### Set a Goal

What do you *really* want to do? Once again, state your goal in a positive manner, beginning with an affirmative—"I will . . ."

### Review the Barriers

There are eight barriers to change. Each has the potential to keep you from getting out of the starting gates or to impede your progress once you get moving. All eight do not necessarily operate in *your* life, however, and the impact a barrier has on you may be quite different from how it affects someone else. As I review the eight barriers, think about their potential influence on *your* proposed change effort.

BARRIER #1 is believing you do not deserve better. It is a by-product of low self-esteem. You know barrier #1 is at work when you believe you are not good enough to have what you want, think you *cannot* accomplish change, or see yourself as lacking the qualities necessary for success.

BARRIER #2 is not seeing your alternatives. When this barrier appears in your life, you think you have no choice except to stay the same, see only the one option that does not appeal to you, reject every available alternative because it is flawed in some way, or cannot decide which avenue of change to pursue. Since you do not know which way to go, you go nowhere.

BARRIER #3 is not knowing what you *really* want and value. When you are blocked by this barrier, you go along with the crowd, let other people choose the direction you travel, or do not communicate your needs and desires. You get stuck because you pursue a goal you do not choose or do not even consider choosing an alternative. When in the grips of barrier #3, you do not prize and cherish or publicly affirm those types of aspirations, and you do not take action at all or do not act repeatedly and consistently.

BARRIER #4 supplies perfectly good reasons *not* to change and encompasses all the "yeah, but"s and excuses you offer to defend the way things are and convince yourself that change is unnecessary. You know you are finding perfectly good reasons *not* to change when you claim things are not so bad or could be worse, build an airtight case for staying the same, or counter every suggestion with a "yeah, but" statement.

BARRIER #5 is cold, raw fear. Like the Three Sillies you read about, you dread a negative outcome that may never come to pass and ignore the probable good that would occur if you did change. You fear possible failure, disappointment, rejection, pain, and a host of other horrors—all of which freeze you in your tracks. In an effort to protect yourself from what you fear, you pass on probable success, accomplishment, acceptance, pleasure, and all the other riches life offers.

BARRIER #6 is a lack of cooperation. When obstructed by this barrier, you try to change alone, think you have to get what you want without anyone else's help, fail to ask for the assistance you need, compete instead of cooperate, and find that your successes have been sabotaged by the people around you. Change can occur without cooperation, but it is slower, and more difficult and painful to achieve.

BARRIER #7 is the curse of perfectionism. Under this barrier's influence you make change an all-or-nothing proposition. You expect perfect answers, perfect change efforts, perfect times and conditions for change, or an ironclad guarantee of perfect results. Your impossibly high expectations cannot be met, but you refuse to accept anything less than exactly what and all you want. Consequently you do and get nothing—when you could achieve excellence.

BARRIER #8 is a shortage of resolve or energy that saps the inner life force you need to take the first step, keep from returning to old habits, or stick to your self-improvement programme. Too little will or energy leads you to procrastinate, give in to temptations, or slide back to square one.

Which of the eight barriers stand in *your* way? What kind of and how much impact can you expect them to have on *your* change effort?

---

## THE OVERALL BARRIER INVENTORY

On a sheet of paper, draw a chart like the one you drew for the Overall Wellness inventory presented in Chapter Two—with one wide column on the left-hand side of the page and seven skinny columns on the right side of the page.

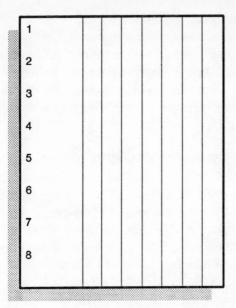

In the wide left column, write key words for each road-block:

#1 – SELF-ESTEEM
#2 – ALTERNATIVES
#3 – VALUES
#4 – EXCUSES
#5 – FEAR
#6 – COOPERATION
#7 – PERFECTION
#8 – WILLPOWER

With your personal goal in mind, answer the following questions:

**Column One:** Which barriers are present in your life RIGHT NOW? *In the narrow first column, place a check mark across from each barrier you feel influences you today.*

**Column Two:** Which barriers do you think will impede your progress *during* your change effort? These may be the same barriers you checked in column one or they may be different, (i.e., you may have the *will* to get started, so barrier #8 is not in your way at the moment. Yet you feel your will could fail you if you had to face temptation somewhere down the line. In that case, barrier #8 could be expected to affect you during your change effort.) *Mark the barriers you may encounter during your change effort by putting an X in the second column.*

**Column Three:** How significant a role does each barrier play in your life? Give each barrier a one, two, three, four, or five rating. A one rating indicates a minimal or relatively insignificant impact on you or the change you plan. A five rating signifies a major obstacle that powerfully blocks your ability to change. *Use the third column for your numerical rating of each barrier.*

**Column Four:** How much will each barrier affect *this particular change effort*? Using the letters *A* through *H*, rank the barriers according to their potential to keep you from getting what you want (based on the goal you have put into writing). An "A" barrier is the one that most powerfully blocks this particular change effort, while an "H" wields the least influence. Each barrier should have a different letter grade. *Use column four to rank them this way.*

**Column Five:** Which barriers must be at least partially dismantled *before* you can take your first step? Do not allow fear or perfectionism to cloud your judgment. Taking into consideration that there are never perfect conditions for change, which barriers do you *really* need to work on before you actually embark upon your change effort? *In the fifth column, mark these with the letter N (for "now").*

**Column Six:** Which barriers must you continue to confront and dismantle *throughout* your change effort? Will you have to confront fear/anxiety again and again? Or once you push through your initial fear will barrier #5 stop influencing you? Will you be done with barrier #2 as soon as you choose your course of action from the available alternatives? Or will you come to numerous crossroads where new alternatives are needed?

If you expect a barrier to reappear periodically during your journey, *write the letter* O *(for "ongoing") in the sixth column.*

**Column Seven:** If there is any barrier you feel you need to know more about, *place an asterisk (\*) in the seventh column* next to it. To learn more about a barrier or how to dismantle it, you can reread the chapter about it and redo the strategies you find there. Or you can do additional research and learn other skills by reading books, listening to audiotapes, or consulting experts.

This Overall Barrier inventory shows you how each of the barriers to change affects you personally. The degree to which each influences your life, the kinds and severity of problems it creates, as well as when and how you will dismantle a barrier, are different for each individual.

For many people, self-esteem is the most powerful obstacle blocking success. Like Steven, you may delay major life changes until you like yourself enough to believe you deserve better. In that case, before conquering a big problem, you should actively build self-esteem and take small steps forward so you can experience some success.

For Jack, on the other hand, perfectionism is a major impediment. He wants it all and he wants it now. So, before he can change, he has to redefine his expectations, break down his ultimate goal into manageable steps, and reward himself for the progress he does make.

Willpower is a significant issue for Karen and continues to be every step of the way. So she has learned to cope by using temptation alternatives she designed herself. In this way she tries to recognize and overcome temptation each time it threatens to halt her progress.

Before Marilyn takes her first step, she needs to stop finding perfectly good reasons *not* to change. To stay on course, she needs cooperation. Therefore, her change effort began by tackling barrier #4. It was only then that she was able to move forward and begin dismantling barrier #6.

From *your* Overall Barrier inventory you too can get a general overview of what you need to do to get unstuck.

---

### DO/GET/BE/ACT

Once you recognize the impact of the eight barriers to change, you can reaffirm your goal and fill in the details of your personal blueprint for change. My longtime friend and colleague Merrill Harmin uses the following strategy to paint a crystal-clear picture of change.

On a sheet of paper held horizontally, draw a four-column chart. From left to right, the columns should be labelled DO, GET, BE, and ACT.

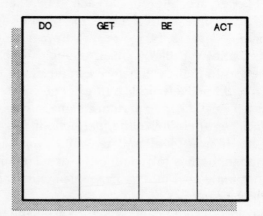

| DO | GET | BE | ACT |
| --- | --- | --- | --- |
| | | | |

In the DO column, write your goal.

Ask yourself what you hope to GET by pursuing and achieving your goal. Your GETs represent your reasons *to* change. List your hopes and expectations in the GET column.

Ask yourself how you will have to BE in order to do and get what you want. The bottom line here is that you have to BE more powerful than the barriers you identify as significant to your change effort. You must BE able to push through your fear of failure. Or you must BE able to see alternatives and choose one to pursue. Or you must BE sure that going back to school is what you want to do and not merely what others are pushing you to do. Using that sort of phrasing, list the barriers to be dismantled in the BE column.

At this point I have added a new item to Harmin's original Do/Get/Be strategy, and that is the word ACT. To do and get what you really want and to be more powerful than the obstacles you face, you must take certain actions. What are they?

If you want to be able to see alternatives and choose one to pursue, your possible actions would include brainstorming, asking three friends for suggestions, calling a meeting of your business colleagues, or using the decision-making strategies found in Chapter Four.

If you want to be able to get more cooperation, your possible actions should include defining what you need, deciding who you need it from, writing out a request, rehearsing, and actually asking for cooperation. Or you might act by validating the people around you or being more open to their ideas and offers.

For each BE you listed, jot down the actions you want to take to do, get, and be what you want.


## My Do/Get/Be/Act Chart

My goal was to write a book about getting unstuck, so that is what I wrote in my DO column.

If you looked at my GET column, you would see the following hopes and expectations. I wanted to get:

. . . the book published and a sense of accomplishment from achieving this goal.

. . . money from the sale of the book (I wouldn't mind if it turned out to be a best-seller).

. . . recognition of the ideas in the book and the work I've devoted myself to for many years.

. . . praise and positive strokes from university colleagues, book reviewers, and readers.

. . . pride and satisfaction from hearing that the book has helped people create better lives for themselves.

How would I have to BE? Well, I had to be able to overcome my fears of rejection and negative criticism. I had to be able to find reasons *to* do what I wanted and counter the excuses I kept making. I had to be able to get cooperation because writing the book would consume time I usually spent with my family and my students. And I had to be able to find the will to persevere with a *big* project. My BEs are listed here in the order of their relative power to keep me from getting and doing what I wanted.

My ACT column was crammed with ways to successfully do, get, and be what I wanted. The work I listed to do on fear alone will give you a good idea of what can go in this column.

I felt I could assuage many of my fears by finding out in advance if the book might "work." Actions in this area included: asking people if they would read a book about getting unstuck; researching what sorts of books on the topic of change had been published recently; and preparing an outline and content summary to elicit the interest of publishers.

I also thought I would work on fear by writing a dozen affirmations about what I was capable of doing and reading them when I got up in the morning and before I went to sleep at night, as well as repeating them after my daily meditation session. If my fears cropped up while I was writing the book, I felt that I could have my wife or a colleague read some of what I had written and reassure me.

All of these steps were ones I ultimately took—and since you are reading the finished product, obviously my plan worked! Do/Get/Be/Act charts can work for you, too.

The Do/Get/Be/Act strategy pulls together the pieces of your change puzzle. It reminds you that barriers do exist and influence you, but it also reveals the actions you can take to keep from getting stuck again at some point in your change effort.

I like to make a typed copy of my Do/Get/Be/Act chart and hang it on the bulletin board in my office. When the going gets tough, I consult my chart, figure out what is happening, and do something about it.

## THE GOAL SQUEEZE

The desire to change becomes a plan when you identify the specific steps you will take to reach your goal and set a tentative deadline for each step. The GOAL SQUEEZE strategy helps you do this and also serves to prevent procrastination.

Once again, state your goal. What do you really want to achieve? Then list *everything* you have to do to achieve your goal. And I do mean everything.

If you want to paint watercolour pictures, for example, your task list should include *everything* you will do, beginning with buying a box of paints, paper, and paintbrushes. My list for writing this book included tasks as seemingly insignificant as buying an ample supply of pens and pencils and asking colleagues for contacts in the publishing world, as well as obviously essential actions such as getting lecture tapes transcribed or going through the letters workshop participants had sent me.

From your list, pull out all the items you can and want to do over the next *six months*. Then make a six-month list, and from that, pull items you can do during the next *month* and make a one-month list. Then, from your one-month list, select tasks you can complete in the next *week* and make a one-week list.

Rank the items on your one-week list according to what you will do first, second, third, and so forth. If you desire, you can assign a day and/or time to each task.

THEN—ONE BY ONE—DO THE TASKS ON YOUR ONE-WEEK LIST.

As each week passes, return to your one-month list and make a new week list. When a month passes, develop a new month list from your six-month list (and take that month week by week). GOAL SQUEEZES really pay off. Before you know it, you will have climbed all the way to your goal.

---

### SELF-CONTRACTS

Any way you look at it, change requires commitment. You have to commit yourself to take the first step *and* you have to commit yourself to pursue your goal until you reach it *and* you have to commit yourself to maintain your new way of life.

A self-contract reinforces that commitment. Even though it is not a legal document and no one will sue you if you do not keep your end of the bargain, a self-contract bolsters your will to change and reminds you of your commitment to change. It encourages you to do the best you can to get what you really want.

If you were indeed entering into a legal contract, you would consider certain questions before drawing up the actual agreement. Going through such preliminaries helps clarify self-contracts, too. Honestly and *realistically* answer the following questions. Then, based on your answers, complete the self-contract form I provide.

1. What is your goal?
2. By what date do you hope to achieve it? (If your goal is a lifestyle change, this date represents the date you hope to adopt your new way of life. It is assumed that you will maintain the effort beyond that date.)
3. What steps must you take?
4. When will you take your first step?
5. Will you need to ... build self-esteem ... increase alternatives ... clarify values ... let go of excuses ... push through fear ... obtain cooperation ... overcome perfectionism ... mount resolve/mobilize energy?
6. Have you started to or made plans to dismantle the barriers in your way?
7. What tangible rewards can you give yourself when you make progress?
8. Will you forgive yourself and get right back on track if, for any reason, you are unable to perfectly comply with your self-contract?

### Self-Contract

I (your name) _____

will (your goal) _____

_____

This contract affirms my commitment to accomplish this goal by (date) _____. I plan to honour my commitment one step at a time. If I should make a mistake or give in to temptation, I promise to forgive myself and get right back on track.

My signature below confirms my intention to get unstuck and go after the life I sincerely desire and richly deserve.

Signed _____

Dated _____

## A FEW MORE ENCOURAGING WORDS

Here you are at the end of the book, facing the question you faced when you read the first word. I could write one hundred more pages without answering that question for you. It is your choice. Will *you* get unstuck?

Before having the last word myself, I will let others who have been where you are now offer you some encouraging words about getting unstuck.

"So much has happened to me since I took my first steps to change," says Cindy. "Not all of it has been good. A year after I got help and got better, my father became ill and then died. I'm not sure the person I used to be would have got through that experience in one piece. I know I wouldn't have made peace with my father or understood that he always did the best he could. I wouldn't have been able to be there for my mum or my younger sister.

"Wonderful things have happened to me, too. The old me would never have been open to them. In the past year I've fallen in love, travelled, written a screenplay. I've met new people and had all kinds of new experiences, and none of it would have been possible if I had not made that first move to get unstuck and change my life for the better."

"Life is pretty darn good," Carol claims. "I wake up in the morning smiling. Okay, not every morning, but some mornings. And that's something when you think that I used to go into the bathroom and cry because I didn't want to face another day at the agency. I actually enjoy my work now. I can't believe I was so scared or that I let myself get so stuck. The only regret I have is that I didn't do something sooner."

"I'm not going to lie about this change business," Jack begins. "It isn't easy. I'm still waiting to get through a whole day without once thinking about chucking the whole programme and going back to my old ways. I *can* say I think about giving up less these days. The better I get, the worse the old Jack looks to me. Basically, I'm happy not to be back where I used to be."

"Do it. Do it. Do it," Harry cheers. "What have you *really* got to lose? If you like what you've got now, then you aren't stuck. If you don't like it, do something. As a buddy of mine likes to say, 'Better to try for *something* and fail, than to try for *nothing* and succeed.' So go for it!"

Karen laughs at Harry's enthusiasm and says, "I'm not *that* excited. But I do agree if what you are doing isn't working, you have to try something else. And give it a chance. Don't be too hard on yourself either. It all comes down to believing in yourself. And as long as we're trading quotations about success, here's one a guy I know gave me. 'Whether you think you *can* or you think you *can't*—you are right.' "

Let *me* leave you with the words of America's dean of psychology, William James. He suggests three steps to take if you honestly want to change. They are:

1. START IMMEDIATELY.
2. START FLAMBOYANTLY.
3. MAKE NO EXCEPTIONS (or excuses).

Because you can recognize the barriers to change and know how to dismantle them, you are now able to do exactly what James suggests. Will you?

I hope you will and that your journey brings you to the places found in your fondest dreams. The possibilities for a better life are out there waiting for you. They are within your grasp as soon as you take your first step to get unstuck. Life is a banquet. Sample its goodness. Life is a gift. Enjoy it. Strive to be more and better. You CAN do it.

# Recommended Reading

*Assert Yourself: How to Reprogramme Your Mind for Positive Action.* Gael Lindenfield. Thorsons, 1986.

*Take Charge of Your Life: How Not to be a Victim.* Louis Proto. Thorsons, 1988.

*Ask for the Moon and Get It! The Secret of Getting What You Want by Knowing How to Ask.* Percy Ross. Thorsons, 1988.

*Staying Ahead: The Secret of Success—Avoiding Self-Sabotage.* John Wareham. Thorsons, 1989.

*Talk and Grow Rich: How to Create Wealth Without Capital.* Ron Holland. Thorsons, 1989.

# Index